An Introduction
To The
New Covenant

GARY GILLEY
DAVID GUNN
DON TREST
CHRISTOPHER CONE
CHARLIE CLOUGH
GEORGE GUNN

CHRISTOPHER CONE
GENERAL EDITOR

An Introduction to the New Covenant

© 2013 Christopher Cone
Published by Tyndale Seminary Press
Hurst, TX

ISBN-10: 193848410X
ISBN-13: 978-1-938484-10-0

All Scripture quotations, except those noted otherwise are from the New American Standard Bible,
©1960,1962,1963,1968,1971,1972,1973,1975,1977, and 1995 by the Lockman Foundation.

CONTENTS

CONTRIBUTORS

GARY GILLEY, TH.D
–Pastor, Southern View Chapel (Springfield, IL)

DAVID GUNN, M.DIV, TH.M
–Professor of Distance Learning Courses, Shasta Bible College
–Ph.D Student, Baptist Bible Seminary

CHARLIE CLOUGH, TH.M, M.S
–Faculty, Chafer Seminary
–Scientist, Author, Former Pastor

DON TREST, M.B.S, D.MIN (CAND.)
–Pastor, Bible Fellowship Church (Pass Christian, MS)
–Director, Tyndale Learning Center, Pass Christian, MS
–Associate Professor of Bible & Theology

GEORGE GUNN, M.DIV, D.D, PH.D (ABD)
–Chair, Department of Bible and Theology, Shasta Bible College
–Dean of Admissions and Records, Shasta Bible College

CHRISTOPHER CONE, TH.D, PH.D
–President, Tyndale Theological Seminary & Biblical Institute
–Professor of Bible & Theology, Tyndale Theological Seminary & Biblical Institute
–Pastor, Tyndale Bible Church (Hurst, TX)

PREFACE

After spending several years researching, writing, and teaching on the literal grammatical–historical method, I began to be aware of some inconsistencies in my own understanding of Scripture. Most prominent, in my estimation, was my understanding that the church was somehow enjoying present blessings of the New Covenant. As I began to examine the covenants more closely I concluded that I had missed some important Biblical concepts in drawing a connection between the New Covenant and the church. I became convinced that such a connection could not be exegetically justified if the literal grammatical–historical method was consistently employed, but was initially unaware of others who agreed with this understanding. As I began interacting on these specific issues with other likeminded thinkers, including pioneering dispensational theologians and exegetes, and with others not so likeminded in this area – including leading Progressive dispensational scholars, I became more convinced that dispensationalism has a consistency problem on the issue of the New Covenant.

In 2008 I was honored to participate in the inaugural Council on Dispensational Hermeneutics, led by Dr. Mike Stallard and supported and hosted by Baptist Bible Seminary in Clarks Summit, Pennsylvania. The discussion included issues related to the New Covenant and led to the 2009 Council being devoted entirely to that topic. At that and subsequent Councils, and through many conversations, I began to discover that a number of other dispensational thinkers viewed the New Covenant similarly, a few of whom contributed to this volume: David Gunn, Gary

Gilley, George Gunn, Charlie Clough, and Don Trest. (Further thanks to Leon Johnson for his participation and encouragement in this project.) Over these past four years, spurred on by much of the research and conversation taking place at the Councils on Dispensational Hermeneutics, at Tyndale Theological Seminary, and at other related and likeminded schools and conferences, this book project was developed and is now finally complete. I am very thankful for each of the contributors, as they have been tremendous encouragement to me personally, and for their participation in this project, as the book is the richer for having each of them involved. Even though we do not all agree on every point, I trust the reader will find a good blend of cohesiveness and independent thought on the part of each writer.

I also appreciate and commend Mike Stallard for his leadership both in the Council on Dispensational Hermeneutics and in his editing of the excellent book – the first of its kind, covering the New Covenant – *Dispensational Understanding of the New Covenant* (Regular Baptist Press, 2012). Because of the usefulness of that volume I commend each of the contributors to that groundbreaking volume: John Master, Dave Frederickson, Roy Beacham, Elliott Johnson, Rodney Decker, and Bruce Compton. Each writer makes an important contribution to dispensational theology, and each gives readers much to consider. Further each of those writers are candid in their discussions and yet do not lack for grace. I applaud this group for modeling brotherly discussion of important issues. Well done, gentlemen. I hope and pray that *An Introduction to the New Covenant* offers the same combination of intellectual rigor and grace.

Whereas *Dispensational Understanding of the New Covenant* presents three leading views (that the church is not related to the NC, that the church is directly related, and that the church is indirectly related) *An Introduction to the New Covenant* is intended to present a broader case for the view that the church is not related to the New Covenant. While Roy Beacham argues in *Dispensational Understanding* to that end (focusing primarily on

ANE covenant aspects), the reader will find the view espoused in this volume to be usually quite agreeable to Beacham's conclusion, even if sometimes argued here on different grounds.

Finally, while each of the writers in this volume are unmistakably convinced of dispensational conclusions, none of us are committed to dispensationalism as a system beyond the point of its agreement with Scripture. We are not dispensationalists first. We are attempting to be Biblicists who – as a result of applying the literal grammatical–historical hermeneutic as consistently as we are able – conclude that the Bible derives many dispensational ideas. Further, we are committed to the Bible over and above any theological system, and we recognize the need for constant evaluation and reshaping of our understandings in the light of His word. It is to that end we humbly present this volume to you, in hopes that it encourages your growth as it has ours. May all that has been written here be for His honor and glory.

Christopher Cone
Spring, 2013

1

LAYING THE GROUNDWORK FOR UNDERSTANDING THE NEW COVENANT

Gary Gilley

A number of years ago I had the privilege of teaching through the book of Jeremiah – my favorite Old Testament prophetic book. One of the outstanding features of Jeremiah's prophecy is its description of the New Covenant found in chapter 31. "'Behold, days are coming,' declares the Lord" the prophecy begins in verse 31, "when I will make a New Covenant with the house of Israel and with the house of Judah." The reader is immediately put on notice that at some point in the future the Lord is going to give a new set of promises to the peoples of Israel and Judah. It will be a different kind of covenant than the Mosaic Covenant, for the people were unable to keep the requirements of the Law and thus suffered the judgment of God (v. 32).

This time the Lord will step up and not only give promises, but also the power for obedience. The Lord takes the initiative at every turn: "I [He vows] will make [the New Covenant] with the house of Israel;" "I will put My law within them and on their heart I will write it." And if that were not enough, "I will be their God, and they shall be My people (v. 33). Later the Lord promises, "I will forgive their iniquity, and their sin I will remember no more" (v. 34). Because of the Lord's provisions within the New Covenant it will be unnecessary for His people to teach one another the Law or the knowledge of God for "they will all know Me" (v. 34).

Such wonderful truth for any occasion, but when this prophecy was given it was especially so. The nation of Israel had long been in exile and Judah was about to be overrun by the Babylonians under Nebuchadnezzar. Life for the Jews was devastating. All the aspirations and dreams that accompanied them into the Promised Land centuries earlier had been dashed and hope for the future was gone. They had wasted God's provisions; they had spurned His love; they had trampled on His grace, and now they were facing His curse as promised (Deut 28:15–68). Contemplating the end of their civilization, as they knew it, at the darkest hour, God offers inspiration to His people in the form of a New Covenant. In Ezekiel's version of the Covenant the Lord pinpoints the timing.

The New Covenant will be put into effect when He takes the Jewish people from the nations in which they had been scattered and gathers them back into their own land (36:24). "Then," we are told, "I will sprinkle clean water on you, and you will be clean..." (v. 25). It is at that time that the Jews will be given "a new heart" and the Lord "will put a new spirit within [them] ..." (v. 26). More than that, the Lord promises, "I will put My Spirit within you and cause you to walk in My statutes" (v. 27). When all of this takes place, they "will live in the land that I gave to your forefathers; so you will be My people, and I will be your God" (v. 28).

To the unbiased mind it seems abundantly clear: The Israelites had failed miserably to keep the Old Covenant of Law and were suffering the consequences. For the sake of the Lord's own glory and because of His unbreakable promises to Israel (Ezek 36:32), He nevertheless makes a New Covenant with Israel. It will be enacted in the future at which time the Lord will bring the Jews back to the Promised Land, change their hearts, give them His Spirit, forgive their sins, place His Law on their hearts, enable them to obey Him, and even remove the curse from their land. Without question Jeremiah and Ezekiel indicate that all of this will take place in a future golden age often referred to as the kingdom.

So far, so good. But then a few years later I taught an extensive series through the book of Hebrews, the only place in the New Testament which fleshes out the meaning of the New Covenant. To be sure, other New Testament passages speak of the New Covenant, but largely in passing; only Hebrews gets down to its meaning in detail. The author of the book quotes the Jeremiah passage, giving explanation and providing several applications. As would be expected, nothing changes from what is found in the Old Testament prophetic passages. Jeremiah 31 is quoted beginning with, "Behold, days are coming, says the Lord, when I will effect a New Covenant with the house of Israel and with the house of Judah." The author of Hebrews still makes clear that a New Covenant with the house of Israel and Judah awaits future fulfillment. As simple as this seems, it is at this point that the students of Scripture break rank offering numerous and varied interpretations of the New Covenant. It is important for our understanding of the New Covenant to briefly identify and explain some of the more prominent of these interpretations:

VIEWS OF THE NEW COVENANT

Conservative theologians differ sharply in their views of the New Covenant, and especially its application to the church. Following is a brief description of some prominent interpretations of the New Covenant.

Two New Covenants
Due to the questions and apparent inconsistencies that will be addressed momentarily, some earlier dispensationalists, such as Lewis Sperry Chafer, sought to find a solution to these problems in the possibility that there were actually two New Covenants –

one for Israel and another for the church. Chafer writes, "Upon entering their [Israel's] kingdom, He [God] will make a New Covenant with the nation which will govern their life in the kingdom."[1] A few pages later he is careful to note that Israel's New Covenant is to be distinguished from the church's: "Reference at this point is to the New Covenant yet to be made with Israel and not to the New Covenant now in force in the Church."[2] Chafer clarifies:

> To suppose that these two covenants – one for Israel and one for the Church – are the same is to assume that there is latitude of common interest between God's purpose for Israel and His purpose for the Church. Israel's covenant, however, is new only because it replaces the Mosaic, but the Church's covenant is new because it introduces that which is God's mysterious land unrelated purpose. Israel's New Covenant rests specifically on the sovereign "I will" of Jehovah, while the New Covenant for the church is made in Christ's blood.[3]

One Covenant for One People

One of the central teachings found within Covenant Theology is that Israel and the church are one undifferentiated people of God. That is, Israel was the people of God under the Old Covenant and the church is the people of God now. Israel was the church under the Law, and the New Testament church is spiritual Israel today. Therefore since there is no real distinction between the two

---

[1] Lewis Sperry Chafer, *Systematic Theology* Vol. IV, (Dallas: Dallas Seminary Press, 1948), 314–5.

[2] Ibid., p. 325.

[3] Lewis Sperry Chafer, *Systematic Theology*, Vol. VII (Dallas: Dallas Seminary Press, 1948), 98–99.

people groups, the issue of whom the New Covenant addresses is moot.

With this understanding, the references to the house of Israel and the house of Judah, as found in Jeremiah and Hebrews, are easily interpreted to refer to the one people of God who have existed throughout time and transcends both Testaments. The only major difference is that the nation of Israel lived under the Mosaic Covenant and the church lives presently under the New Covenant. Also all the land and physical promises associated with the New Covenant are stripped of any literal meaning and given spiritual significance. Thus God's pledges concerning Israel being returned to her land (Jer 31:8–11, 15–17), increase in herds and flocks (Jer 31:23–24), and rebuilding cities (Jer 31:38–40) are not interpreted as literal promises but are given allegorical meanings. This is necessary, for as Reformed theologian Charles Hodge writes, "The literal interpretation of the Old Testament prophecies relating to the restoration of Israel and the future kingdom of Christ, cannot   possibility be carried out...Neither is there the slightest suggestion that the future kingdom of Christ is to be of earthly splendour."[4]

Those holding to the New Covenant Theological view (a recent development which offers a blend between dispensationalism and Covenant Theology) have the same understanding. Larry Pettegrew writes:

> Though making some significant steps forward, NCT takes a step back toward Covenant Theology and teaches that the New Covenant is ultimately fulfilled with the church rather than with the nation of Israel. New Covenant Theologians admit that Jeremiah 31:31 teaches that the New Covenant was originally made with Israel. According to Lehrer, "If you read the verses that surround this text...,

---

[4] Charles Hodge, *Systematic Theology*, Vol III,(Hendrickson, 2003), 809, 811.

it is crystal clear that this New Covenant, in its Old Testament context, is promised to the geopolitical nation of Israel at some point in the future." Nonetheless, "Israel in the Old Covenant era was a temporary, unbelieving picture of the true people of God, the church. There always existed a small remnant of believers within unbelieving Israel." Thus, in both Covenant Theology and NCT, the church replaces Israel, and God has no special future for the nation other than as individual Jews become a part of the church.[5]

One New Covenant Made with Israel but Participated in by the Church
Among leading dispensationalist today, the majority take the view that the Lord cut the New Covenant with Israel and ratified it with the blood of Christ. The New Covenant is therefore specifically for Israel and the physical promises within the Covenant will be fulfilled with the Jews in the future Millennial Kingdom. However, the church (composed of both Jewish and Gentile Christians) participates in the spiritual blessings of the Covenant now. Renald Showers writes, "Saved Gentiles are members of the Church. They are grafted into the place of covenant blessing in the sense that they partake of the spiritual blessings of the New Covenant, as do the remnant Israelite members of the Church."[6]

Thomas Ice states, "Israel, not the church will fulfill the New Covenant as prophesied in the Old Testament. The church does partake of the spiritual blessings of the Abrahamic and New Covenants, but does not fulfill those promises as given for Israel

---

[5] Larry D. Pettegrew, "The New Covenant," *The Master's Theological Journal*, Vol. 2, issue #2, Fall, 1999, 191.

[6] Renald Showers, *There Really Is a Difference*, (Bellmawr, NJ: The Friends of Israel Gospel Ministry, 1990), 110.

(Rom 15:27)."[7]   The reasoning behind this position is well represented by Larry Pettegrew: "Terminology and provisions spelled out in the NT indicate that Christ inaugurated the New Covenant at His first advent. Though the New Covenant will not be fulfilled with Israel until her future repentance, the church through Spirit baptism into Christ participates in that covenant."[8]

One New Covenant Made with Israel Alone
Larry Pettegrew, in his article on the New Covenant, admits that "an enormous problem arises in approaching the New Covenant in the Old Testament. The promises of the New Covenant direct themselves to Israel, and that leaves non–Israelites on the outside looking in."[9] He is correct; all Old Testament passages touching on the New Covenant are directed to the nation of Israel. When we move to the New Testament Gospels Jesus is offering the kingdom, which will function under the stipulations of the New Covenant, to Israel.   The Jews, sadly, reject their Messiah and therefore Christ did not enact the New Covenant during His lifetime. He did, however, fulfill the necessary requirements to ratify the Covenant through His blood on the cross.

The question is what has become of the New Covenant now? Some, such as John Master, believe, "The church is united to the mediator of the New Covenant. The New Covenant has been cut. The actualization of the New Covenant in the lives of believers, however, is yet future, when Christ returns and the house of Israel and the house of Judah are transformed by God's grace to obey completely the commands of God."[10] Others take a

---

[7] Thomas Ice, *Pre–Trib Perspectives*, Vol. V, Issue #10, February, 2001, 8.

[8] Larry D. Pettegrew, 251.

[9] Ibid., 252.

[10] John R. Master, "The New Covenant," *Issues in Dispensationalism*, Wesley R. Willis and John R. Master, eds, (Chicago: Moody, 1994), 108.

different stance. Pettegrew writes, "After His ascension, Christ inaugurated the New Covenant by pouring out the Holy Spirit on the day of Pentecost. The New Testament thus becomes a New Covenant document...All the teaching about the Holy Spirit in the New Testament (especially about the 'promise of the Spirit'; (Eph 1:13; Gal 3:14) is evidence that the New Covenant has been inaugurated."[11] Still Pettegrew sees more to come: "The church participates in the New Covenant, but the New Covenant will not be finally fulfilled until Israel comes into a right relationship with God at the end of the Tribulation."[12] Bruce Ware agrees,

> It seems clear that the promised new age, in which the New Covenant would finally be realized would come only when God's king would liberate Israel from its oppressors and when God's Spirit would inhabit the whole company of the people of God.   Consequently, in Old Testament perspective, while the time of the New Covenant's enactment was uncertain, one thing was certain, namely, that when God would bring to his people the promised spiritual transformation, it would also be accompanied by the promised physical, national, and geographic blessings.[13]

As Ware, and many others see it, the church can presently be participating in Israel's New Covenant through the *already not yet* eschatological framework. He sees the problem solved "when we permit the fulfillment of such eschatological promises to take

---

[11] Pettegrew, 267.

[12] Ibid., 269.

[13] Bruce A. Ware, "The New Covenant the People(s) of God," *Dispensationalism, Israel and the Church: The Search for Definition,* Craig A. Blaising and Darrell L. Bock,eds (Grand Rabids: Zondervan, 19992), 84.

both a preliminary and partial ('already') fulfillment as well as a later full and complete ('not yet') realization. And such in fact seems to be the case in regard to the New Covenant."[14] Under this view only the spiritual aspects of the New Covenant promises are now inaugurated in this age, with the physical/land promises awaiting the return of Christ.[15]

TOWARD A SOLUTION

As we attempt to analyze and work through the various views we must first establish our hermeneutic. As dispensationalists we take a grammatical/historical approach to Scripture and thus do not add allegorical meanings to the texts. While we recognize symbolism, metaphor and the like, we read the text through a normal interpretative lens and do not change the obvious, literal meaning of Scripture. In addition, we believe the Old Testament writings stand on their own and are not dependent on the New Testament for their meaning. Although the doctrine of progressive revelation allows for additional insight, fulfillment, and revelation as the Bible marches toward completion, the New Testament does not actually change the original meaning of Old Testament teaching. Specifically, in this regard I would agree with John Master,

> A dispensational understanding of the New Covenant assumes that the New Testament writers do not change the meaning of the original prophecy, as correctly understood in its historical context. They may, however, provide additional information concerning "fulfillment"

---

[14] Ibid., 94.

[15] Ibid.

not found in the Old Testament prophecy as it was originally understood in its context.[16]

This means we begin with the meaning of the Old Testament passages dealing with the New Covenant, and as we do so what do we discover? There is little question, from the prophecies of Jeremiah and Ezekiel, that the New Covenant is a unique promise to the house of Israel and the house of Judah. It is a replacement for the Old Covenant of law that the Jewish people failed to keep resulting in their judgment and exile. There is also little doubt that the New Covenant has a starting point and that is when the Lord has gathered His people from the nations in which they have been scattered bringing them back to the land He had promised them as an inheritance. Ezekiel 36:24 reads, "For I will take you from the nations, gather you from all the lands and bring you into your own land."

That this prophecy concerning bringing His people home is not a reference to the returning exiles under Zerubbabel, Ezra, or Nehemiah, is obvious from the description of the spiritual renewal that will accompany their physical return. Ezekiel 36:25–27, immediately after promising a physical gathering of Israel to their land, reads, "Then I will sprinkle clean water on you, and you will be clean; I will cleanse you from all your filthiness and from all your idols. Moreover, I will give you a new heart and put a new spirit within you; and I will remove the heart of stone from your flesh and give you a heart of flesh. I will put My Spirit within you and cause you to walk in My statutes and you will be careful to observe My ordinances."

The very next verse (v. 28) returns to the promise of being restored to the land: "You will live in the land that I gave to your forefathers..." The type of spiritual renewal being portrayed in both Jeremiah 31 and Ezekiel 36 has yet to be seen among the people of Israel and obviously awaits the future. From the Old

---

[16] John Master, 94.

Testament narratives it becomes clear that the New Covenant promises, both physical and spiritual, will be fulfilled when the kingdom of God is established on earth by Jesus Christ Himself.

Reading exclusively from Old Testament it would be most difficult to honestly find another interpretation. The problem comes when we turn to the New Testament. It is possible – even likely – that the Holy Spirit has chosen to supplement our understanding of the Old Testament depiction of the New Covenant. This would not imply that what the prophets wrote was wrong but that it was not complete. It is conceivable that the Lord has other applications for the New Covenant that He did not reveal in the Old Testament. The only way to know is to turn to the New Testament and see what it says.

I will leave the detailed exegesis of these texts to the other authors of this volume, but it would be helpful to take a brief look at what lies ahead. Turning to the New Testament we find that the New Covenant does not play a major role in either the teachings of Jesus or the apostles. Jesus mentions the New Covenant only three times: Matthew 26:28; Mark 14:24 and Luke 22:20. Upon closer examination, however, these three statements are all simply different accounts of the same occasion – the Lord's Supper with His disciples on the night before His crucifixion. What we learn, in relationship to the New Covenant, is that Jesus' death, and the shedding of His blood, was needed to ratify the New Covenant (see Heb 9:16). However, because a covenant has been ratified does not necessarily mean that it has been placed into operation (this will have to be determined by further revelation in the epistles). From the information given in the Gospels, as far as we know Jesus never mentioned the New Covenant but once – on the night before His death.

None of John's writings reference the New Covenant, nor do Peter's. Paul mentions it three times (Rom 11:27; 1 Cor 11:25; 2 Cor 3:6) but never develops its meaning. In 1 Corinthians 11:25 Paul is merely repeating what Jesus said at the Supper. Romans 11:27 is a passing quote from Isaiah 59:21. In 2 Corinthians 3:6

Paul speaks of himself and others as being ministers of the New Covenant, but does not say specially what that means. In none of these passages are we told that the New Covenant is now being fulfilled.

This leaves the book of Hebrews to provide supplemental material to the Old Testament concept of the New Covenant. The New Covenant is dealt with extensively in Hebrews 8:7–9:28, and mentioned in 10:16–17 as well. We are not surprised to discover that there are many opinions concerning what the author of Hebrews is saying, but as for the place the New Covenant plays in the life of the believer today we can be confident of certain things.

First, it is apparent that the author of Hebrews envisioned the possibility of some of his readers returning to current Jewish practices. To do so, the author argues, is to go backwards spiritually, leaving behind the superiority of Christ for the inferiority of the Law. When the book of Hebrews addresses the New Covenant, it quotes from Jeremiah's prophecy (8:8–12) (the only such quote found in the New Testament). Yet the author never says that the New Covenant is being fulfilled presently. He does imply that once the New Covenant was announced by Jeremiah the Old Covenant began the process of becoming obsolete and growing old (8:13). With the coming of the church age, the Old Covenant has been placed on the shelf as God deals with His church through His Spirit rather than the Law (see 2 Cor 3:4–18). When Christ returns He will not resurrect the Old Covenant of Law but will enact the New Covenant, which He has already ratified with His blood. Rather than the church age people of God returning to the Old Covenant of Law, they should live in the power of the indwelling Holy Spirit as they look forward to the full manifestation of the New Covenant in the kingdom age. This is the message of Hebrews to the church–age believer.

As we examine the Epistle to the Hebrews we must draw the conclusion that the New Covenant is relevant to the church in some manner, through the Mediator, Christ Jesus (Heb 8:6; 9:15;

12:24). The New Covenant has been cut, or ratified by the blood of Christ, yet it seems obvious that the full actualization of the New Covenant awaits the return of Christ at which time the houses of Israel and Judah will be transformed by the power of God, will be gathered to their Promised Land, and will enjoy the blessing of the kingdom of God on earth.

QUESTIONS AND INCONSISTENCIES

Before I studied in depth the books of Jeremiah and Hebrews, I accepted without hesitation the common dispensational view that the New Covenant was made with Israel, not the church, and that Israel, not the church will fulfill the New Covenant during the Millennial Kingdom. The church did, however, partake of the spiritual blessings now as a result of the Christian being saved by the blood of Christ and placed into Christ, who is the Mediator of the New Covenant. In this interpretation the physical and land promises are reserved for the future, primarily with Israel, but the spiritual promises are being experienced now by the church.

This seems to make good sense, after all, there appears to be much overlap between the spiritual promises within the New Covenant and the realities of the Christian life. The indwelling of the Holy Spirit is part of the New Covenant and is true of the Christian; full forgiveness of sin is a key component of the New Covenant and is made possible because of the cross-work of Christ, and it is also a reality for the church age saint; regeneration, or the new birth, is promised in the New Covenant and for the present disciple of Christ as well. Since these blessings are promised in the New Covenant and also experienced by the Christian surely they are the result of the Christian participating in the New Covenant now. A complete fulfillment of the New Covenant is yet to come but an apparent partial fulfillment is happening in the meanwhile, so goes the argument.

Yet, as I looked more closely, these conclusions seemed to be more logical deductions than Biblical revelation. I found myself faced with a dozen or so questions and inconsistencies with the common dispensational view. Here they are in no particular order:

- Under the New Covenant the "Law" plays a vital role. This is to be expected when one considers that the Old Covenant of Law was given specifically to the Jews and will be replaced by the New Covenant. It does not seem to me that the role of the Law is minimized under the New Covenant, what is different is the place and power of the Law. First, Israel was given the Law in written form – beginning with the Decalogue followed by over 600 accompanying rules and regulations covering the civil, ceremonial and moral life of the Jews. When the New Covenant is enacted there appears to be no diminishing of the Law (and no indication that the Law has changed). What will change is that the Law will be written in the hearts of God's people. Rather than being written on stone or paper, the Law then will be internalized.

   Secondly, the Old Covenant failed, not because of any inherit weakness in the Law, but because the people defied the Law and rebelled against God. While the Jews knew what was right and what pleased the Lord they seem to have no power to obey. They relied on self-restraint and will-power ultimately resulting in spiritual failure. But under the New Covenant the Lord will change His people's hearts (Ezek 36:26) and empower them with the Holy Spirit so that they will be capable of obeying God. As a matter of fact obedience will be the norm with disobedience swiftly judged (Isa 66:20).

   However, all of this Law-talk sounds a dissonant note for the church age. Believers in this dispensation are specifically told that they are not under the Mosaic Law (Gal 2:29; 3:23-26). We have died to the Law (Rom 7:1-

6) and live in newness of life through the power of the Holy Spirit (Gal 5:16–25). It is for this reason that the apostle Paul tells the Christians in 2 Corinthians 3:6–11 not to return to the way of the letter but to live by the Spirit.   Under the New Covenant the believer is characterized by the Law being written in their hearts, and enabled to live in obedience to the Law by the power of the Spirit.   By contrast, the New Testament epistles claim that the church–age believer has been freed from the Law of Israel. In what sense, therefore, could the Christian be participating now in the New Covenant? If the New Covenant era will be characterized by keeping the Law and if the Christian is freed from the Law, it seems most difficult to conclude that the church is now under the New Covenant spiritual provisions. The differences seem irreconcilable.

This is a difficult dilemma, one which some have tried to get around by claiming that the Law under the New Covenant is not the same Law as under the Old Covenant. But I have a hard time drawing this conclusion for a couple of reasons. First, there is no statement found in Scripture that makes this claim. The Law was such a central feature under the Old Covenant that it would seem to me additional and clear revelation that the New Covenant is speaking of anything but the Mosaic Law would be needed to come to a different conclusion. Secondly, the natural assumption on the part of the Jews when they heard the word "law" would be to understand the Mosaic Law being referenced – unless there was good reason to redefine the word. No good reason is given to redefine the Mosaic Law or replace the Law with different laws. I must conclude then that the New Covenant is a covenant based upon the Old Covenant of Law, which the epistles specifically state the Christian is no longer under obligation to keep.

- Is God's Law being written on our hearts and minds today? If one could somehow navigate around the first concern they would still be faced with this question. I think it would be a mistake to trivialize the importance of the question by claiming the answer is found in that the Holy Spirit brings to our hearts and minds God's truth. This statement by the prophets is much stronger than that as the next question will show. At this point we are all in agreement that the Holy Spirit plays a vital role in our understanding of the ways of God. Without His ministry none of us would come to Christ for none would seek Him (Rom 3:11) and none would comprehend His glory (2 Cor 3:18; 4:6). But today the Holy Spirit teaches through the written Word of God, which He has inspired (2 Pet 1:20–21). Apart from the Scriptures we would have only the knowledge of God that we find in natural revelation (Ps 19:1–6). We would have no comprehension of His person, the need of mankind, the salvation found in Christ or the path of righteousness He wants us to walk. Today the Word of God is written in a book; but under the New Covenant it is written on our hearts and minds. Apparently Bibles will not be needed in the kingdom as Christ will rule personally from the throne of David and the Law of God will be directly written on our hearts. The functioning ministry of the Word of God in our lives today is vastly different than under the New Covenant. This leads to the reason for my next question.

- How can the Great Commission idea of "teaching" be reconciled with the New Covenant statement that "they shall not teach again, each man his neighbor and each man his brother..." (Jer 31:34)? The implication is because the

Law of the Lord is placed in the minds and written on the hearts under the New Covenant, instruction concerning the things of God will be unnecessary. Yet Jesus sent His followers out to make disciples by teaching people to "observe all I commanded you" (Matt 28:20). Throughout the book of Acts the apostles taught the gospel and the commandments of Christ, and Acts 2:42 tells of the early church meeting specifically to devote "themselves to the apostles' teaching." The epistles not only contain the essence of New Testament truth but repeatedly call for the leaders of the church to teach. Paul's last inspired admonishment was to Timothy to "preach the word" (2 Tim 4:2). If, in fact, the Law of God is written in our minds and hearts, there would be no need for the sort of instruction exemplified and commanded in the New Testament. This New Covenant provision does not harmonize well with what we find true of the church age in Scripture.

- Do all know the Lord today? One of the great results of the Lord placing His Law in minds and writing it in hearts under the New Covenant is that He will at that time "be their God and they shall be [His] people" (Heb 8:10). And the reason given for why teaching others to know the Lord is unnecessary is because, "All will know Me, from the least to the greatest of them" (Heb 8:11). Just as the Law of God will be directly implanted within His people, so too will be the knowledge of the Lord – and this promise is for the least to the greatest of people (Jere 31:34).

    In no stretch of the imagination is this true today. The world continues in full rebellion against the Lord. But someone might counter, "This is a reference to Christians, all of whom know the Lord." To some degree this might make sense, as all believers "know" the Lord. However, when coupled with the first part of the sentence indicating that under the New Covenant none will have need of instruction concerning the Lord, we have a problem. The New Testament church gathered to be instructed in the way of the Lord. Perhaps the apostle Paul's highest personal goal was to know Christ (Phil 3:10), something he affirmed he had not attained in his lifetime (Phil 3:12–14). Once again, there is incongruence between the provisions of the New Covenant and both the personal experience of the Christian and the teachings of the New Testament about life during the church age.

• Even the spiritual promises of the New Covenant do not appear to be operable today. Those living in the New Covenant era are promised some pretty astounding spiritual blessings: a new heart and a new spirit (Ezek 36:26), the indwelling of the Holy Spirit (Ezek 36:27), the laws of God placed in their hearts and written on their minds so that teaching the ways of the Lord will be unnecessary (Jer 31:33–34), complete forgiveness of sin (Jer 31:34), full knowledge of God (Jer 31:34), and a hatred of their past sins (Ezek 36:31). Other prophecies indicate that the kingdom age will be one of obedience and holiness (Isa 35:8–10). If the church is enjoying these spiritual blessing now I must say I am disappointed. While Christians have been forgiven, regenerated and Spirit-indwelt (all blessings much like those promised in the New Covenant), the depth of spiritual life and obedience pictured under the New Covenant seems much greater than what is being witnessed today within the church. Surely those who have God's laws written on their hearts and minds to such an extent that everyone knows the Lord would evidence more of the holiness of God than is witnessed today.

- The New Covenant is major proof of God's faithfulness to Israel. Romans 9–11 is written primarily to offer confirmation that although Israel had rejected the Lord and their Messiah, He would nevertheless remain faithful to them because His "gifts and calling are irrevocable" (Rom 11:29). Within this context the New Covenant is referenced (11:26–27) as a time in which "'the Deliverer will come from Zion, He will remove ungodliness from Jacob. This is my covenant with them, when I take away their sins." The purpose of the Covenant directly points to Israel and her sins – sins the Lord will remove when Christ comes again ("out of Zion"). In the context of Romans 9–11, Israel is being used as an object lesson of the faithfulness of the Lord and in that sense has direct application to the church. But the example given is of God's faithfulness to Israel, not to the church; and God's Covenant is to Israel not the church.

- Israel is the direct recipient of the New Covenant, rather than the church. The New Covenant is only mentioned by this name once in the Old Testament, in Jeremiah 31:31. This passage is quoted in the only detailed explanation of the Covenant in the New Testament – Hebrews 8. However, all careful Bible students recognize that it is presented in several other prophetic passages, most predominately Ezekiel 36:24–38. In all of the texts, in either Testament, it is Israel that is addressed and it is Israel that is being described and given promises. Ezekiel 36:24 can only be speaking of Israel, "For I will take you from the nations, gather you from all the lands and bring you into your own land." Jeremiah 31:31 reads, "'Behold, days are coming,' declares the Lord, 'when I will make a New Covenant with the house of Israel and the house of Judah.'" The result of these statements is clear: that the New Covenant is promised to Israel, not to the church.

However, in accordance to the hermeneutical principle of progressive revelation it is very possible that a promise given to Israel in the Old Testament could be given fuller meaning and understanding in the New Testament. That is, the Lord may have intended to include the church in on all, or portions of, the Covenant all along but simply did not reveal that truth until a later date. The problem we have with this idea is that *we are never given additional revelation that includes the church.* There are some New Testament texts that seem to imply church involvement, but implication is not direct teaching, and as I will mention below, those tests are not as clear as many think in describing how the church relates to the New Covenant. Without additional revelation it is presumptuous to believe the church is presently enjoying the spiritual benefits of the New Covenant. This leads to another question.

• On what basis is it assumed that the church participates in only the spiritual benefits of the New Covenant? Whenever the New Covenant is presented in Scripture it is presented as a whole. That is, both physical and spiritual promises make up the Covenant and there is no revelation stating that the spiritual aspects precede the physical. As it is often interpreted, the spiritual promises such as complete forgiveness, the indwelling of the Holy Spirit and perhaps regeneration, are presently in force and being enjoyed by the church today; but the physical promises such as Israel being gathered back to the land, fruitful harvests, rebuilding of desolate and ruined cities, and increased flocks (see Ezek 36:24–38) await Israel in the kingdom age. I have to ask: Where is the revelation that teaches this two–part enactment of the New Covenant?

- The New Covenant is promised to be fulfilled at a particular point in time. Not only is the New Covenant specifically given to Israel, its commencement date is specifically given as well. Jeremiah 31:31 says, "Behold days are coming... when I will make a New Covenant with the house of Israel and with the house of Judah." Hebrews 8:10 says that the Covenant will be made with Israel "after those days." Turning to Ezekiel 36:24 we discover the New Covenant will be enacted at the time when the Lord draws the Jews back to their land from all the nations in which He has scattered them. But it is not merely a physical move, for at that time He "will sprinkle clean water on [them], and [they] will be clean... Moreover, [He] will give [them] a new heart and put a new spirit within [them]" (v. 25). In other words, physical blessings will be accompanied by spiritual renewal. The Old Testament texts indicate that the physical and spiritual aspects of the New Covenant will be placed into service at the same time. It will be a time yet in the future when the people of Israel will be brought back to their land of promise and given hearts and lives which will be in tune with God. Nothing in the New Testament teaching on the New Covenant changes the Old Testament timeline. The New Covenant promises await the return of Christ and the setting up of His kingdom on earth. Again, I have to ask what right do we have (apart from additional revelation) to say that the physical/land promises of the New Covenant are future while the spiritual promises are applicable to the church today?

ON THE OTHER HAND

Given these objections, why do so many insist that the church is presently participating in the spiritual benefits of the New Covenant? There are several arguments commonly given to support this idea that I want to mention and briefly make an objection or two to each:

- The similarities between spiritual blessings.   As mentioned above, both those under the New Covenant and the church age believers are promised complete forgiveness of sins. Both received this forgiveness on the basis of the work of Christ on their behalf on the cross. But the Christian is given forgiveness at the moment of salvation; Israel, as a nation will receive forgiveness when Christ returns and gathers His people home. Romans 11:26–27 confirms this: "And so all Israel will be saved; just as it is written, 'The deliverer will come from Zion, He will remove ungodliness from Jacob.' This is my covenant with them, *when* I take away their sins."

    Similarly both Christians and Israel are promised regeneration, but again the timing is distinct. The Christian is regenerated at the time of conversion while the people of Israel receive new hearts when the Lord sets up His kingdom (Ezek 36:24–26). Also, both the church age saint and New Covenant Israel will be Spirit indwelt but the moment in which the believer is indwelt is simultaneous with his spiritual regeneration while Israel is indwelt at the return of Christ. Ezekiel 36:27 states, "I will put My Spirit within you and cause you to walk in My statutes, and you will be careful to observe My ordinances." And when will this take place? When "you will live in the land that I gave to your forefathers..."

- Christ is the Mediator of the New Covenant (Heb 9:15; 12:24). Christ's death is efficacious and necessary for sins under all covenants and for all people. Without the cross sins from Adam to the end of time could not be cleansed. There is no question that on the basis of Christ's death He is the Mediator of the New Covenant. But there also is no question that Christ's death is the basis for the forgiveness of sins under the Old Covenant and even before. With this reasoning it does not seem much of a stretch to see that Christ's death accomplished more than one thing. It provided the means of redemption for those in previous dispensations including those under the Old Covenant as well as those in the church age. At the same time His blood was necessary to ratify the New Covenant and provide forgiveness for those in the coming kingdom age.

• Jesus confirmed that His blood ratified the New Covenant. In Luke 22:20 Jesus states, "This cup which is poured out for you is the New Covenant in My blood." When writing to the church at Corinth the apostle Paul reminds the believers of this truth (1 Cor 11:25). As a result of such passages everyone is in agreement that Jesus' blood was necessary to authorize the New Covenant. But because a covenant has been cut, does that necessarily mean that it is in force. John Master says it this way, "Because a covenant has been 'cut' does not mean that it is fully operational. God 'cut' a covenant with Abraham regarding the land (Gen 15), which has not yet been fulfilled. There may or may not be a period of time between the cutting of the covenant and its realization in human experience, when it becomes functional."[17]

Neither Jesus nor Paul specifically stated that the New Covenant was placed into effect immediately. As a matter of fact virtually everyone, including those who believe the New Covenant is fully operational today, recognizes at least some time lapse between the ratification of Covenant at the cross, and the time it was

---

[17] Ibid., 99.

placed into service (usually at Pentecost) 50 days later. That is, no one believes the Covenant became operational at the Last Supper when the Lord said "this cup is the New Covenant in My blood" (1 Cor 11:25). Nor does anyone believe that such took place on the cross. Even those who accept the positions of Covenantal Theology would not understand the New Covenant beginning to function until the Holy Spirit was poured out at Pentecost.

In order to take the stance that the New Covenant became active at Pentecost, one has to interpret the pouring out of the Spirit in Acts 2 as a fulfillment of one of the New Covenant promises. While neither Jeremiah 31 nor Hebrews 8 mentions it, Ezekiel 37:27 promises, "I will put my Spirit within you." Could this be a reference to Pentecost and the coming of the Spirit to indwell the believer? This would seem unlikely, for the next line of the verse reads, "And cause you to walk in My statutes, and you will be careful to observe My ordinances." While the church age saint is empowered by the Holy Spirit and thus Spirit enabled to live in obedience to the Lord, nevertheless it is rather obvious that all believers sin and many fail miserably. It would seem to go too far to think that the Spirit is really "causing" us today to walk in the Lord's statutes. On the other hand, this promise fits well with the description of life in the kingdom in which righteousness reigns and any defiance against the Lord will evoke immediate judgment (Ps 2:9; Is 11:4; 66:20).

- Paul claimed to be a minister of the New Covenant (2 Cor 3:6). This is perhaps the strongest verse supporting the idea that the New Covenant is fully in force presently. If Paul, an apostle to the Gentiles, calls himself a "servant of a New Covenant," it is conceivable that he is affirming his role as an apostle under the administration of the New

Covenant. This is one possible interpretation. However there is another plausible interpretation – could he not simply be saying that he is ministering in light of the future enactment of the Covenant? *Just as Paul preached the kingdom of God (Acts 28:30) while not physically being in the kingdom, so he could be a minister of the New Covenant, while not actually living under the New Covenant.* Paul preached the kingdom as something yet to come; so he could preach the New Covenant as something yet to be placed into operation. This seems to fit better the overall teaching concerning the New Covenant in the rest of Scripture.

CONCLUSION

The New Covenant contains a glorious set of promises that can only be realized because of the blood of Christ. That Christ's crucifixion ratified the Covenant is not in question – that the Covenant is presently *in force* is. Covenantal theologians believe the church operates under the conditions and assurances of the New Covenant. Most dispensationalists reject this view, seeing the full enactment of the Covenant awaiting the future, when Christ sets up His kingdom on earth. At that time the Lord will fulfill both the physical/land promises with Israel, as well as bring about the full enjoyment of the spiritual promises.

However, the majority of dispensationalists believe there is presently a partial fulfillment of the New Covenant until the Lord returns and establishes the kingdom age, at which time the Covenant will be completely operational.   But where in the Scriptures is revelation given teaching a partial fulfillment during the church age? Even the concept of a partial fulfillment, in which the spiritual, but not the physical, promises are actively enjoyed, is suspect. The New Covenant promises full obedience, not fractional. It promises all the power of the Spirit which brings about compliance to God's ordinances, not the inconsistency we often experience. It promises comprehensive knowledge of the Lord, not the dim view we presently possess (1 Cor 13:12). It promises that we will no longer need teachers, while today teachers are an important part of Christian life. If the New Covenant is being partially fulfilled today, it seems to be very partial indeed.

My understanding is that just as the nation of Israel functioned under the auspices of the Old Covenant between the giving of the Law and the coming of the Spirit at Pentecost, so Israel, and those who join with her in serving the Lord during the Millennium (Is 58) will function under the auspices of the New Covenant. The New Covenant is specifically for the kingdom age, not the church age. The church today has nothing directly to do with the New Covenant; she operates under the law of Christ (Gal 6:2).

2

AN OVERVIEW OF NEW COVENANT PASSAGES, OSTENSIBLE AND ACTUAL

David Gunn

One of the most acute challenges to doing exegesis well is the propensity of our preconceptions to get in the way and bungle the entire enterprise – especially when those preconceptions are informed by theological positions long championed by many and challenged by few. When involved in exegetical pursuits, we must always remind ourselves precisely of what is the goal of our pursuit. Exegesis seeks above all else to uncover the meaning of the text of Scripture, and that requires that we stick to the text with unremitting tenacity. "Is this what the text *really means*?" is the question of the exegete, and it is a question of supreme importance to the issue addressed by this book.

For centuries, the Christian Church has held certain beliefs about the New Covenant that have enjoyed virtual unanimity from generation to generation, with only minor variations here and there. Now, the contributors to this book are gazing at those beliefs with a critical eye and asking the question, "Is this what the text of Scripture *really means*?" It is of course no easy task to challenge theological views that have long enjoyed ascendency, largely because of the comfort of the familiar, which takes us back to those preconceptions again.

Because of the complexity of the task at hand, it is of preeminent importance that we ground ourselves firmly in the texts of Scripture from the outset, rather than allowing preconceptions and long–favored viewpoints to win the day solely on the basis of familiarity. This chapter offers a bird's–eye view of all the major texts that are most frequently taken to refer to the New Covenant. In many cases, the application of specific texts to discussions on the New Covenant is justified; in some cases, it is not. Therefore, an attempt will be made to identify which of these Biblical texts truly concern the New Covenant, and which of them have been frequently misattributed. The aim of this chapter is therefore twofold: first, to provide an overview of the scriptural texts most likely to occupy a discussion on the New Covenant; and second, to make some preliminary judgment as to which of those texts do or do not actually refer to the New Covenant. For the purposes of simplicity and ease of reference, we will begin with Jeremiah's passages (since he offers the clearest and most paradigmatic teaching on the New Covenant), and proceed according to canonical order thereafter.

Methodologically, my strategy will be first to determine what the defining characteristics of the New Covenant are according to Jeremiah.[1] Then, the remaining passages in question will be measured against those characteristics. The higher degree of overlap there is between a passage and the characteristics of the New Covenant as revealed by Jeremiah, the greater the likelihood that it is a New Covenant passage. The objection might be raised that this strategy cedes too much authority to *similarity*, given the fact that *similarity* can never conclusively establish *identity*. The observation is granted, but keep in mind that this chapter is intended to be introductory and to furnish a survey-view of the texts in question, not to provide meticulous, detailed,

---

[1] Jeremiah is granted paradigmatic status because his passages are probably the most detailed on the subject, and because his first New Covenant passage (31:31–34) constitutes the *locus classicus* of Old Testament teaching on the New Covenant. That is also the passage wherein the term "New Covenant" was first coined.

and definitive exegesis. The conclusions reached about each of these passages will therefore be somewhat tentative by necessity. Nevertheless, it is hoped that they will be helpful in establishing a basic framework or "starting point" from which more detailed investigation of the various passages may proceed.

Jeremiah 31:31–34
[31] "Behold, days are coming," declares the LORD, "when I will make a New Covenant with the house of Israel and with the house of Judah, [32] not like the covenant which I made with their fathers in the day I took them by the hand to bring them out of the land of Egypt, My covenant which they broke, although I was a husband to them," declares the LORD. [33] "But this is the covenant which I will make with the house of Israel after those days," declares the LORD, "I will put My law within them and on their heart I will write it; and I will be their God, and they shall be My people. [34] They will not teach again, each man his neighbor and each man his brother, saying, 'Know the LORD,' for they will all know Me, from the least of them to the greatest of them," declares the LORD, "for I will forgive their iniquity, and their sin I will remember no more."[2]

That this passage is foundational to the Bible's teaching on the New Covenant is accepted by virtually everyone. It was evidently Jeremiah who coined the expression "New Covenant," as this is the only passage in the Old Testament that uses it. While little need be said therefore about whether or not Jeremiah 31:31–34 refers to the New Covenant, a brief examination of the passage is nonetheless essential to the primary aim of this chapter. Since our objective is to determine which passages do or do not refer to the New Covenant, this passage serves well as a sort of "control passage." That is, since the actual phrase "New Covenant" is used only rarely in Scripture, the legitimacy or illegitimacy of an

---

[2] All English Bible references are from *New American Standard Bible: 1995 Update* (LaHabra, CA: The Lockman Foundation, 1995).

alleged reference to the New Covenant must be determined by a comparison of the content of the passage in question to the characteristics of the New Covenant, which have been clearly described by Jeremiah the prophet.

At least seven characteristics of the New Covenant are described by Jeremiah in this passage. First, it is to be a *New Covenant*, i.e. distinct from and dissimilar to (see v. 32) the old covenant, which Jeremiah identifies as the Sinaitic Covenant. The mention of the historical breaking of the old covenant in verse 32 suggests that not only will the covenant's content be somewhat different this time around (it will "not be like [כ אֹל]" the old one), but so will the other party's fidelity to it. It is therefore "new" in more than one sense: new terms, and new results.

Some interpreters have suggested that the New Covenant is not actually new at all, but constitutes rather a *renewing* of the old covenant.[3] This interpretation is a rather difficult one to hold, given the sharp contrast drawn between the two in verse 32a. Indeed, that sharp contrast would seem to imply, quite to the contrary, that the two covenants are qualitatively distinct and that the enactment of the latter presupposes the obsolescence of the former.[4]

Second, the New Covenant is to be made with the "house of Israel and with the house of Judah." Precisely what that means will no doubt differ from interpreter to interpreter. Chances are, this interpretive decision will be determined in part by whether one begins his interpretive endeavor with the Old Testament or

---

[3] Bernard P. Robinson, "Jeremiah's New Covenant: Jer 31,31–34," *Scandinavian Journal of the Old Testament* 15, no. 2 (2001): 188.

[4] W. L. Holladay, *Jeremiah 1–25*, Hermeneia (Philadelphia: Fortress Press, 1986), 9.

with the New.[5] In any case, there can be little doubt that Jeremiah himself, and those to whom he prophesied, would have understood the "house of Israel" and the "house of Judah" to refer to those two literal political units that together composed the divided Jewish nation. That the perpetuity of that people is guaranteed shortly thereafter, in 31:35–37, supports this contention.

Third, the period in which the New Covenant will be enacted is the eschaton. The phrase introducing this passage ("days are coming," יָמִים בָּאִים) as well as possibly the phrase "after those days" (אַחֲרֵי הַיָּמִים) in verse 33 are eschatological formulae, denoting a remote future timeframe for the fulfillment of this prophecy.[6]

Fourth, it will result in Yahweh putting His law "within" His people and writing it "on their heart."[7] Note the contrast between the internalization of God's law under the New Covenant and the breaking of God's law under the old covenant (v. 32). This is a crucial difference between the two covenants: laws inscribed on stone tablets may be broken just as surely as the stone tablets themselves may be dashed to pieces when hurled to the ground in a flash of golden-calf-inspired rage, but laws inscribed on the human heart are another matter entirely. This placing of the law

---

[5] Timothy M. Willis, "'I Will Remember Their Sins No More': Jeremiah 31, the New Covenant, and the Forgiveness of Sins," *Restoration Quarterly* 53, no. 1 (January 2011): 4.

[6] Walter C. Kaiser Jr., "The Old Promise and the New Covenant: Jeremiah 31:31–34," *Journal of the Evangelical Theological Society* 15, no. 1 (Wint 1972): 19.

[7] Whether or not this law referred to by Jeremiah should be identified with the Mosaic Law is disputed. A good case can be made that the law of the New Covenant is distinct from the Mosaic Law. See Femi Adeyemi, "What Is the New Covenant 'Law' in Jeremiah 31:33?" *Bibliotheca Sacra* 163, no. 651 (July 2006): 312–321.

within God's people appears to be the means by which fidelity to the terms of the New Covenant will be achieved.

Fifth, it will result in covenantal fellowship between Yahweh and His people: "I will be their God, and they shall be my people." Obviously, this was the goal of the old covenant as well (cf. Ex 29:45–46; Lev 26:12), but since that covenant was broken it appears that the goal was never fully realized. The almost utopian language used by Jeremiah to describe the New Covenant suggests that where the old covenant failed, the new will succeed.

Sixth, the scope of application will be universal in some sense: "they will all know me, from the least of them to the greatest of them." Potter's analysis is worthwhile: "This then is what is new about the covenant: it will no longer be mediated by scribes and the elite, but will be universally apprehended by one and all, from the greatest to the least. God and ordinary men are linked at last."[8]

Seventh, the forgiveness of sins is central to the operation of the New Covenant. The barrier of sinfulness that continued to separate God from His people throughout their history will finally be removed.[9]   The covenantal relationship envisioned will therefore be one of full and unrestrained fellowship between God and man.

These seven characteristics likely do not describe the New Covenant exhaustively, but they do provide us with a general and multifaceted picture of what that covenant will look like. In the present chapter, these characteristics serve as a kind of measuring standard by which the legitimacy of posited references to the New Covenant may be evaluated.

---

[8] Harry D. Potter, "The New Covenant in Jeremiah 31:31–34," *Vetus Testamentum* 33, no. 3 (Jul 1983): 353.

[9] Bernard P. Robinson, "Jeremiah's New Covenant: Jer 31,31–34," 201.

Jeremiah 32:37–40

³⁷ Behold, I will gather them out of all the lands to which I have driven them in My anger, in My wrath and in great indignation; and I will bring them back to this place and make them dwell in safety. ³⁸ They shall be My people, and I will be their God; ³⁹ and I will give them one heart and one way, that they may fear Me always, for their own good and for the good of their children after them. ⁴⁰ I will make an everlasting covenant with them that I will not turn away from them, to do them good; and I will put the fear of Me in their hearts so that they will not turn away from Me.

The parallels between this passage and Jeremiah 31:31–34 are immediately evident. "They shall be my people and I will be their God" in verse 38 is conceptually identical to "I will be their God and they shall be my people" in 31:33, characteristic #5. The impartation of "one heart" likely describes the same phenomenon as characteristic #4 (Yahweh writing His law "on their heart"). This also seems to be reflected in the perpetual fear of God resulting from this covenant (i.e., perpetual fidelity). These parallels with 31:31–34—including nearly verbatim language in some cases—strongly support a New Covenant referent for this passage.

Verse 37 makes mention of the eschatological regathering of the people of Israel to their historic homeland. While this verse clearly connects the passage to the eschatological timeframe of the New Covenant (characteristic #3), it would probably be overreaching to include the regathering of Israel as one of the features of the New Covenant. Although the two will apparently be executed almost simultaneously, it seems preferable to see Israel's regathering as a prerequisite condition necessary for the fulfillment of the New Covenant rather than part and parcel with it.[10]

Verse 40 introduces an important characteristic to the description of the New Covenant features: it will be an *everlasting covenant* (ברית עולם) just like the Abrahamic Covenant (cf. Gen. 17:7). Unlike the Sinaitic Covenant, which was temporary and passed into obsolescence after the coming of Christ (Rom 6:14; 7:6; 10:4; Gal 6:15; Col 2:16–17), the New Covenant will endure forever. This, then, constitutes an eighth New Covenant characteristic from Jeremiah.

Jeremiah 50:4–5
[4] *"In those days and at that time," declares the LORD, "the sons of Israel will come, both they and the sons of Judah as well; they will go along weeping as they go, and it will be the LORD their God they will seek.* [5] *They will ask for the way to Zion, turning their faces in its direction; they will come that they may join themselves to the LORD in an everlasting covenant that will not be forgotten."*

The context in which this passage occurs is Jeremiah's prophecy of Babylon's destruction (which occupies all of chapters 50–51). Contrary to the commonly–held view that this prophecy has already been fulfilled (the dates given for fulfillment tend to vary, but most agree that the destruction in view here was concluded by 20 B.C.), a good case can be made that Babylon has *never* been destroyed in a manner consistent with the details of Jeremiah's prophecy, and that the fulfillment of Jeremiah 50–51 is yet future.[11] The destruction of Babylon envisioned by Jeremiah is

---

[10] This is somewhat analogous to the Sinaitic Covenant. The emancipation and exodus of the Israelites from Egypt were not strictly speaking features of that covenant, but were rather prerequisites for the covenant's establishment.

[11] Charles H. Dyer, "The identity of Babylon in Revelation 17–18," *Bibliotheca Sacra*, 144 no. 575 (Spring 1987): 444–445.

therefore probably the very same Babylonian destruction predicted in Rev. 18. This would necessarily assign to 50:4–5 an eschatological timeframe for fulfillment, thereby paralleling characteristic #3. Most likely, the return of Israelites to Zion is the same phenomenon as the eschatological regathering discussed in Jeremiah 32:37.

Two more New Covenant characteristics are also evident in this passage. The second party to the covenant is identified as "sons of Israel" and "sons of Judah," paralleling characteristic #2. Furthermore, this covenant is identified as an "everlasting covenant," precisely the same verbiage used to express characteristic #8 in Jeremiah 32:40. The covenant referred to in this passage is therefore almost certainly the New Covenant.

At this point, we will depart from Jeremiah and treat the remainder of the alleged New Covenant passages in canonical order for ease of reference. Before we do, however, it will be helpful to list succinctly the eight New Covenant characteristics of Jeremiah for easy consultation. They are as follows:

1.) It will be new (i.e., separate from and superseding the old covenant).
2.) It will be made with the House of Israel and the House of Judah.
3.) It will be enacted in the eschaton.
4.) It will involve Yahweh's putting his law "within" His people, and writing it "on their heart."
5.) It will result in a proper covenantal relationship between Yahweh and His people.
6.) The scope of application will be universal in some sense.
7.) Central to its operation is the forgiveness of sins.
8.) It will be an everlasting covenant.

Genesis 12:1-3
[1] Now the LORD said to Abram, "Go forth from your country, and from your relatives and from your father's house, to the land which I will show you; [2] and I will make you a great nation, and I will bless you, and make your name great; and so you shall be a blessing; [3] And I will bless those who bless you, and the one who curses you I will curse. And in you all the families of the earth will be blessed."

This passage constitutes the first iteration of the Abrahamic Covenant. The question at hand is precisely what degree of continuity may be established between this covenant and the New Covenant. Some have felt that the New Covenant is nothing more than a *renewing* of the Abrahamic Covenant, and therefore that these two covenants should not be seen as completely disparate. For at least three reasons, this interpretation is unsatisfactory.

First, both covenants are everlasting covenants (cf. Gen 17:7; Jer 32:40; 50:5). Although this might be seen as a commonality between the two covenants, and therefore grounds for conflating the two, an even greater case can be made for discontinuity from this observation. That is, if the Abrahamic Covenant is truly an everlasting covenant, then why would it ever need to be renewed? This point is especially poignant when paired with the unconditional nature of the Abrahamic Covenant (Gen 15:12, 17). If it were possible for an everlasting, unconditional covenant like this one to fall into such a state that renewal was necessary, then in what sense was it ever truly everlasting or unconditional in the first place?

Second, the New Covenant evidences several characteristics (such as the internalization of the Law, the remission of sins, and the giving of the Spirit) that are completely absent from any clear iteration of the Abrahamic Covenant. So if the New Covenant is simply a renewing of the Abrahamic Covenant, then why the new terms? Such would seem far better suited to an entirely distinct and fresh covenant than to a renewing of an old covenant. Additional support for this point comes from Paul, according to whom covenants may neither be annulled nor added to once ratified (Gal 3:15).

Third, the grounds on which continuity between the Abrahamic and New Covenants may be established are fairly shaky. The premise for such an establishment seems to be rooted in the importance of the Abrahamic Covenant to New Testament soteriology, which admittedly cannot be overstated. Thus, if one assumes that God's salvific arrangement with the Church is related in some way to the New Covenant (which many do), then it is easy to see how Genesis 12:1-3 might be taken to refer in some sense to it. After all, Paul identified the "seed" promise in the Abrahamic Covenant[12] as directly referential to Jesus Christ (Gal 3:16), and the atoning blood of Jesus is said to be the "blood of the New Covenant" (Matt 26:28; Mark 14:24; Luke 22:20; 1 Cor. 11:25). Furthermore, as we have seen, one of the central purposes of the New Covenant is redemptive in nature. So might there be a connection to be made here? Perhaps so, but such a connection would be indirect at best. The trajectory seems forced: *Promised seed -> Jesus Christ -> Jesus' blood of the New Covenant -> New Covenant.* Since the Abrahamic Covenant itself makes no mention of the Seed's blood, it would seem heavy-handed to make such a direct connection between these two covenants. Besides, as Walton has argued, the primary purpose of the Abrahamic Covenant appears to be not redemptive, but revelatory.[13] Or, in his nomenclature, it is not designed to "resolve the Eden problem (sin)," but to "resolve the Babel problem (deity falsely construed)."

---

[12] The "seed promise" is not explicitly mentioned in 12:1-3, but it begins to rise to the surface just a few verses later in v. 7, and it is generally regarded to be implicit in the promise to "make of Abraham a great nation." Furthermore, the promises made to Abraham in vv. 1-3 are frequently taken to extend also to his offspring, and ultimately to Jesus Christ.

[13] John H. Walton, *Genesis*, The NIV Application Commentary (Grand Rapids: Zondervan, 2001), 401.

That redemptive undertones necessarily accrue to the (primarily revelatory) Abrahamic Covenant is unsurprising, as the God revealed thereby is a God who has devised and ordained a grand plan to save sinners, and the universal blessing envisioned in verse 3 – at least from the perspective of systematic rather than Biblical theology – is difficult to divorce from what we now know of God's redemptive plan for the ages. So are there continuous elements between the two covenants? Of course! They are established between the same God and the same ethnic group of people, they both involve Jesus Christ (as the New Testament explicates), and both appear to be unilateral (or unconditional) covenants, in contradistinction to the conditionality of the Sinaitic Covenant. But that does not establish any overt continuity between the two covenants *per se.* One might well propose that the Abrahamic Covenant will reach its ultimate fulfillment at the same time the New Covenant is enacted (evidently the promise of worldwide blessing via Abraham's seed will reach fruition during the Millennium, which comports well with the New Covenant's eschatological timeframe – other passages will attest to this as well),[14] but that is not the same as recognizing a New Covenant reference in Genesis 12. In the final analysis, no such connection between the two covenants is supportable.

Isaiah 55:3
³ "Incline your ear and come to Me. Listen, that you may live; and I will make an everlasting covenant with you, according to the faithful mercies shown to David."

---

[14] Alva J. McClain, *The Greatness of the Kingdom* (Winona Lake: BMH Books, 1959), 212.

As we approach this verse, we should take notice that it is written to Israelites,[15] that the utopian undertones with which the immediate context is saturated are suggestive of an eschatological (more specifically, a *Millennial*) fulfillment timeframe, and that the covenant mentioned here is said to be everlasting. Those three factors constitute occurrences of New Covenant characteristics #2, #3, and #8, so the odds that this verse refers to the New Covenant are good. But what are we to make of the (somewhat startling) reference to King David?

The exegetical problems posed by חסדי דוד are impossible to deal with in a chapter of this length. However, if we accept the standard view (namely, that this construction is an objective genitive),[16] then we would seem to have good warrant in classifying Is 55:3 as a New Covenant passage. The faithful mercies shown to (lit. "of") David, if an objective genitive, would be the blessings promised to David in the Davidic Covenant. We know that the Davidic Covenant is ultimately fulfilled by Jesus Christ, who will "reign over the house of Jacob" and whose kingdom "will have no end" (Luke 1:33). Furthermore, Jesus is inextricably connected to the New Covenant: His blood ratifies it (Luke 22:20; 1 Cor 11:25), He is said to be its mediator (Heb 9:15; 12:24), and He, it would seem, will be the one to establish it at His Second Coming.

So, although sparse in details, Isaiah 55:3 does apparently refer to the New Covenant. The Davidic Covenant is related to the New Covenant not in that the two are identical, but in that the one who fulfills the former will also establish the latter. Thus, two covenants are referenced in this passage: the New Covenant

---

[15] The audience is identified as Israelites in 52:1–2, and no shift in addressees is apparent anywhere in the intervening chapters.

[16] Peter John Gentry, "Rethinking the 'Sure Mercies of David' in Isaiah 55:3," *Westminster Theological Journal* 69, no. 2 (Fall 2007): 279.

("everlasting covenant,"), and the Davidic Covenant ("the faithful mercies shown to David").

Isaiah 59:20-21

[20] *"A Redeemer will come to Zion, and to those who turn from transgression in Jacob," declares the LORD.* [21] *"As for Me, this is My covenant with them," says the LORD: "My Spirit which is upon you, and My words which I have put in your mouth shall not depart from your mouth, nor from the mouth of your offspring, nor from the mouth of your offspring's offspring," says the LORD, "from now and forever."*

The covenant mentioned in verse 21 is most likely the New Covenant, for four reasons. First, the Apostle Paul connected this passage with the New Covenant in Rom. 11:26–27. Second, the covenant's eternal perpetuity depicted in v. 21 by means of the continuous fidelity of Israel's successive generations comports well with the eighth New Covenant characteristic. Third, the scope of this covenant's fulfillment is clearly nationalistic (cf. "Zion" and "Jacob" in v. 20), paralleling Jeremiah's second characteristic. Fourth, this passage introduces a ninth New Covenant characteristic (the giving of the Spirit) which, as we shall see, will be repeated in several other New Covenant texts. The first-person singular suffix on "Spirit" (רוּחִי) strongly suggests that the Holy Spirit is in view. Whether or not the giving of the Spirit directly *causes* eschatological Israel's perpetual fidelity is not entirely clear from the grammar of the text, but as Church-age believers with a more robust understanding of the Spirit's work of regeneration, we are perhaps justified in speculating that the two are indeed causally connected.

In this passage, Isaiah has contributed an important ninth New Covenant characteristic to the original list of eight derived from Jeremiah's prophecies. That list may therefore be revised as follows:

1.) It will be new (i.e., separate from and superseding the old covenant).
2.) It will be made with the House of Israel and the House of Judah.
3.) It will be enacted in the eschaton.
4.) It will involve Yahweh's putting his law "within" His people, and writing it "on their heart."
5.) It will result in a proper covenantal relationship between Yahweh and His people.
6.) The scope of application will be universal in some sense.
7.) Central to its operation is the forgiveness of sins.
8.) It will be an everlasting covenant.
9.) It will involve the giving of the Spirit.

Ezekiel 11:17–20
[17] Therefore say, 'Thus says the Lord GOD, "I will gather you from the peoples and assemble you out of the countries among which you have been scattered, and I will give you the land of Israel."' [18] When they come there, they will remove all its detestable things and all its abominations from it. [19] And I will give them one heart, and put a new spirit within them. And I will take the heart of stone out of their flesh and give them a heart of flesh, [20] that they may walk in My statutes and keep My ordinances and do them. Then they will be My people, and I shall be their God."

In this revelation given to Ezekiel, it appears that more than one covenant is referred to. The giving of the land of Israel in verse 17 would seem to be a fulfillment of the land–promise element of the Abrahamic Covenant, but the actions described in verses 18–20 seem to relate more to the New Covenant. Several of Jeremiah's descriptive characteristics of the New Covenant may be seen in these verses. First, the audience addressed here comprises Israelites (cf. vv. 15–16), which parallels characteristic #2. Second, the reference to replacing their "heart of stone" with a "heart of flesh" parallels characteristic #4 (the writing of God's law in "their heart"), as does the prediction that they will keep God's statutes and ordinances (since the law has now been internalized, it presumably will not be broken as the external law of the Sinaitic Covenant had been). Third, the latter part of verse 20 parallels characteristic #5, "they will be My people, and I shall be their God" being identical in Hebrew to Jeremiah 32:38.

Furthermore, Isaiah's ninth New Covenant characteristic, the giving of the Spirit, makes an appearance here (v. 19). Note that the placement of this item directly between Jeremiah's third and fifth New Covenant characteristics strongly suggests that the giving of the Spirit is not an event separate from (though simultaneous with) the New Covenant's enactment, but is actually an integral part of the New Covenant proceedings. In light of all these parallels, it is safe to say that this verse seems clearly referential to the New Covenant. Bear in mind that the juxtaposition of Abrahamic and New Covenant fulfillments does not imply that the two covenants are meant to be conflated, merely that they will be fulfilled in the same general timeframe (the eschaton, cf. Jeremiah's characteristic #3).

Ezekiel 16:59–62

59 For thus says the Lord GOD, "I will also do with you as you have done, you who have despised the oath by breaking the covenant. 60 "Nevertheless, I will remember My covenant with you in the days of your youth, and I will establish an everlasting covenant with you. 61 Then you will remember your ways and be ashamed when you receive your sisters, both your older and your younger; and I will give them to you as daughters, but not because of your covenant. 62 Thus I will establish My covenant with you, and you shall know that I am the LORD, 63 so that you may remember and be ashamed and never open your mouth anymore because of your humiliation, when I have forgiven you for all that you have done," the Lord GOD declares.

Whereas Ezekiel 11:17–20 referred to two covenants (Abrahamic and New), this passage seems to refer to three: the Sinaitic in verse 59 (which Israel broke), the Abrahamic in v. 60a (which was made "in the days of [Israel's] youth"), and the New in verses 60b and 62 (which is yet to be established in the future). That the third covenant is in fact the New Covenant is supported by several parallels between its description in this passage and what we know to be characteristic of the New Covenant from passages already surveyed.

First, this covenant is to be established in the future (New Covenant characteristic #3).[17]   Note that the "everlasting covenant" (ברית עולם) in v. 60 is not identified with the covenant made "in the days of [Israel's] youth," but appears alongside it as a separate covenant.[18]   Although the establishment-language is admittedly reminiscent of Genesis 17:7, here that establishment is cast as yet future, which would seem to indicate a covenant separate from the Abrahamic (which has already been established). Furthermore, the "sisters" mentioned in verse 61 (Sodom and Samaria) are future *restored* versions of the ancient cities which had received God's wrath (cf. vv. 53, 55). Many have noted the difficulty of identifying any such historical restoration of Sodom,[19] so a yet future fulfillment (even from our perspective) to Ezekiel's prophecy comports best with the details of the situation described. That being the case, the New Covenant is most likely the one in view.

---

[17] Actually, futurity by itself does not necessitate an eschatological frame of reference. But the fact that these verses have not been obviously fulfilled at any point in Ezekiel's future right up to the present is strongly suggestive of an eschatological frame of reference.

[18] Some have attempted to identify this covenant with the Abrahamic, but the grammar of v. 60 as well as the overall thrust of the passage renders such an identification rather dubious.

[19] Marten H. Woudstra, "Everlasting Covenant in Eze 16:59–63," *Calvin Theological Journal* 6, no. 1 (April 1971): 35.

Second, Jeremiah's seventh characteristic (the forgiveness of Israel's sins) makes an appearance in v. 63. So this covenant is both future to Ezekiel's time (and, as we have seen, to ours) and it involves the forgiveness of sins; does this not sound like the New Covenant? It certainly seems more likely that Ezekiel here refers to the New Covenant than that he is discussing a future covenant entirely distinct from any other mentioned in Scripture. Therefore, we are justified in classifying this text as a *bona fide* New Covenant text.

Ezekiel 36:25–32
24 "For I will take you from the nations, gather you from all the lands and bring you into your own land. 25 Then I will sprinkle clean water on you, and you will be clean; I will cleanse you from all your filthiness and from all your idols. 26 Moreover, I will give you a new heart and put a new spirit within you; and I will remove the heart of stone from your flesh and give you a heart of flesh. 27 I will put My Spirit within you and cause you to walk in My statutes, and you will be careful to observe My ordinances. 28 You will live in the land that I gave to your forefathers; so you will be My people, and I will be your God. 29 Moreover, I will save you from all your uncleanness; and I will call for the grain and multiply it, and I will not bring a famine on you. 30 I will multiply the fruit of the tree and the produce of the field, so that you will not receive again the disgrace of famine among the nations. 31 Then you will remember your evil ways and your deeds that were not good, and you will loathe yourselves in your own sight for your iniquities and your abominations. 32 I am not doing this for your sake," declares the Lord GOD, "let it be known to you. Be ashamed and confounded for your ways, O house of Israel!"

In this passage, which is probably the single most detailed text on regeneration in the Old Testament, New Covenant language abounds. Verse 22 reveals that the addressee is national Israel (characteristic #2). Furthermore, the phenomena predicted include the giving of a new heart and the concomitant internalization of God's law in verses 26–27 (characteristic #4), the giving of the Spirit in verse 27 (characteristic #9), the establishment of proper covenantal relationship between God and the nation in verse 28 (characteristic #5), and the forgiveness of sins in verse 29 (characteristic #7). Moreover, a good case can be made for the eschatological timeframe of this passage. For one thing, the regathering in verse 24 is very possibly the same eschatological regathering mentioned in other confirmed New Covenant texts (Jer 32:37; 50:4–5). For another, the land's bountiful produce in verses 29–30 is reminiscent of other prophetic descriptions of the eschatological Messianic Kingdom, such as Micah 4:4 (cf. Mic 4:1 for proof of an eschatological timeframe). So it is altogether likely that an eschatological timeframe is also implied in this text (characteristic #3).

But might it not be proposed that the regathering mentioned here is actually the historical regathering following the Babylonian Captivity, and that the forgiveness of sins and restoration of proper fellowship with God actually refer to the reinstitution of the Mosaic system in Ezra 3 and following? Perhaps, but such an interpretation runs into problems quite quickly. The sweeping forgiveness of sins and national regeneration depicted by Ezekiel was rather grossly exaggerated if the post-exilic years are in view. After all, Ezekiel's language seems ill-suited to, say, the late sixth century B.C., when the prophets Haggai and Zechariah had to castigate the people for neglecting the Lord's affairs. (Evidently the people were none too responsive, given the similar indictments delivered by Malachi about a century later.)

Besides, if this passage is to be applied to the post-exilic years, then what are we to make of the giving of the Spirit? Surely the Spirit was not given prior to the glorification of Jesus, as John 7:39 attests. That being the case, perhaps we could connect Ezekiel's prophecy to the Day of Pentecost in Acts 2 and apply the New Covenant to the Church, just subsequent to Christ's death, burial, resurrection, and ascension! But that will not do either, for to do so we must neglect the national regathering in verse 24, the occupation of the Holy Land in verse 28, and the abundant harvest in verses 29–30, none of which can be construed as descriptive of the Church's inception. A far better interpretive option is to see the timeframe as eschatological (i.e., Millennial) and the application of the New Covenant as to a freshly reconstituted Israel, newly regathered into her historic homeland in the wake of an earlier eschatological dispersion (cf. Rev 12:14ff.).

Ezekiel 37:14, 23, 26
[14] "I will put My Spirit within you and you will come to life, and I will place you on your own land. Then you will know that I, the LORD, have spoken and done it," declares the LORD. . . . [23] "They will no longer defile themselves with their idols, or with their detestable things, or with any of their transgressions; but I will deliver them from all their dwelling places in which they have sinned, and will cleanse them. And they will be My people, and I will be their God. . . . [26] I will make a covenant of peace with them; it will be an everlasting covenant with them. And I will place them and multiply them, and will set My sanctuary in their midst forever."

For the sake of simplicity, these three verses have been singled out when in fact the entire chapter constitutes one lengthy discourse, most of which could be said to refer to the New Covenant. Essentially the same comments made of the previous passage may also be made of this one. The giving of the Spirit (characteristic #9) is evident in verse 14, as well as possibly a change of heart/internalization of the law (i.e. regeneration), assuming "you will come to life" is meant to be understood in terms of spiritual rather than physical life. In any case, the national regeneration is finally explicated in verse 23, along with the restoration of proper covenantal relationship (characteristic #5). The covenant itself is mentioned in verse 26, and it is designated an everlasting covenant (characteristic #8). Further-more, verse 16 of this chapter specifies that the addressees are Israel and Judah (characteristic #2). Once again, the timeframe is likely eschatological even though these two verses do not say so explicitly. The references to national regathering in the immediate context imply as much (vv. 21–22), as do the unfulfilled prophecies in the course of the text. Ezekiel says that the twelve tribes will be reunited under one king (v. 22), that they will thereafter live in the land forever (v. 25), and that the temple established at that time will stand forever (v. 26). Only by extreme leaps of logic can these statements make any sense in a historical post–exilic Israel, since those years saw Israel's monarchy ended, her temple destroyed, and her people dispersed! It would seem clear, then, that this passage is indeed a New Covenant passage, and that its fulfillment awaits a future occasion.

Hosea 1:9–11
⁹ And the LORD said, "Name him Lo-ammi, for you are not My people and I am not your God."   ¹⁰ Yet the number of the sons of Israel will be like the sand of the sea, which cannot be measured or numbered; and in the place where it is said to them, "You are not My people," it will be said to them, "You are the sons of the living God." ¹¹ And the sons of Judah and the sons of Israel will be gathered together, And they will appoint for themselves one leader, And they will go up from the land, For great will be the day of Jezreel."

This passage is quite sparse on details when it comes to the New Covenant, which makes dogmatism difficult. Nevertheless, the contrast between the present state of alienation between God and Israel and the future state of a restored relationship in these verses sounds quite a lot like New Covenant characteristic #5. As with other New Covenant texts, we see the establishment of the covenant and the regathering of national Israel into the land intertwined. Again, this probably bespeaks an eschatological timeframe (characteristic #3). The reference to Israel's sons being immeasurable and innumerable also bespeaks Yahweh's covenant faithfulness, but with this item it would appear to be faithfulness to the Abrahamic rather than to the New Covenant. This is not problematic, however; several passages surveyed in this chapter have already made reference to two or more separate covenants (including the New Covenant) in the space of a few verses. So, it is quite likely that this passage does refer to the New Covenant, but it is difficult to be as certain as we might be with other passages.

Before we move on to other passages, however, a word of caution concerning the application of this verse is in order. Commentators have long observed an interpretive conundrum connected with Paul's quotation of this passage in Romans 9:26. The oddity is that Hosea clearly addressed his remarks solely to Israelites, but Paul quotes the verse when discussing the inclusion of Gentiles in God's salvific plan.[20] Many have capitalized on this observation, concluding that Hosea 1:10 does indeed apply directly to Gentile Christians,[21] so the inspired New Testament text has expanded the scope of Hosea's addressees after the fact. This, in turn, is taken as clear apostolic endorsement of complementary hermeneutics.

I feel burdened to stress that this interpretation is unnecessary, and serves only to muddy the entire enterprise of Biblical interpretation. The language used by Paul in Romans 19:25–26 is not the language of application, but of comparison (ως και εν τω Ωσηε λεγει). His intention is therefore not to draw a 1:1 application as though this prophecy were directly fulfilled by the Church, but rather to illustrate his point with a Biblical

---

[20] Douglas J. Moo, *The Epistle to the Romans*, The New International Commentary on the New Testament (Grand Rapids: Eerdmans, 1996), 613.

[21] E.g. Luke Timothy Johnson, *Reading Romans: A Literary and Theological Commentary* (Macon: Smyth & Helwys Pub., 2001), 164; James R. Edwards, *Romans*, New International Biblical Commentary (Peabody: Hendrickson Publishers, 1992), 242.

principle much in the same way that we use sermon illustrations in our pulpits today. So, if this passage is taken to refer to the New Covenant (which is certainly plausible), keep in mind that Romans 9:26 does not necessitate an extension of that covenant beyond the scope of Hosea's original addressees.

Hosea 2:18–23
[18] "In that day I will also make a covenant for them with the beasts of the field, the birds of the sky and the creeping things of the ground. And I will abolish the bow, the sword and war from the land, and will make them lie down in safety. [19] I will betroth you to Me forever; yes, I will betroth you to Me in righteousness and in justice, in lovingkindness and in compassion, [20] And I will betroth you to Me in faithfulness. Then you will know the LORD. [21] It will come about in that day that I will respond," declares the LORD. "I will respond to the heavens, and they will respond to the earth, [22] And the earth will respond to the grain, to the new wine and to the oil, And they will respond to Jezreel. [23] I will sow her for Myself in the land. I will also have compassion on her who had not obtained compassion, and I will say to those who were not My people, 'You are My people!' And they will say, 'You are my God!'"

At first glance, this passage appears to make reference to the New Covenant. The addressees are Hosea's "mother" and her "children of harlotry," (vv. 2, 4) a clear reference to unbelieving Israel (otherwise the language of an injured marital relationship to be restored in the future by the husband's – Yahweh's – faithful pursuit, makes little sense). This is clearly in line with New Covenant characteristic #2, so we are on firm ground from the very beginning. Furthermore, the restoration of a proper covenantal relationship (characteristic #5) can be seen in verses

19–20, 22,[22] and an eschatological timeframe (characteristic #3) can be seen in the language of peace (v. 18, cf. Mic 4:3), and of bountiful harvest (vv. 21–22, cf. Mic 4:4; Ezek 36:29–30). Furthermore, if we take "she is not my wife, and I am not her husband" in verse 2 to refer to the dissolution of Israel's "marriage" to Yahweh (which marriage was presumably established with the enactment of the Sinaitic Covenant) and the reconciliatory language of verses 19–20 as the future "remarriage" of Israel and Yahweh, then there would appear to be New Covenantal undertones in that the obsolete old marriage covenant is superseded by the new marriage covenant (characteristic #1).

So a strong argument can be built for the New Covenant reference of this passage. On the other hand, a problem arises when we consider the usage of "covenant" (בְּרִית) in verse 18. While Israelites are the addressees of this discourse, the covenant in verse 18 does not seem to be enacted between Yahweh and Israel. On the contrary, Yahweh establishes (or mediates)[23] the covenant, but the two parties specified are Israel on the one hand and the animal kingdom on the other! While there is good prophetic precedent for the pacification of the animal kingdom in the Millennium (Is 11:6–8; 65:25; Ezek 34:25; cf. Rom 8:19–22), there is no clear indication that it is directly connected to the New Covenant, or that the animal kingdom will constitute an

---

[22] Admittedly, it is valid to question just how much overlap there can be between the actual historical and future covenants enacted between Yahweh and His people on the one hand, and the metaphorical marriage covenants employed rhetorically in this discourse on the other. That being said, however, note that the interchange at the end of v. 23 is descriptive of a divine–human rather than a husband–wife relationship, and that it mirrors quite closely the New Covenant language of Jer 31:3, 32:38; Ezek 37:27.

[23] Robert B. Chisholm Jr., "Hosea," in *The Bible Knowledge Commentary*, edited by John F. Walvoord and Roy B. Zuck, 1377–1407, Old Testament ed. (Wheaton: Victor Books, 1985), 1386.

additional interested party to that covenant. So while characteristic #3 garners even further support and characteristic #5 is unaffected, characteristic #2 must fall (at least insofar as the covenant of verse 18 is concerned), and with it any certainty that this passage is in fact a New Covenant passage.

What are we to make of this? In the final analysis, perhaps we should conclude that while this passage does seem to refer *indirectly* to the New Covenant (several of its elements are clearly seen in this discourse), it does not do so *directly*, and in fact the only covenant explicitly mentioned is a different covenant altogether. This passage discusses in broad, sweeping strokes several eschatological blessings that will attach to Israel in the Millennium. As such, New Covenant blessings are mentioned, but so are other blessings not directly connected to that covenant.

As an aside, it seems likely that the "covenant" that is mentioned in verse 18 is used merely rhetorically to refer to the establishment of a new (non–violent) relationship between Israel (and mankind in general) on the one hand and the animal kingdom on the other. We need not conclude that there will be a literal covenant established between these two parties (as though animals were granted sentience), complete with a covenantal sign, covenantal oath, and enactment ritual! Such a literalistic interpretation is of course possible, but probably not necessary in this case, given the rhetorical nature of the discourse and the somewhat absurd requirements necessitated by such an interpretation.

Joel 2:28–29
[28] *"It will come about after this that I will pour out My Spirit on all mankind; and your sons and daughters will prophesy, your old men will dream dreams, your young men will see visions.* [29] *even on the male and female servants I will pour out My Spirit in those days."*

Pettegrew concludes from this passage (and others) that "the outpouring of the Spirit was an important part of a series of events that would initiate the eschatological period."[24] From our survey of Isaiah's and Ezekiel's New Covenant texts, we have already arrived at the same conclusion, and have furthermore identified the eschatological giving of the Spirit as one of the terms of the New Covenant. It is immediately evident that this characteristic (#8) is the main thrust of Joel 2:28–29. It is not, however, the only New Covenant characteristic mentioned. Verses 23 and 26–27 indicate that the addressees are Israelites (characteristic #2), and the repetition of "the Day of Yahweh" in vv. 1, 11, and 31 marks the timeframe as eschatological (characteristic #3).

Furthermore, it should be pointed out that "all flesh" (the NASB's "all mankind" is probably a poor translation of כָּל בָּשָׂר in this case) most likely refers not to all people in the world but rather to all people in Israel. This is the most natural reading as the immediate surrounding context gives every indication that Israel alone is under consideration for the duration of this discourse. The sense is not so much "all flesh everywhere [cutting across ethnic lines]," but rather "all flesh [in Israel] without distinction." In other words, unlike in Israel's former days when only select individuals received the Spirit (such as David the king, Balaam the prophet, and Samson the judge), the days following the establishment of the New Covenant will herald the giving of the Spirit to all Israelites without distinction. This is evident in the three merisms (1. sons and daughters; 2. old men and young men; 3. male and female servants) as well as in the contrast between the servants in verse 29 and the (presumably free) recipients of the Spirit in verse 28. Note that if this reading is correct, then that constitutes yet another New Covenant characteristic: #6.

So, chances are very good that Joel's prophecy is indeed predictive of the New Covenant. As for the somewhat thorny issue of how this passage's meaning in its original context relates to its

---

[24] Larry D. Pettegrew, *The New Covenant Ministry of the Holy Spirit*, 2nd ed. (Grand Rapids: Kregel, 2001), 40.

quotation by Peter on the Day of Pentecost, that will be addressed shortly.

The Last Supper (Matt 26:28; Mark 14:24; Luke 22:20; 1 Cor 11:25)

Matt 26:28 for this is My blood of the covenant, which is poured out for many for forgiveness of sins."

Mark 14:24 And He said to them, "This is My blood of the covenant, which is poured out for many."

Luke 22:20 And in the same way He took the cup after they had eaten, saying, "This cup which is poured out for you is the New Covenant in My blood."

1 Cor 11:25 In the same way He took the cup also after supper, saying, "This cup is the New Covenant in My blood; do this, as often as you drink it, in remembrance of Me."

During the Last Supper, as He passed the cup of wine to His disciples, Jesus made a clear connection between His blood and the New Covenant (η καινη διαθηκη). Therefore, these passages should definitely be regarded as relating directly to the New Covenant. That being said, the question of *whether or not* they relate to the New Covenant is far more easily answered than the question of *what precisely they say* about it. To say that Jesus' blood is directly connected to the New Covenant, and even perhaps that Jesus' blood ratifies the New Covenant, is fully supportable from (and possibly even demanded by) these passages.[25]

---

[25] Robert A. Peterson, *Salvation Accomplished by the Son: The Work of Christ* (Wheaton: Crossway, 2011), 217.

On the other hand, to assert (as most do)[26] that the New Covenant was enacted, established, or inaugurated at the time of Jesus' crucifixion, does not appear to be a necessary conclusion from these passages. They do assert that Jesus's blood is the blood of the New Covenant, and even that it is to be poured out for many for the remission of sins,[27] but they do not directly connect the New Covenant to the "many" whose sins are being remitted, save of course for the obvious fact that the blood accomplishing the remission just so happens to be the same blood that ratifies the covenant. Does that imply that the remission to which Jesus refers is to be identified specifically and exclusively with the particular redemption described in Jeremiah 31:34? That is a *possible* conclusion (and the question undoubtedly warrants further exegetical attention), but it would not seem to be a *necessary* conclusion, since Jesus Himself does not make any such identification explicit.

Acts 2:16–18

[16] but this is what was spoken of through the prophet Joel: [17] 'AND IT SHALL BE IN THE LAST DAYS,' God says, 'THAT I WILL POUR FORTH OF MY SPIRIT ON ALL MANKIND; AND YOUR SONS AND YOUR DAUGHTERS SHALL PROPHESY, AND YOUR YOUNG MEN SHALL SEE VISIONS, AND YOUR OLD MEN SHALL DREAM DREAMS; [18] EVEN ON MY BONDSLAVES, BOTH MEN AND WOMEN, I WILL IN THOSE DAYS POUR FORTH OF MY SPIRIT and they shall prophesy."

We have already determined that Joel 2:28–29, which Peter quotes here, is a New Covenant passage, so it would seem a

---

[26] E.g., L. Morris, *Luke* (Downers Grove: IVP Academic, 1974), 334–335; D.L. Bock, *Luke* (Downers Grove: InterVarsity Press, 1994), 350; J. Reiling and J. L. Swellengrebel, *A Translator's Handbook on the Gospel of Luke* (Leiden: Brill, 1971), 688.

[27] Luke further seems to identify the "many" with the disciples in his somewhat peculiar rendering of the sentence.

simple matter to conclude that this, too, is a New Covenant passage. After all, Peter establishes a link between Joel's prophecy and the Day of Pentecost, and Joel's prophecy – as we have seen – concerns the New Covenant, so the conclusion appears to be a simple one. Unfortunately, in this case such an interpretive approach is simplistic to the point of deficiency. It is one thing to say that Peter connects Joel's prophecy to the Day of Pentecost; it is another thing entirely to determine the precise relationship between the two that Peter posited.

The interpretation of the passage ultimately turns on the meaning of the introductory formula, τουτο εστιν το ειρημενον (literally, "this is that which has been spoken"). One option is that Peter sees in the events of the Day of Pentecost a direct fulfillment of some or all of Joel's prophecy. This is the view espoused by the majority of interpreters.[28] The second option, which I find much more exegetically satisfying, is that Peter is drawing a comparison between the Spirit's activity in Joel's prophecy and the Spirit's activity on the Day of Pentecost, without actually establishing a one to one fulfillment. While this is definitely a minority opinion, it is not without scholarly support.[29]

---

[28] E.g. Darrell L. Bock, *Acts*, Baker Exegetical Commentary on the New Testament (Grand Rapids: Baker Academic, 2007), 112; Richard N. Longenecker, "The Acts of the Apostles," in *The Expositor's Bible Commentary*, edited by Frank E. Gaebelein, 9:206–573 (Grand Rapids: Zondervan, 1981), 275; I. Howard Marshall, *Acts*, The Tyndale New Testament Commentaries (Grand Rapids: Eerdmans, 1980), 74; Pettegrew, *The New Covenant Ministry of the Holy Spirit*, 104–105.

[29] E.g. Arnold G. Fruchtenbaum, "Rabbinic Quotations of the Old Testament and How It Relates to Joel 2 and Acts 2," Paper presented to the Pre-Trib Study Group, Dallas, TX (December 2002), 5–7; Thomas Ice, "Peter's Quotation of Joel in Acts 2," *Midnight Call* (April 2007), 22–26; Russell L. Penney, "Joel, Eschatology Of," in *Dictionary of Premillennial Theology*, edited by Mal Couch, 213–216 (Grand Rapids: Kregel, 1996), 215.

Several considerations are noteworthy. First, the language of the introductory formula does not demand a literal fulfillment of Joel's prophecy. Pettegrew argues that "this is that" is regularly used to express fulfillment, selectively citing Acts 4:11 and 7:37–38. But other usages of this formula in the New Testament indicate loose comparison rather than direct correspondence (Matt 26:26; Mark 14:22–24; Luke 22:19; 1 Pet 1:24–25), so literal fulfillment is not necessitated on grammatical grounds.

Second, it should be fairly obvious upon reflection that the events of Joel's prophecy simply were not fulfilled in Acts 2. The wonders manifested on the Day of Pentecost were a sound like a mighty rushing wind and the appearance of tongues of fire (Acts 2:2–3), not blood, columns of smoke, the darkening of the sun, and the reddening of the moon (Joel 2:29–30). The manifestation of the Spirit's power comprised speaking in tongues (Acts 2:4), not prophesying, dreams, and visions (Joel 2:28–29). Furthermore, the Spirit was apparently only poured out on the twelve apostles on the Day of Pentecost (Acts 2:1), not on "all flesh" (Joel 2:28). So if Peter really did believe that Joel's prophecy was being fulfilled on the Day of Pentecost, then it must be said that that assessment was objectively and demonstrably incorrect.[30]

Third, as we have already seen, the timeframe set by Joel for the fulfillment of his prophecy is the Day of the LORD (Joel 2:1, 11, 31). But about twenty years after Peter's sermon on the Day of Pentecost, Paul explicitly denied in his second epistle to the Thessalonians that the Day of the LORD had already arrived (2

---

[30] Remember that prophecies must be fulfilled precisely as they were initially stated by God's prophet; there is no margin for error or exaggeration. For example, Jesus was literally virgin–born, He actually rode into Jerusalem on a donkey, soldiers really did cast lots for His garments, and He was indeed "pierced for our transgressions" and "crushed for our iniquities." This principle is paradigmatic of true prophecy to the point that any prophecy that does not come true exactly as prophesied, did not originate from God (Deut 18:21–22).

Thess 2:2–3). Thus, it is exceedingly problematic to see a literal fulfillment of Joel's prophecy on the Day of Pentecost, as doing so would necessitate pitting one inspired text against another, and severely muddling the eschatological scheme presented by the New Testament.

Most likely, Peter's point in quoting Joel is this: "Men of Judea, this phenomenon [speaking in tongues] is not the product of drunkenness as you mistakenly suppose. Rather, it is the product of the outpouring of the Spirit. Just as Joel foretold signs and wonders effected by the Spirit's outpouring, so also these signs and wonders are effected by the Spirit's outpouring." Peter thus applies an aspect of Joel's prophecy (the giving of the Spirit bringing about miraculous signs) to his present situation without applying the entirety of the prophecy itself. Acts 2:16–18 is therefore most likely *not* a New Covenant text, despite the fact that it quotes one.

Romans 9:25–26
[25] *As He says also in Hosea, "I WILL CALL THOSE WHO WERE NOT MY PEOPLE, 'MY PEOPLE,' AND HER WHO WAS NOT BELOVED, 'BELOVED.'* [26] *AND IT SHALL BE THAT IN THE PLACE WHERE IT WAS SAID TO THEM, 'YOU ARE NOT MY PEOPLE,' THERE THEY SHALL BE CALLED SONS OF THE LIVING GOD."*

See comments made under the section on Hosea 1:9–11. Much like the previous passage (Acts 2:16–18), this quotation of an Old Testament text entails comparison rather than fulfillment. Romans 9:25–26 should not be regarded as referential to the New Covenant, except as a sort of "sermon illustration" to Paul's main point (the inclusion of Gentiles in God's salvific plan).

Romans 11:26-27

26 *and so all Israel will be saved; just as it is written, "THE DELIVERER WILL COME FROM ZION, HE WILL REMOVE UNGODLINESS FROM JACOB."* 27 *THIS IS MY COVENANT WITH THEM, WHEN I TAKE AWAY THEIR SINS."*

At this point in his epistle to the Romans, Paul is seeking to answer the question "has God rejected His people [Israel] (11:1)?" After all, if (as Paul has asserted) justification renders a sinner absolutely just before God, and if living in a manner consistent with that justification yields a life of sanctification, and if the guaranteed end result of justification is majestic glorification, then how does one explain the fact that Israel has apparently been cast aside by God? Paul's answer is that God indeed has *not* rejected Israel (v. 1). Rather, the nation of Israel has been temporarily set aside insofar as God's economy is concerned, but it will be taken up again after the "fullness of the Gentiles" has been completed (vv. 15-25). This is the context in which verses 26-27, the climax of Paul's discourse on Israel's future, occur.

Immediately, then, we begin to see commonalities with the characteristics of the New Covenant. From the *future* restoration of Israel, it is no great stretch to posit the *eschatological* restoration of Israel, which would comport with New Covenant characteristic #3. Note also that the object of salvation is "all Israel" (πας Ισραηλ), likely reflecting characteristics #2 and #6. The salvation itself is defined in terms of the forgiveness of sins (v. 27), characteristic #7. Furthermore, the primary Old Testament text quoted here (Is 59:20-21) is one that we have already identified as a New Covenant passage. The weight of evidence, then, strongly suggests that the New Covenant is indeed in view in Romans 11:26-27.

2 Corinthians 3:6
⁶ who also made us adequate as servants of a New Covenant, not of the letter but of the Spirit; for the letter kills, but the Spirit gives life.

Two factors strongly suggest that this is indeed a New Covenant passage. First, the actual usage of the phrase "new coven- ant" (καινης διαθηκης) is obviously significant (aside from 1 Cor 11:25, this is the only occurrence of the expression in Paul's writings).[31]   Second, the language in which Paul couches his discussion is reminiscent of at least two New Covenant characteristics in that he contrasts the New Covenant with the old (vv. 6–11, characteristic #1) and alludes to the contrast between letters written on stone and letters written on the heart (vv. 2–3, characteristic #4). Because these two factors are so persuasive, virtually no commentator has disputed the New Covenant reference in this verse. Neither do I.

That being said, it is questionable whether this passage can be construed to apply the New Covenant to the church. Paul almost certainly does not include the entirety of the Church in the first-person plural pronoun (ημας), that signifies those who have been made servants (or ministers) of the New Covenant. The referent of ημας is almost certainly Paul and his ministerial companions, not the church of Corinth, let alone the universal Church.[32]

One possible understanding of this passage is that Paul's ministry is a "New Covenant ministry" insofar as his ministerial goal is to provoke his fellow Jews to jealousy and thereby bring them to salvation (Rom 11:13), the ultimate expression of Jewish salvation being, of course, the New Covenant. Another view is that

---

[31] William R. Baker, *2 Corinthians*, The College Press NIV Commentary (Joplin, MO: College Press, 1999), 141.

[32] Jarvis Williams, *One New Man: The Cross and Racial Reconciliation in Pauline Theology* (Nashville: B&H Publishing Group, 2010), 53.

"servants (or ministers) of a New Covenant" (διακονους καινης διαθηκης) is a descriptive rather than an objective genitive, and that Paul is therefore describing his ministry as a "New-Covenant-like ministry," not purporting that he actually administers the New Covenant. This view is bolstered by the fact that "New Covenant" is anarthrous in this verse, and by the somewhat loose, informal manner in which Paul customarily uses Old Testament quotations throughout 2 Corinthians. In either case, it is not exegetically necessary to deduce a direct application of the New Covenant to the Church from this passage, even though it clearly does make reference to the New Covenant.

New Covenant Passages in Hebrews
(7:22; 8:7–13; 9:15; 10:8–9; 12:22–24)

7:22 so much the more also Jesus has become the guarantee of a better covenant.

8:7-13 For if that first covenant had been faultless, there would have been no occasion sought for a second. 8 For finding fault with them, He says, "BEHOLD, DAYS ARE COMING, SAYS THE LORD, WHEN I WILL EFFECT A New Covenant WITH THE HOUSE OF ISRAEL AND WITH THE HOUSE OF JUDAH; 9 NOT LIKE THE COVENANT WHICH I MADE WITH THEIR FATHERS ON THE DAY WHEN I TOOK THEM BY THE HAND TO LEAD THEM OUT OF THE LAND OF EGYPT; FOR THEY DID NOT CONTINUE IN MY COVENANT, AND I DID NOT CARE FOR THEM, SAYS THE LORD. 10 FOR THIS IS THE COVENANT THAT I WILL MAKE WITH THE HOUSE OF ISRAEL AFTER THOSE DAYS, SAYS THE LORD: I WILL PUT MY LAWS INTO THEIR MINDS,
AND I WILL WRITE THEM ON THEIR HEARTS. AND I WILL BE THEIR GOD, AND THEY SHALL BE MY PEOPLE. 11 AND THEY SHALL NOT TEACH EVERYONE HIS FELLOW CITIZEN, AND EVERYONE HIS BROTHER, SAYING, 'KNOW THE LORD,' FOR ALL WILL KNOW ME, FROM THE LEAST TO THE GREATEST OF THEM. 12 FOR I WILL BE MERCIFUL TO THEIR INIQUITIES, AND I WILL REMEMBER THEIR SINS NO MORE." 13 When

He said, "A New Covenant," He has made the first obsolete. But whatever is becoming obsolete and growing old is ready to disappear.

9:15 For this reason He is the mediator of a New Covenant, so that, since a death has taken place for the redemption of the transgressions that were committed under the first covenant, those who have been called may receive the promise of the eternal inheritance.

12:22-24 But you have come to Mount Zion and to the city of the living God, the heavenly Jerusalem, and to myriads of angels, 23 to the general assembly and church of the firstborn who are enrolled in heaven, and to God, the Judge of all, and to the spirits of the righteous made perfect, 24 and to Jesus, the mediator of a New Covenant, and to the sprinkled blood, which speaks better than the blood of Abel.

The epistle to the Hebrews contains the highest concentration of New Covenant passages in the New Testament. We have identified five primary texts that are taken to have some bearing on the doctrine of the New Covenant. Of those five, the four quoted above are indisputably referential to the New Covenant. All but 7:22 contain the term "New Covenant" (διαθηκη καινη), and the direct quotation of Jeremiah 31:31–34 (the *locus classicus* on New Covenant teaching in the Old Testament) in Hebrews 8:8–12 guarantees that this is precisely the covenant that the author of Hebrews has in mind.

Furthermore, the usage of New Covenant language in this epistle resonates with New Covenant characteristic #1: the New Covenant is repeatedly contrasted with the old so as to highlight the superiority of the new and the obsolescence of the old. This strategy is used all throughout the epistle, and not just with covenantal language; contrasts are drawn between Christ and the angels, Christ and Moses, Christ's Melchizedekian priesthood and the old Levitical priesthood, and so on. The goal in all of this is to highlight the superiority of Jesus Christ over all other authorities and cherished religious figures or institutions. Thus, in invoking New Covenant language, the author contrasts Moses's covenant (the Sinaitic Covenant) with Christ's covenant (the New Covenant), stressing the superiority of the latter over the former. Unquestionably, these four texts are New Covenant passages.

A word of caution, however: the presence of New Covenant passages in Church–age scripture is by itself insufficient warrant to establish the Church's participation in the New Covenant. In the four passages surveyed above, there is no indisputable exegetical warrant for concluding that the New Covenant applies to the Church. The statement in 7:22 that Jesus is the guarantee (or "guarantor") of the New Covenant has no direct bearing on precisely who the second party to that covenant is (Israel or the Church, or both). Hebrews 8:7–13 establishes the superiority of the New Covenant and the obsolescence of the old, but makes no application of the New Covenant to the Church. In fact, the use of a third–person plural (αυτους) rather than a first-person plural pronoun in verse 7 along with the unqualified quotation of Jeremiah 31:31 ("I will effect a New Covenant *with the house of Israel and with the house of Judah*," emphasis mine) would seem evidence against such a position.

If the author wished to apply the New Covenant to the Church, why would he identify Israel and Judah as the second party to the covenant without any additional word of explanation or qualification? Finally, the identification of Christ as the mediator of the New Covenant in 9:15 and 12:24, again, has no direct bearing on the relationship of the Church to that covenant. It is *Christ's* relationship to the New Covenant that is described here, not the Church's. While we cannot help but see that the New Covenant is discussed in these passages, it would be overreaching to conclude that a connection between the Church and the New Covenant is thereby implied.

10:8-9 After saying above, "SACRIFICES AND OFFERINGS AND WHOLE BURNT OFFERINGS AND sacrifices FOR SIN YOU HAVE NOT DESIRED, NOR HAVE YOU TAKEN PLEASURE in them" (which are offered according to the Law), ⁹ then He said, "BEHOLD, I HAVE COME TO DO YOUR WILL." He takes away the first in order to establish the second. ¹⁰ By this will we have been sanctified through the offering of the body of Jesus Christ once for all.

This passage has been separated from the other four passages in Hebrews because no explicit New Covenant language is present in this case. While the sanctification in verse 10 might seem at first blush a solid example of the New Covenant's application to the Church, it would first need to be established that this is in fact a New Covenant passage. Although the strategy of contrasting new and old is used in both this passage and the four New Covenant passages in Hebrews, it is also used in plenty of other passages that have nothing to do with the New Covenant whatsoever (contrasts between Christ and Moses, the Melchizedekian and Levitical priesthoods, etc.). The similarity in the author's strategy is therefore insufficient evidence to establish a New Covenant reference for this passage.

The sacrifices and offerings as well as the Law in verse 8 are obviously elements of the Sinaitic Covenant, but the contrast here is between the Mosaic sacrifices and Christ's sacrifice, not the Sinaitic and New Covenants. Of course the sacrifice of Christ is related to the New Covenant in that His is the blood that ratifies it (cf. the discussion on the Last Supper passages above), but that does not mean that any passage referring to Christ's sacrifice is therefore automatically a New Covenant passage. Dispensationalists of all stripes concur that Christ's sacrifice both effects the salvation of Christians and ratifies the New Covenant, but there is no good reason to collapse the distinction between the two, prior to exegesis of the germane texts. Since the contrast in this passage centers on sacrifices rather than on covenants, Hebrews 10:8–9 is not a New Covenant passage.

CONCLUSION

This chapter has endeavored both to survey the major texts identified (sometimes rightly, sometimes wrongly) as New Covenant passages, as well as to issue a preliminary judgment on which ones can and cannot be legitimately regarded as referencing the New Covenant. Obviously, this chapter makes no pretensions of having exegeted those passages deeply; such would be impossible in a work of this scope and length. Nevertheless, it is my hope that the foregoing discussion furnishes a good starting place from which deeper and more meticulous exegetical work can be launched.

As we have seen, many of these texts are indeed New Covenant passages while some of them are not. However, when it comes to classification, such a simple dichotomy is ultimately too broad and fails to capture the full range of differences between the various passages surveyed insofar as the subject of the New Covenant is concerned. Therefore, I find it helpful to divide these passages into four categories: 1.) Passages that clearly refer to the New Covenant; 2.) Passages that refer to the New Covenant, but should not necessarily be applied as they commonly are (i.e. with reference to the Church's relationship to the New Covenant); 3.) Passages that *may* refer to the New Covenant; and 4.) Passages that do not refer to the New Covenant, or do so only indirectly. According to that fourfold categorical scheme, the conclusions of this chapter are summarized as follows:

Passages that clearly refer to the New Covenant	Jer. 31:31–34; 32:27–40; 50:4–5; Isa. 55:3; 59:20–21; Ezek. 11:17–20; 16:59–62; 36:25–32; 37:14, 23, 26; Joel 2:28–29; Rom. 11:26–27
Passages that refer to the New Covenant, but should not necessarily be applied as they commonly are	Matt. 26:28; Mark 14:24; Luke 22:20; 1 Cor. 11:25; 2 Cor. 3:6; Heb. 7:22; 8:7–13; 9:15; 12:22–24
Passages that may refer to the New Covenant	Hos. 1:9–11
Passages that do not refer to the New Covenant, or do so only indirectly	Gen. 12:1–3; Hos. 2:18–23; Acts 2:16–18; Rom. 9:25–26; Heb. 10:8–9

Obviously, these categories do not constitute entirely watertight compartments, and there may be some degree of overlap between them (especially as regards the last three categories). Nevertheless, they provide a helpful framework for thinking through which passages are and which are not relevant to a discussion on the New Covenant.

3

HERMENEUTIC RAMIFICATIONS OF APPLYING THE NEW COVENANT TO THE CHURCH[1]

Christopher Cone

PREFACE

Allow me first to acknowledge that this is not an easy matter for me personally to discuss, for the simple reason that I appeal in this study to the works and positions of great and godly men who have in many cases had a direct and personal bearing on my own spiritual growth and understanding, and yet on this vital topic I find myself at odds with nearly all of them. Nonetheless, if they have taught me anything they have taught me that I must rely on His word as authoritative, and that we must be willing to challenge each other to accuracy in our handling of the word of truth – even contending earnestly for the faith which was once delivered to the saints.

---

[1] Initially Addressed to The Council on Dispensational Hermeneutics at Baptist Bible Seminary, September 24, 2009, and later published as "Hermeneutical Ramifications of Applying the New Covenant to the Church: An Appeal to Consistency" in *Journal of Dispensational Theology*, Dec 2009: 5–24.

I hope and pray that none would perceive my challenges herein to the views of these men as anything but an attempt to honestly evaluate their views in the light of Scripture. As dispensationalists living in this age, we stand on the shoulders of giants – imperfect giants, but giants nonetheless. It is fitting that we show our gratitude and appreciation, honoring them as fathers and fellow servants who have brought us far in our quest for a more Biblical theology. It is likewise fitting that we be unwilling to squander the rich heritage they have afforded us and which reminds us that, as one dear father in the faith has so succinctly phrased it, "The Biblical data gives us the correct doctrine. Everything must be tested against those data."[2]

INTRODUCTION

In his very thorough handling of the development of replacement theology in the history of the church, Ronald Diprose recognizes that misunderstanding the role of Israel in God's plan has a ripple effect on every aspect of theology. He says,

> ...ecclesiology and eschatology are not the only areas of Christian theology to have been affected by the Church's views concerning Israel. In fact, the omission of Israel in Christian theology has had detrimental, yet deterministic effects on a wide variety of theological issues.[3]

He concludes with even greater emphasis,

> *Failure to reflect seriously on Israel in light of the relevant Biblical data has serious consequences for the entire*

---

[2] Charles C. Ryrie, *Basic Theology* (Wheaton, IL: Victor Books, 1986), 76.

[3] Ronald Diprose, *Israel and the Church: The Origin and Effects of Replacement Theology* (Waynesboro, GA: Authentic Media, 2004), 3.

enterprise of Christian theology. It was the neglect of relevant Biblical data concerning the place of Israel in God's plan which permitted replacement theology to develop during the early centuries of the Christian era.[4]

As Diprose correctly observes, we can trace much faulty doctrine to the improper handling of the Biblical teaching regarding the nation of Israel. This faulty doctrine often, though not always, manifests itself in the behavior of believers. Arnold Fruchtenbaum goes a bit further when he (correctly, I believe) asserts that while replacement theology does not cause anti-Semitism, the two are not uncomfortable with one another.[5] The history of the church at times reflects a storied distortion of God's plan for Israel and at other times the revolting consequences of such distortions. Theological method results in theological conclusions, and theological conclusions generally give birth in their likeness to the fruit of behavior.

In an evenhanded consideration of dispensational conclusions we must turn to the devices that derive the conclusions. Have we maintained a purity of method necessary for the accurate handling of the word of truth or have we fallen prey to devices we would otherwise consider wholly inadequate? The answer is directly evidenced in our understanding of how the New Covenant will be fulfilled. Be certain that this matter of the New Covenant and the nation with whom He made it remains no small concern to God, as He indicates that the fixed order of His created world hangs in the balance (Jer 31:35–36). On matters of such importance to God we might expect to find near universal agreement among His people, but alas we find nothing of the kind. Postmillennialism, amillennialism, and covenant premillennialism

---

[4] Ibid., 171.

[5] Arnold Fruchtenbaum, *Israelology: The Missing Link in Systematic Theology* (Tustin, CA: Ariel Ministries, 1993), 836–837.

offer explanations that we find unacceptable. But even within the dispensational tradition the understandings are varied and disparate. At least three major views are readily discernible upon examination of dispensationalism's development. (1) The *Multiple New Covenant* view (here referenced as MC) – this was the view of Chafer and Walvoord, for example, who believed there to be an Old Testament covenant for Israel, to be fully and literally fulfilled by Israel, and a New Testament covenant for the church, fulfilled presently and in the future by the church. (2) The *Single Covenant Multiple Participants* view (here referenced as SCMP) – this was the view of Scofield, for example, who believed that the church participates during the present age in aspects of Israel's New Covenant, though the covenant will be fulfilled literally with Israel in the future. A variation of this view was presented by Pentecost and has come to be perhaps the most accepted of all dispensational views on the New Covenant. (3) The *Single Covenant Israel Only* view (here referenced as SCIO) – Darby was one of the few to espouse this view, as he believed the church to be totally unrelated to the New Covenant, yet having a relationship with the One who ratified the New Covenant.

The three views each require the utilization of distinct hermeneutic devices for their derivation, and upon review of these devices it seems clear that the devices are as incompatible as the conclusions themselves. Which conclusion is correct – or nearest correct? Which hermeneutic device is to be employed? As Diprose observed, these are not simply matters of ecclesiology or eschatology, rather these matters cut to the core of the very character of God and how we are to approach His word. In light of the importance of this issue, what follows is an attempt to evaluate the three basic views and the legitimacy of the three devices applied to derive them.

THREE VIEWS, THREE DEVICES

The Multiple New Covenant View (MC)
Lewis Sperry Chafer suggests that the church is "sheltered under a New Covenant made in His blood."[6] Further, he distinguishes between "the New Covenant yet to be made with Israel and...the New Covenant now in force with the church."[7] In agreement, Walvoord says, "Most premillenarians (Darby excepted) would agree that *a* New Covenant has been provided for the church, but not *the* New Covenant for Israel."[8] Walvoord believes the MC view has two significant advantages. First, he says,

> It provides a sensible reason for establishing the Lord's supper for believers in this age in commemoration of the blood of the New Covenant. The language of 1 Corinthians 11:25 seems to require it...It hardly seems reasonable to expect Christians to distinguish between the cup and the New Covenant when these appear to be identified in this passage.[9]

It seems that this argument misses the revealed purpose of the ordinance – at least as it pertains to Paul's immediate audience. Paul adds a postscript to Jesus' words, saying "For as often as you eat this bread and drink the cup, you proclaim the Lord's death until He comes" (1 Cor 11:26). If the New Covenant was a significant aspect of the cup *for the Corinthians' application*, then

---

[6] Lewis Sperry Chafer, *Systematic Theology, Volume IV* (Grand Rapids, MI: Kregel, 1993), 49.

[7] Ibid., 325.

[8] John Walvoord, *The Millennial Kingdom* (Grand Rapids, MI: Zondervan, 1959), 214.

[9] Ibid., 218–219.

why were they not told to proclaim the New Covenant? Why did Paul say nothing more of the matter in his letter? The ordinance focuses on His death, not on the covenant.

Second, Walvoord appeals to one of Paul's two other direct references to the New Covenant, saying,

> In 2 Corinthians 3:6, Paul speaking of himself states: "Our sufficiency is of God: who also made us sufficient as ministers of a New Covenant." It would be difficult to adjust the ministry of Paul as a minister of the New Covenant if, in fact, there is no New Covenant for the present age.[10]

This argument is based on the premise that in order for one to serve a covenant that covenant must be in effect. That premise seems flawed, however, in light of Paul's stated hope of Israel's national salvation (e.g., Rom 11:13–15). Notice he uses the same term here (*diakonous*) as he does in Romans 11:13 (*diakonian*). He magnifies his service that Jews might be saved. Additionally, the covenant can be ratified and awaiting fulfillment without being in effect or presently fulfilled, and one can be serving it even as he hopes for its future fulfillment.

Another writer explains that the theological framework of dispensations understood in a particular way requires multiple New Covenants. He says,

> Each dispensation is, in fact, a covenantal arrangement that establishes the stewardship required of each dispensation. The dispensations of "human government" and of the "Mosaic Law," or any dispensation including the "church age," involve "New Covenants." By definition, a change in dispensations results from a change in stipulations (with the implied or specifically articulated

---

[10] Ibid., 219.

blessings and cursings). The former covenant relationship is replaced with an updated and revised covenant. In some cases this involves the updating of the historical prologue section of the covenant as well. *Every new dispensation involves some "New Covenant," not only the present church age"* [emphasis mine].[11]

Here, the theological hermeneutic is employed. The writer cannot identify specifically and precisely identified covenants in Scripture that would characterize each dispensation. This is the same device used to derive the covenants of redemption, works, and grace. If we are to have any credibility in our assertions that we as dispensationalists are *uniquely* literal grammatical-historical in our handling of the text, then we cannot engage in such maneuvers.

The writer adds, "When the New Covenant and the Melchizedekian priesthood have begun to function, there is no going back to the Aaronic priesthood and the Mosaic Law (Heb. 7:17–19)."[12] While there is no return to the Mosaic Law, the continuation of the Levitical priesthood is demanded by God's eternal salt-covenant with Aaron (Num 18:19) and a literal fulfillment of an addendum to the Davidic covenant (Jer 33:12–23) and is to be fulfilled literally through the Zadokian line (Ezek 43:19ff). The writer crystallizes the issue when he says,

> The New Covenant specifically mentioned in the Scriptures is yet future for a redeemed and sanctified Jewish people. Theologically there are many New

---

[11] John Master, "The New Covenant," *Issues in Dispensationalism*, Wesley Willis and John Master, eds. (Chicago, IL: Moody Press, 1994),102.

[12] Ibid., 104.

Covenants because each dispensation is a New Covenant.[13]

Many admirable thinkers would agree with this statement, at least in part. Note for example, the observation of Eugene Merrill:

> ...the "New" Covenant of Jeremiah is not precisely the same as the New Covenant of most New Testament texts but that nonetheless both flow from the Abrahamic Covenant. Jeremiah's covenant is made explicitly with a renewed, eschatological Israel and Judah (cf. Jer. 31:1, 17, 23, 27, 31) whereas the New Covenant of the New Testament is universalized to include not only Israel but also all the nations who turn to the Lord in repentance and faith.[14]

In this view, Jeremiah's New Covenant then is not for the church, but there is a theologically derived New Covenant that is necessitated by the basic theological understanding of how God works in each dispensation. Note this understanding builds upon the premise that dispensations are soteriological outworkings of God rather than doxological ones. It cannot be overstated how destructive the soteriological centered understanding is, since the logical and theological requirements of such grounding force us to

---

[13] Ibid., 108.

[14] Eugene Merrill, "The Covenant with Abraham: The Keystone of Biblical Architecture," *Journal of Dispensational Theology* (Volume 12, Number 36, August 2008), 16.

handle the text as creatively as our covenant–theology brothers.[15] To say that "Church saints have a covenantal relationship with God"[16] by way of the New Covenant demands either that we identify a passage in which God directly makes a New Covenant (and consequently an old one) with the church or that we relinquish the high ground of consistency in applying literal grammatical–historical hermeneutics, recognizing as John Gerstner did, that "far from determining dispensational theology, the dispensational literal hermeneutic (with all its inconsistencies), is in fact the direct result of that theology."[17]

How can we criticize the covenants of redemption, works, and grace as being unBiblical and artificial when we likewise refer to, for example, an Adamic[18] covenant and an Edenic covenant, when nothing is ever so called in Scripture? After all, if we adopt the view that every dispensation represents some kind of New Covenant, then these "covenants" are indeed logically and theologically necessitated, thus we defend our characterization of

---

[15] For sake of brevity I will not address here the importance of recognizing God's doxological purpose rather than soteriological purpose as the central factor in defining a dispensation. Nonetheless, I believe this to be the greatest single issue that dispensational theology must rectify if we would hope to maintain a truly Biblical theology. I do address this in some detail in *Prolegomena: Introductory Notes on Bible Study & Theological Method* (Tyndale Seminary Press, 2009), 94–96.

[16] John Master, "The New Covenant," *Issues in Dispensationalism*, Wesley Willis and John Master, eds. (Chicago, IL: Moody Press, 1994), 109.

[17] John Gerstner, *Wrongly Dividing the Word of Truth* (Morgan, PA: Soli Deo Gloria, 2000), 111.

[18] Though Hosea 6:7 may be best understood to reference Adam directly (it could reference men in general, as in the KJV), the passage references the severity of offense by way of analogy and does not provide explicit evidence that God made a covenant with Adam. If one were to hold that such a covenant was made, there would be difficulty in demonstrating the location and content with specificity.

some promises as covenants based on something other than exegetical necessity. Our hermeneutics become "a very shaky affair indeed."[19] Regardless of the grand heritage and tradition of the multiple New Covenant   view, we cannot stand upon it, as the cost to do so is nothing less than our very feet. Consider the following statements:

> Accordingly, the best solution to the problem is to recognize that Christ introduced by His death on the cross this covenant of grace which has many applications.

And

> The covenant of grace, accordingly, is extended principally to Israel in the Old Testament, to the church in the present age...

Are these the comments of Zacharias Ursinus? Johannes Cocceius? O.T. Allis? Louis Berkhof? John Gerstner? R.C. Sproul? None of the above. They come from an affirmation of MC by John Walvoord.[20] Contrast Walvoord's words with Berkhof's on dispensationalism's "Adamic covenant," and a near stunning role reversal is observed. Berkhof says,

> The first revelation of the covenant is found in the protoevangel, Gen. 3:15. Some deny that this has any reference to the covenant; *and it certainly does not refer to any formal establishment of a covenant.* [emphasis mine] The revelation of such an establishment could only follow after the covenant idea had been developed in history. At

---

[19] Gerstner, Op. Cit., 110.

[20] John Walvoord, *The Prophecy Knowledge Handbook* (Wheaton, IL: Victor Books, 1990), 503.

the same time Gen. 3:15 certainly contains a revelation of the essence of the covenant.[21]

The covenant theologian argues that the text does not refer to the formal establishment of a covenant, and that deriving such a covenant requires reading theology back into the text. And while he doesn't protest too vehemently (as he cannot with any great consistency), his methodology seems in this instance more characteristically dispensational than that of the dispensational theologian.

The Single Covenant, Multiple Participants View (SCMP)
C.I. Scofield, in his *Study Bible Notes* on Hebrews 8, summarizes what he identifies as eight Biblical covenants, and says that the New Covenant "secures the eternal blessedness, under the Abrahamic Covenant of all who believe." Elsewhere he says that "Christians are now partakers"[22] of the New Covenant. J. Carl Laney in similar fashion believes that "Under the New Covenant, spiritual blessings are secured for all believers through the redemptive work of Christ."[23] He emphasizes the point further saying, "Virtually all the blessings we have in Christ are based on spiritual provisions of the New Covenant."[24] He adds that

---

[21] Louis Berkhof, Systematic Theology (Grand Rapids, MI: Eerdmans, 1974), 293.

[22] C.I. Scofield, *Scofield Bible Correspondence Course Volume I: Introduction to the Scriptures* (Chicago, IL: Moody Bible Institute, 1959), 70.

[23] J. Carl Laney, "God's Plan of the Ages" in *Understanding Christian Theology*, Charles Swindoll and Roy Zuck, gen. eds. (Nashville, TN: Thomas Nelson, 2003),249.

[24] Ibid., 228.

Believers today are living between the first and second advents of Christ under the provisions of the New Covenant. They are participating in a form of God's kingdom, but are yet awaiting its full consummation when Christ will establish His reign on the earth.[25]

This understanding of the New Covenant shows a reliance on the hermeneutic device of "already not yet." John Witmer recognizes the slight furthering of this device in PD, which he says "identifies the spiritual blessings of the New Covenant with God's promises to David in the Davidic Covenant."[26]   Witmer distinguishes between spiritual blessings of the New Covenant and physical blessings of the Davidic covenant. But can we draw distinctions between spiritual blessings and physical ones within the framework of a covenant offered to specifically named recipients? Consider that the fulfilling of the spiritual blessing is immediately to be followed by the granting of the physical blessing (Ezek 36:27–28).

In similar fashion, Paul Benware, seemingly voicing his agreement with SCMP says,

The church, then, is a partaker of the spiritual blessings of the New Covenant, enjoying regeneration, the forgiveness of sin, and the presence and ministry of the Holy Spirit.[27]

While it is wholly appropriate to say that the church partakes of spiritual blessings, why the need to connect the spiritual blessings

---

[25] Ibid., 231.

[26] John Witmer, "Christ's Present Ministry at the Right Hand of God the Father," *Understanding Christian Theology*, Charles Swindoll and Roy Zuck, gen. eds. (Nashville, TN: Thomas Nelson, 2003),361.

[27] Paul Benware, *Understanding End Times Prophecy* (Chicago, IL: Moody Press, 2006), 77.

to the New Covenant? The Abrahamic covenant promises blessing for those who are not Abraham's physical descendants (Gen 12:3). Likewise, the ministry of the Holy Spirit to gentiles is promised outside of the context of the New Covenant (cf. Joel 2:28ff and Acts 2, etc.). Additionally, there is significant revelation regarding salvation of gentiles outside of the context of the New Covenant (Gen 12:3, Is 11:10; cf. Gen 15:6 and Jon 3:5; Is 42:6; 49:6; etc.). It should also be noted the regeneration spoken of in Jeremiah 31 is not only related to the forgiveness of sins, but also to the planting of Israel in the land (v. 33), the writing of God's law on the heart (v. 33), and the needlessness of any further teaching about God (v. 34). None of these things are ever said to accompany the regeneration of church age believers. Additionally, the sins to be forgiven in the New Covenant are "their" sins (note in v. 34, the third person plural pronominal suffix: *la'avonam*). Following standard rules of grammar we must look for the antecedent to which the third person plural refers. It is *they* who also broke the old covenant – the house of Israel and the house of Judah.

Stanley Toussaint acknowledges that Christ, in the upper room (Mt 26:27; Mk 14:24; Lk 22:20) was most assuredly referencing the Jeremiah 31 New Covenant. He says,

> It seems that the King is looking back to the prophesied New Covenant also known as the everlasting covenant and the covenant of peace (Jeremiah 31:31–34; 32:37–40; Ezekiel 34:25–31; 37: 26–28). This is what would immediately flash into the mind of the average Jew. *In fact, it could refer to no other covenant since no other covenant was still unconfirmed.* [emphasis mine][28]

---

[28] Stanley Toussaint, *Behold the King: A Study of Matthew* (Portland, OR: Multnomah Press, 1980), 299.

Toussaint adds that the New Covenant was "clearly and definitely made with the nation of Israel exclusively."[29] However, as he critiques the view that the "New Covenant is with Israel only and has no relationship to the church,"[30] he says, "to assert that there is one New Covenant with Israel only having no relationship to the church is erroneous for several reasons."[31] He acknowledges an exclusive audience with a still yet future fulfillment, while at the same time he suggests that "the New Covenant must be in effect today."[32] Again, this seems to be at the very least a flirtation with Ladd's "already not yet" hermeneutic device. But is it justified by the New Testament references to the New Covenant? Clearly, the admirable Toussaint and others holding to SCMP believe so, as Toussaint offers four justifications.

> First, Paul in 2 Corinthians 3:6 clearly states that he is a minister of a New Covenant. It is certain that his ministry was not confined to Israel only. He was the minister of a New Covenant then in effect which was applicable to Jew and Gentile alike.[33]

Unfortunately, it appears this is a non sequitur. Paul references himself and those serving with him as *diakonous kaines diathekes* – servants of a New Covenant. Note that Paul was *serving* a New Covenant, not *administering* it. Thus his audience (whether Jew or Gentile, or both) is irrelevant as it relates to this point. How then does he serve a New Covenant? Perhaps insofar as he magnified his ministry in order that the Jews might be moved to jealousy

---

[29] Ibid., 300.

[30] Ibid., 301.

[31] Ibid.

[32] Ibid.

[33] Ibid.

and be saved (Rom 11:13–14). By so doing he is certainly seeking to hasten the fulfillment of the covenant. Perhaps that is not sufficient and there remains more to consider, but nonetheless, the term Paul used (*diakonous*) does not provide or even imply any connection of the New Covenant or the blessings of the New Covenant to the church.

> Second, in 1 Corinthians 11:25, Paul quotes the Lord in saying, "This cup is the New Covenant in my blood." Therefore the New Covenant must be in effect today, and it must sustain some relationship to the church.[34]

Again, this seems not an entirely accurate conclusion. The first premise is (apparently) that the moment the blood of the covenant was shed, the covenant became effective. Compare this with the ratification of the Abrahamic covenant which did not see any of its specific aspects specifically fulfilled until much later. Perhaps it would be better to say the covenant was ratified but not fulfilled. If Toussaint means that the covenant stands ratified, I must concur, but if he means that it is in effect, or that it is underway, then if we expect a literal fulfillment of the covenant we would expect it to be fulfilled in the order it was given. Notice the first aspect of the New Covenant proclaimed by God is the writing of God's laws on the hearts of those of the house of Israel and the house of Judah. Is this in effect or has this already happened? Again, note the order of the covenant reiterated in Ezekiel 36:24ff.

The first event proclaimed is a national ingathering. Even if one argues that 1948 fulfilled that (I do not believe it did in any way, though it might serve as a precursor or a preparation), were we to understand that the New Covenant was not in effect before that? Of course not. We must be careful not to parse the things necessary for fulfillment using the *already not yet* device. Further,

---

[34] Ibid.

if Christ's death served as a ratification rather than a "putting into effect" of the covenant, then we would see a clear delineation of the church's (non) relation to the New Covenant: the church would be related to the Mediator, and not to the covenant.

Nothing in 1 Corinthians 11:25 offers any indication either that the covenant is in effect today or that it is related to the church. The church is to remember Him, not the covenant. His death then met (at least) two purposes related to this present discussion: (1) He died to ratify the New Covenant with the house of Israel and the house of Judah – the covenant cannot be fulfilled unless it is first ratified. His death accomplished that. Notice that all in the room were only Jews, and the church had not been inaugurated yet. (2) He died to enable the fulfillment of the final component of the Abrahamic covenant (Gen 12:3) – that all the families of the earth would be blessed through Abraham. It is the Lord's death we proclaim through the ordinance, not the covenant.

> Third, advocates of the view that there is one covenant only with one application to Israel argue that Jeremiah 31 is addressed to the Jews. This is true. *However this does not hinder the possibility of participation of the church in its blessings* [emphasis mine].[35]

The emphasized statement is true, but it is no less an argument from silence: nothing indicates that such participation is impossible, thus it is possible. We could argue anything is possible, but how do we move from possibility to actuality? The literal grammatical–historical hermeneutic does not permit us to make such a move based on a theological framework, but instead requires that it be exegetically warranted. Note how Saucy uses an argument from silence to justify aspects of Davidic covenant fulfillment in the present age. He says first,

---

[35] Ibid.

It would appear, therefore, that either Psalm 110 is a reference to heaven or Peter was giving a new interpretation to the psalm. As we have seen, the right hand of God was not spatially thought of as being in heaven. In fact, it was not primarily a spatial concept at all, but a metaphor for the supreme position of authority next to the king. *Thus Peter's teaching that Christ assumed this position through the ascension added something that was probably not recognized in earlier interpretations of the Psalm* [emphasis mine]. But this should not lead to the conclusion that Peter was denying the original meaning.[36]

He argues that key aspects regarding David's throne and the right hand of God were not limited by the Old Testament terminology, and thus left room for later re-interpretation. This is the maneuver (the complementary hermeneutic) whereby PD derives its "already not yet" device. Using this device, Saucy concludes that the Davidic covenant is at least partially being fulfilled at present:

> That this present salvation is not the complete fulfillment of these promised blessings to the world is clear from Paul's statement that when Israel returns to her God, the riches for the Gentiles will be far more than they are even today (Ro 11:12). The Gentiles, however, are being blessed with messianic salvation at present because the Messiah has come and has accomplished salvation...the evidence dealing with the restoration of the Davidic kingship

---

[36] Robert Saucy, *The Case for Progressive Dispensationalism* (Grand Rapids, MI: Zondervan, 1993), 71.

reveals only an initial fulfillment of the covenant promises during the present age. [37]

It seems that Toussaint's defense here of the SCMP is not only consistent with the methodology of many other traditional dispensationalist thinkers, but it is surprisingly consistent with that of progressive dispensationalists as well.

Toussaint offers a fourth argument against the one covenant one recipient view:

> Finally, in Hebrews 8:6 and 9:15, Christ is said to be the mediator of a new and better covenant now. If His mediatorship is present, then the covenant upon which His mediatorship is based must be present.[38]

This argument offers a conclusion (the covenant must be present) based on a single premise (His mediatorship is present). First, the distinction between being "in effect" and being presently ratified (past action with existing results) must be considered. It appears Toussaint intends the former, yet the latter would seem to meet the condition of the argument well enough. To argue specifically for "in effect" rather than presently ratified would require a more thorough argument with stated premises rather than assumed ones. In other words, if the structure of Toussaint's fourth argument is accepted, it could just as easily be stated as follows: If His mediatorship is present then the covenant upon which His mediatorship is based must stand presently ratified. If restated in this way, then the argument would favor the single covenant, single recipient view.

Also note that inseparable from His role as Mediator of the covenant He is a priest in the order of Melchizedek (6:20). That is

---

[37] Ibid., 80.

[38] Stanley Toussaint, op. cit., 302.

to say that He is a priestly King. If we apply "already not yet" to
one aspect of Christ's mediatorial role, by saying that His
mediatorship is present and thus the (new) covenant is present,
we cannot with integrity dismiss such application to other
aspects. Is Christ reigning as a Melchizedekian king now? PD
answers without hesitation in the affirmative: "...Jesus'
resurrection–ascension to God's right hand is put forward by
Peter as a fulfillment of the Davidic covenant...As the Davidic heir,
Jesus sits in and rules from heaven."[39] The problem of consistency
is readily apparent: how can I apply "already not yet" to the New
Covenant and yet argue that it should not be applied to the
Davidic covenant? Eliott Johnson observes a nuance in PD
methodology that might sound familiar. He says, "Craig Blaising
relates an inaugural or present fulfillment due to Christ's
mediation of the covenants with the church after His first
advent."[40] The subtle distinction here between PD and SCMP is
that PD applies "already not yet" to the covenants (plural) while
SCMP applies it only to the New Covenant. Further, the
hermeneutic which derives "already not yet" is grounded in the
silence of the Old Testament. Darrell Bock describes the PD
argument as follows:

> The progressive argument is that the New Testament
> treats a wide scope of provisions as realized in the current
> era, while also noting the fundamental shifts in the
> administrative structure and operation of God's promise
> in this era. These provisions and shifts are proclaimed in
> terms that point to the realization and advance of the

---

[39] Darrell Bock, "The Reign of the Lord Christ," *Dispensationalism, Israel
and the Church: The Search for Definition* (Grand Rapids, MI: Zondervan,
1992), 49–50.

[40] Elliott Johnson, "Covenants in Traditional Dispensationalism," *Three
Central Issues in Contemporary Dispensationalism* (Grand Rapids, MI:
Kregel, 1999), 122.

> promises of God. They show that *a covenantal stage has been reached as a result of Jesus' coming that is directly connected to the promises of old. In sum, some of what was promised in the covenants has come and has been instituted.* [emphasis mine] The sheer scope of this covenantal language points to initial realization.[41]

The silence of the Old Testament on certain matters pertaining to the covenants has apparently become the fertile ground for expansion and "already not yet" fulfillments.

Finally, it should be noted that the focus of Hebrews is the qualification and superiority of Jesus Christ, and that none of the sixteen appearances of *diatheke* show any exegetical connection whatsoever to the church. On the contrary, the New Covenant is repeated verbatim with the distinct recipient language completely intact (8:8–12).

Dismissing then (1) the non–literal view, (2) the single covenant, single recipient view, and (3) the multiple covenant view, Toussaint offers a fourth option he considers more tenable:

> It asserts that the New Covenant was made with Israel and will ultimately find its fulfillment in that nation, but in the meantime the church enters into certain blessings of the New Covenant.[42]

He explains further that

> It must be concluded, therefore, that the church benefits from certain spiritual blessings of the New Covenant such

---

[41] Darrell Bock, "Response: Covenants in Traditional Dispensationalism," *Three Central Issues in Contemporary Dispensationalism* (Grand Rapids, MI: Kregel, 1999), 157.

[42] Stanley Toussaint, op. cit., 302.

as regeneration and the forgiveness of sins, but all the blessings will be Israel's as manifested in the future earthly kingdom.[43]

A glaring problem remains. On what basis is regeneration and forgiveness of sins for church age believers tied to the New Covenant? The argument from silence is not sufficient. There must be a clear and definite exegetical connection, and yet there is none. Note for emphasis that John's Gospel is the only one of the four that references regeneration (specifically, being born again), and it is the only one of the four that ignores entirely the ratification of the New Covenant, as John's record of the upper room discourse does not include the ordinance of the cup. This is not a clumsy omission on John's part.

The church bearing a relationship to the Mediator has strong exegetical grounding, but the church participating in any aspects of God's New Covenant with the house of Israel and the house of Judah can only be defended by an abandonment of the literal grammatical-historical hermeneutic in favor of the complementary hermeneutic and the "already not yet" device so eagerly embraced by PD. Once again, should we hold to this view, we find ourselves on the low ground with no room to criticize "development" using the "already not yet" device. Particular hermeneutic methods result in particular conclusions. If we are accepting of the methods, we are forced to likewise approve of the conclusions derived from consistently applying the methods. *PD simply does with the Davidic covenant what SCMP has done with the New Covenant.* Perhaps this is one reason that only a handful of "traditional" dispensationalists have mounted meaningful arguments against PD.

---

[43] Ibid.

It should be noted at this point that Fruchtenbaum,[44] Decker,[45] and others have identified a dispensational view closely related to SCMP, highlighting a distinction between this view that the church participates in some way in the New Covenant, and the view (SCMP) that the church has a preliminary part in the New Covenant. Fruchtenbaum, for example, identifies Pentecost as a representative of this better perspective. Despite this endorsement, it seems that this view uses the same device as SCMP, and really isn't significantly different after all. Pentecost, though representing that the church is not under or fulfilling the New Covenant, asserts that the church is receiving New Covenant blessings. He says,

> Since the church receives blessings of the Abrahamic covenant (Gal. 3:14; 4:22-31) by faith without being under or fulfilling that covenant, so the church may receive blessings from the New Covenant without being under or fulfilling that New Covenant.[46]

What seems to be missed is a critical factor in this discussion: that gentile believers during the church age *are indeed under and fulfilling directly* the seventh aspect of the Abrahamic covenant (Gen. 12:3, cf. Gal. 3:14), an assertion which if true would remove the Abrahamic covenant from consideration as a proof text for an "already not yet" approach to covenant blessings. This view, though emphasizing primarily (if not only) soteriological shared blessings, nonetheless relies entirely on the "already not yet"

---

[44] Arnold Fruchtenbaum, *Israelology*, 366–369.

[45] Rodney Decker, "New Covenant, Dispensational Views of the," *Dictionary of Premillennial Theology* (Grand Rapids, MI: Kregel, 1996), 280–282.

[46] J. Dwight Pentecost, *Things to Come* (Grand Rapids, MI: Academie/ Zondervan, 1964), 127.

device. For this reason, I do not consider it to be distinct from SCMP, but rather a more subtle form of the same.

The Single Covenant, Israel Only View (SCIO)

Bernard Ramm makes an astute and troubling observation when he suggests " to say that we are under the benefits of the covenant without actually being under the covenant is to clandestinely admit what is boldly denied."[47] Connecting the church directly to benefits promised specifically to Israel requires any one of three maneuvers: (1) the application of the allegorical hermeneutic to the end that Israel and the church are not viewed as completely distinct, (2) the employment of the theological hermeneutic to the end that a covenant is artificially derived outside the parameters of exegetical warrant, and (3) the utilization of the "already not yet" device to show some degree of present fulfillment or present application of the New Covenant. I can discover no legitimacy whatsoever in any of these three options, as all three supplant literal grammatical–historical hermeneutics in favor of other hermeneutic devices, which, if applied consistently, would distort the Biblical text beyond recognition and undermine its perspicuity beyond comprehension. There must be a simpler way, and one that allows a greater degree of consistency in hermeneutic method. It would seem that SCIO is the view most consistent with a literal grammatical–historical hermeneutic, and no special–case hermeneutic device is required to derive it.

Examining the New Testament record we discover that the synoptic gospels point to the ratification of the New Covenant (Mt 26:28; Mk 14:24; Lk 22:20), and each delineate clearly that ratification taking place at his death – an event that necessarily precedes the inauguration of the church. Likewise, Jesus' audience was entirely Jewish (and not yet members of the church), and it would not have been at all out of place for Him to discuss an

---

[47] Bernard Ramm, *Protestant Biblical Interpretation: A Textbook of Hermeneutics* (Grand Rapids, MI: Baker Book, 1970), 264.

entirely Jewish covenant. Finally, there is *nothing in these passages that would imply the covenant is related in any fashion to the church*. Thus the New Covenant referenced here is not a covenant with an as of yet non-existent church. Paul's later inclusion of the ordinance in 1 Corinthians 11:25-26 tells us the purpose for the ordinance in the church: to proclaim the Lord's death until He comes. The emphasis is not on the covenant He ratified but is rather on His own death – a death that Paul characterizes later as a critical part of the gospel (15:3), yet with no relation to or mention of the covenant.

Furthermore, though John makes exclusive Gospel reference to blessings of the same (or at least similar) kind as those identified in the New Covenant – i.e., regeneration (Jn. 3) and near exclusive (only elsewhere specifically discussed in Lk 12:12; and 24:49) reference to the future ministry of the Holy Spirit (Jn 14-16), he excludes the ordinance entirely, and makes no mention of any covenants in any of his letters.

Similarly, Paul returns to the theme of regeneration in Titus (3:5) without any mention of the covenant in that all-important pastoral letter. He discusses the ministry of the Spirit in all of His epistles but Philemon, yet mentions the covenant directly on only three occasions (Rom 11:27; 1 Cor 11:25 and 2 Cor 3:6). Even the forgiveness of sins cited in Romans 11:27 references specifically the sins of Israel and forgiveness for Israel. Note the distinct usage of second person (you, your, vv. 25 and 28) and third person pronouns (them, their, v. 27). Israel and Jacob directly are directly identified in 11:26 and are clearly the antecedents for the third person pronouns of 11:27. Paul's final mention of the covenant in 2 Corinthians 3:6 is an assertion that he (and those serving with him) are servants of the New Covenant – presumably to the extent that the church is intended in part to move Jews to jealousy in order that they might call upon their Messiah (Rom 11:13-15). He does not connect the New Covenant with the church in any way. In fact, he offers no definition of the New Covenant nor does he relay any of its content. This is a reality that suggests he expected his readers to understand the covenant from already existing revelation.

Though Paul does not in these passages invoke either a new and separate covenant with the church nor a shared application of the previously revealed one, some argue that he does the latter in Ephesians 2:11–3:6, a passage in which gentiles are described as, among other things, "strangers to the covenants." (2:12) In 2:12 Paul presents five conditions of unsaved gentiles, and he does not assert that all of these conditions are reversed at the time of salvation. Notice the remedy he diagnoses: those formerly far off have been brought near (2:13), having access through Him in one Spirit to the Father (2:18). Believing gentiles have been made fellow citizens with the saints (believing Jews) (2:19). But fellow citizens of what? Are we now partakers of Jewish covenants? Are we now of the commonwealth of Israel? Have we now become "spiritual" Jews? No on all counts. The mystery is precisely identified in 3:6 that we are fellow members of the body and fellow partakers of the promise (note, not promises). We are brought near to the Jews by virtue of our oneness in the body of Christ, but nowhere in this grand section are we co-partakers or fellow citizens in any aspect outside of that body. This is according to promise. Paul's first mention of the promise in Ephesians appears in 1:13 referencing the Holy Spirit. We could also consider the seventh aspect of God's covenant with Abraham (Gen 12:3) and compare this with John's concise description of the promise – eternal life (1 Jn. 2:25). Whether the promise here references the related aspects of the ministry of the spirit, gentile blessings under the Abrahamic covenant, or eternal life, there is no stated or implied connection between the church and the covenants of Israel. Paul says we were once strangers to the covenants of promise and that now we have been brought near (*eggus*). *Near* is not *in*side or *upon*.

Peter also considers the concept of new birth (1 Pet 1:23) and does not reference any related covenant – in either of his letters. Nor does Jude mention the covenants, though he considers the present ministry of the Holy Spirit (v. 20). This leaves remaining unconsidered only the author of Hebrews, who references the New Covenant more frequently than all other New Testament writers combined.

The New Covenant is first mentioned in Hebrews by implication in 7:22 as "a better covenant." The clear contrast is between the Law (the inferior covenant), referenced also as the first covenant (8:7; 9:1), and the second (8:7), also tabbed the New Covenant (8:13; 9:15; 12:24) and the eternal covenant (13:20). At least three major points can be made in argument that the New Covenant discussed in Hebrews does not in any way pertain to the church.

First, the purpose of the Epistle is primarily to extol the superiority of the Person of Christ (1:3-14), and secondarily to ensure the readers do not neglect in position or practice the great salvation that He provides (2:1-4). That the New Covenant, of which He is the Mediator, is contrasted with the old is only one of numerous contrasts in the Epistle (e.g., Levitical priesthood vs. Melchizedekian priesthood; Angels vs. Christ; copies of things vs. the things themselves; sacrifices vs. the Sacrifice; Moses vs. Christ, etc.) serving as means to support the primary theme. We would not and should not assume that because the writer appeals to a particular role of Christ, that such a role is necessarily and immediately applicable to the church. For example, note that the superiority of Christ's priesthood is clarified as being identified with Melchizedek – the priestly king. Is Christ reigning today? Is there an expectation that Christ will be King of the church? Applying any aspect of Christ's work discussed in this context directly to the church requires us to extend not only beyond the scope and stated purpose of the text, but it also requires that we reconsider *every* role of Christ identified in this context. Again, as in other contexts (e.g., 1 Cor 11:25ff), the focus is the Mediator, not the covenant He mediates, which is simply raised in this context as a means whereby we can understand the Mediator to be superior and sufficient. It is by one offering, not one covenant that he has perfected for all time those who are sanctified (Heb 10:14).

Second, the distinction of pronouns used and inclusion of original-recipient language in the New Covenant passages indicate that there has been no changes or additions to the original and directly identified recipients of the New Covenant. Note in 10:15 the Holy Spirit bears witness to "us," yet in 10:16 the covenant will be made with "them", and He will put His laws upon "their" heart and will write them on "their" mind, and "their" sins will be forgiven. *Us* is not *them*. The pronouns maintain the distinction between the readers of Hebrews and those with whom the covenant is made and to whom it is fulfilled. Likewise, 8:8–12 offers a retelling of Jeremiah 31:31–34, and includes the original-recipient language ("with the House of Israel and with the House of Judah," 8:8). There is absolutely no indication of a redefining or an altering in any way of the recipients. We cannot assume that since the passage appears in a letter to church age believers (at least in part) that we can thus arbitrarily apply what is quoted to the church or the church age. It cannot be overstated that there is no language here, directly or implied, that would indicate a shift or expansion of the recipients of the New Covenant, on the contrary, the pronouns and names included tell us *there is to be no expansion or redefinition*.

Third, there is no new content added to the covenant that would imply any possibility for expansion or redefinition. It is not insignificant that the covenant is recounted in full without any alterations. This would confirm that the reader is rightly to understand the New Covenant of Hebrews as the New Covenant of Jeremiah, and thus neither as a second New Covenant nor an alteration of the first to accommodate the church's blessing.

It would seem certain blessings had by the church that are often associated by interpreters with the (or, a) New Covenant are discussed regularly by the New Testament writers with either no mention of the covenant or with no view to applying the New Covenant to the church in any way. If this is so, then we must ask the question, "from whence comes the blessings of the church?" If those blessings are not derived from the New Covenant then from what are they derived? It is critical to the SCIO premise that the present day blessings of the church are derived from the seventh aspect of the Abrahamic covenant (Gen 12:3) – an aspect that would anticipate and include the substitutionary atonement of Christ on behalf of not only Jews but gentiles as well. While it is observed that there is no exegetical warrant for relating the New Covenant to the church, SCIO is encumbered by no theological necessity to do so. By method of the literal grammatical–historical hermeneutic, SCIO is able to uniquely maintain – unlike the other views considered here – the *complete* distinction of Israel and the church, and the complete, literal, and *only* literal fulfillment of the provisions of God's New Covenant with Israel.

CONCLUSION

Allow me a bit of wordplay akin to Pascal's wager, though such will no more prove the superiority of SCIO as Pascal's wager does the existence of God. And though I typically bristle at such utilitarian considerations, perhaps this one might spark us to a reconfiguring and a reexamination of some theological premises that call for reconfiguring and reexamination. So, I pose two questions.

First, what do I have to gain by applying the New Covenant to the church? I would suggest nothing at all. Each of the blessings that the church presently enjoys fits neatly within God's revealed plan as an aspect of the Abrahamic covenant. (Perhaps I might gain the approval of certain of my peers, though with all due love and respect I must count that as nothing worthy of pursuit.)

Second, what do I have to lose by applying the New Covenant to the church? I lose the theological method on which I depend – the literal grammatical–historical device. I can no longer claim consistency, as I must utilize other devices wholly foreign to literal grammatical–historical. Having lost my method and my consistency, I would soon expect to lose my confidence in the veracity of the text and the theology that it reveals. I would expect no more to stand firmly in sound doctrine nor to recognize error when it manifests itself in doctrines mine or externally held, for I would have no more standard for understanding written language. What benefit is inerrancy, inspiration, or infallibility without a standard by which to interpret what has faithfully been recorded? Like Nietzsche, I would expect that even if there were truth or meaning I would be incapable of ascertaining it, and thus it would be lost to me. In short, if I lose consistency in hermeneutic method, I have lost the text and all for which it stands.

George Peters marveled at those who, by applying kingdom elements of the Davidic covenant to the church, traded in the greatness of God's revealed plan for an artificial theological construct. Peters laments,

> It is *strange* and *sad,* that some of the most eminent and talented men of the church, *blinded by a subtle theory*, cannot and will not see how antagonistic such a theory is to God's faithful promises. No wonder that we are so carefully cautioned to beware of mere human wisdom.[48]

Perhaps we might consider that an error of the same kind – even if made with regard to a different covenant – produces equally strange and sad results.

[48] George N. H. Peters, *The Theocratic Kingdom, Vol. I* (Grand Rapids, MI: Kregel, 1978), 657.

4

THE HOLY SPIRIT, THE CHURCH, AND THE NEW COVENANT:

CHALLENGING A POINT OF METHODOLOGICAL SIMILARITY BETWEEN CLASSICAL DISPENSATIONALISM, COVENANT THEOLOGY, PROGRESSIVE DISPENSATIONALISM, AND NEW COVENANT THEOLOGY [1]

Christopher Cone

ABSTRACT

Classical dispensationalists generally invoke the relationship of the Holy Spirit to the church during the present dispensation as an aspect of present application (though not fulfillment of) the New Covenant (NC) to the church. Progressive dispensationalists have cited this classical understanding (of the Holy Spirit's present function in relation to the church as directly connected to the NC) as an instance of Classical dispensationalist employment of the *already not yet* (ANY) hermeneutic device. Consequently, progressives perceive no departure from classical hermeneutic methodology on their own part in applying ANY to the Davidic Covenant.

---

[1] Addressed to The Council on Dispensational Hermeneutics, at Baptist Bible Seminary, September 21, 2011, as "Considering the Relationship of the Holy Spirit to the Church in Connection With the New Covenant."

This paper examines the Covenant, Classical dispensational, Progressive dispensational, and New Covenant Theology perspectives of the relationship between the NC and the contemporary ministry of the Holy Spirit, and concludes by exegetical analysis that His relationship to the church is not directly connected to the NC. Further, it is argued here that ANY is not an appropriate hermeneutic device to be employed in this context (the Holy Spirit, the NC, and the church). Consequently, in some cases Classical dispensationalist interpreters have been inconsistent in hermeneutic methodology by employing ANY as a hermeneutic device, and in those cases Classical dispensationalist interpreters have operated from a Covenant framework and inadvertently justified the hermeneutic methodology of Progressive dispensationalism.

SECTION I

INTRODUCTION

Elsewhere I argued that ANY is not a legitimate hermeneutic device within the literal grammatical–historical method. In support of that thesis I asserted that the NC was not in any way currently being fulfilled in the church, and further, that the church was not presently enjoying the blessings of the NC. Additionally, I suggested that church–age blessings were anticipated in the Abrahamic covenant (particularly in Gen 12:3), and that church–age forgiveness of sin and the corresponding indwelling by the Holy Spirit are not in any way connected to the NC (nor is such a connection necessary, or even beneficial), except that the One who ratified it also and at the same time accomplished the necessary condition for the fulfillment of Genesis 12:3 – He paid for the sins of all the families of the earth (1 Jn 2:2).

That the current church–age ministry of the Holy Spirit is unconnected to the NC is a necessary condition for the legitimacy of this supporting argument, and yet many in the dispensational camp would not agree with this discontinuity. Larry Pettegrew is representative of dispensational perspective on this matter as he observes, "when the New Covenant is fulfilled with Israel in the future kingdom, the Gentiles will receive 'trickle down' blessings."[2]

Pettegrew adds, "The disciples were told to wait in Jerusalem until the final provision of the New Covenant in the church age was inaugurated...some fifty days after Passover, Christ inaugurated the New Covenant by pouring out the Holy Spirit."[3] He says, "Clearly, the provisions of the New Covenant are also operative and observable beginning on the day of Pentecost."[4] He cites specifically "the law in the heart, a personal relationship with God, forgiveness of sins, and even the ministry of the Holy Spirit on believers,"[5] and posits "the New Testament documents should be viewed as instruction on how to live out the New Covenant in the present age."[6] While acknowledging tensions in such an interpretation (in light of the original recipients of the New Covenant promises), he suggests "the most Biblically informed solution is that the church participates in the New Covenant but that the New Covenant will not be finally fulfilled until Israel comes into a right relationship with God and its Messiah at the end of the Tribulation."[7]

---

[2] Larry Dean Pettegrew, The New Covenant Ministry of the Holy Spirit (Grand Rapids, MI: Kregel, 2001), 32.

[3] Pettegrew, 35.

[4] Ibid.

[5] Pettegrew, 36.

[6] Ibid.

[7] Ibid.

REFORMED PERSPECTIVES

Pettegrew is neither original nor alone in his assertion that the Holy Spirit's ministry to the church is an NC blessing. In contrasting Old and New Covenants, John Calvin observes, "The Old Testament is of the letter, for it was published without the working of the Spirit. The New is spiritual because the Lord has engraved it spiritually on men's hearts [II Cor 3:6a]."[8] He clarifies that the New is operative, saying, "The New is the ministry of righteousness because it reveals God's mercy, through which we are justified [II Cor 3:9]."[9]

Abraham Kuyper, while recognizing that the Spirit had been active in "the Church of the Old Covenant,"[10] he notes that, in light of the prophecies of Numbers 11:29, Isaiah 32:14–17, Ezekiel 11:19 and 36:25, Joel 2:30–31, Luke 24:49, John 14:16–17 and 15:26, 16:7–8, and Acts 1:4–8 "it can not be doubted that the Holy Scriptures means to teach and convince us that the outpouring of the Holy Spirit on Pentecost was His first and real coming into the Church."[11] Especially notable is Kuyper's understanding that Ezekiel 36:22ff – a restatement of NC restoration promises of Jeremiah 31 – is fulfilled at Pentecost.

O.T. Allis, in discussing the role of law in the current age, asserts succinctly the connection between the NC and the present ministry of the Holy Spirit: "For the gospel age in which we are living is that day foretold by the prophets when the law of God shall be written in the hearts of men (Jer. Xxxi. 33) and when the

---

[8] John Calvin, *Institutes of the Christian Religion*, trans., Ford Lewis Battles, ed., John T. McNeill (Philadelphia, PA: Westminster Press, 1940), 2:11:8.

[9] Calvin, 2:11:8.

[10] Abraham Kuyper, *The Work of the Holy Spirit* (Grand Repids, MI: Eerdmans,1975), 113.

[11] Kuyper, 115.

Spirit of God abiding in their hearts will enable to keep it (Ezek. Xi. 19, 26f.). The gospel age is the age of the New Covenant…"[12]

Louis Berkhof observes that "the covenant" [he means the covenant of grace] is only fully realized in the elect, citing Jeremiah 31:31–34 as a proof.[13] Berkhof adds, "The New Testament Dispensation of the covenant may be called universal in the sense that in it the covenant is extended to all nations, and is no more limited to the Jews as it was in the old dispensation."[14] The elect to whom Berkhof refers are those who are "called to be children of God and heirs of eternal life."[15] Thus, for Berkhof, the ministry of the Spirit in and to the elect constitutes a covenant relationship.[16] While the idea that the church's present blessing did not, of course, originate with Calvin, Kuyper, Allis or Berkhof, either, theirs is representative of a Reformed position that has been (I argue) borrowed by dispensational thinkers.

CLASSICAL DISPENSATIONAL PERSPECTIVES

Lewis Sperry Chafer says on the one hand (correctly, I suggest), "Now Israel is dormant and all that is related to her covenants and promises is in abeyance."[17] He adds "it is made certain that the present age has been marked off as one of peculiar privilege and

---

[12] Oswald T. Allis, *Prophecy and the Church* (Phillipsburg, NJ: Presbyterian & Reformed, 1947), 42.

[13] Louis Berkhof, *Systematic Theology* (Grand Rapids, MI: Eerdmans, 1949), 276.

[14] Berkhof, 276.

[15] Berkhof, 114.

[16] Berkhof, 426.

[17] Lewis Sperry Chafer, *Systematic Theology, Volume VI: Pneumatology* (Grand Rapids, MI: Kregel, 1983), 83.

benefit for Gentile peoples."[18] He characterizes this present time
(in which he observes everything related to Israel's covenants are
dormant) as "this age of the Church...properly styled the
dispensation of the Holy Spirit."[19]

It is evident from these comments that Chafer, in this
context, draws a complete distinction between the ministry of the
Holy Spirit in the present age and the NC. While Chafer does
contrast the present indwelling of the Holy Spirit and previous
Old Testament ministry by citing 2 Corinthians 3:6,[20] and he
further considers circumcision of the heart as discussed in Ezekiel
44:7,[21] nowhere in Chafer's chapters devoted to the work of the
Holy Spirit in the church–age believer does he in any way connect
the present ministry of the Holy Spirit to the NC.[22]

Elsewhere, however, Chafer identifies two NC's – one for
the church and one for Israel. He defines and contrasts the two as
follows:

> (11) The New Covenant for the Church (Luke 22:20),
> which incorporates ever promise of saving and keeping
> grace for those of the present age who believe. Its many
> blessings are either possessions or positions in Christ.
> (12) The New Covenant for Israel (Jer. 31:31–34; Heb.
> 8:7–12), which covenant is "new" in the sense that it
> supersedes as a rule of life the Mosaic Covenant that Israel
> broke, but it does not alter or conflict with the Palestinian
> Covenant, the Abrahamic Covenant, or the Davidic
> Covenant. Its blessings are fourfold and all yet future,

---

[18] Chafer, 84.

[19] Chafer, 100.

[20] Chafer, 123.

[21] Chafer, 146.

[22] See Chafer, *Vol VI*, 80–298.

though assured unconditionally on the unfailing faithfulness of God.[23]

Notably, there is no exegetical weight behind Chafer's claim that there is a New Covenant made with the church. His citing of Luke 22:20 as supportive of such a covenant ignores at least two important textual factors. First, the reference to the NC is articulated in the Greek of Luke 22:20 (ἡ καινὴ διαθήκη), and would have been understood by the disciples as referring to a specific covenant previously announced.[24] Second, when Paul quotes the statement in 1 Corinthians 11:25, he notes only one application of the event for the church: "you proclaim His death until He comes."

Why then does Chafer follow in the path of Covenant theologians in identifying covenants that are not so identified in Scripture? Why does Chafer depart from the literal grammatical-historical hermeneutic in favor of a theological hermeneutic in this context? It seems an attempt on the one hand to counter Covenant theology's merging of Israel with the church while at the same time accommodating a central tenet in Covenant theology – that the church has a present covenant relationship with God (a tenet entirely unnecessary, as Chafer demonstrates by writing an entire volume on the Holy Spirit without once connecting His ministry to the NC).

The keen observer will note that in Chafer's volume on Pneumatology, of all secondary sources cited, Chafer leans most heavily upon John Walvoord, who also describes a separate New Covenant for the church:

---

[23] Lewis Sperry Chafer, *Systematic Theology Volume I: Prolegomena, Bibliology and Theology Proper* (Grand Rapids, MI: Kregel, 1993), 43.

[24] Pentecost observes this also, see Dwight Pentecost, *Things to Come* (Grand Rapids, MI: Academie, 1964), 126.

Just as Israel will be graciously forgiven under the New Covenant, so also the church in the present age receives grace. All grace systems stem from the death of Christ, whether applied to Israel or other peoples. Hence the church in the present age also participates in a New Covenant. This can be best explained as one New Covenant of grace made possible by the death of Christ, whether applied to Israel in Jeremiah or the church as in the New Testament.[25]

While Chafer at least offers a proof–text, Walvoord bases his NC on a simple syllogism:

P1:The church in the present age receives grace
P2: All grace systems stem from the death of Christ
C: Hence, the church participates in a NC

This is easily recognizable as a *non sequitur*, and invites the question of why such brilliant and godly men as Chafer and Walvoord would compromise their theological methods to the point of proof texting and poor logic. I propose that they were attempting to concurrently counter and accommodate certain aspects of Covenant theology.

I do not here intend to suggest that deliberate accommodation of Covenant theology is an epidemic in dispensational thought. However, I do assert that dispensational thought has been so strongly influenced by Covenant grounding that we struggle to extricate ourselves, and in some aspects don't even realize the trap in which we are caught. I think that such is the case with those who hold that the current blessings enjoyed by the church – including the present ministry of the Holy Spirit – are connected to the NC.

[25] John Walvoord, *The Prophecy Knowledge Handbook* (Dallas, TX: Dallas Seminary Press, 1990), 140.

While Dwight Pentecost does not attempt in *Things to Come* a resolution of conflicting theories among dispensationalists pertaining to the NC,[26] he offers some commentary very relevant to the discussion. First, he notes that Hebrews does not indicate that Israel's NC is operative with the church.[27] Second, he suggests that the New Testament references to *the* NC would all have been understood as referencing *the* NC of Jeremiah 31.[28] Finally, he adds this telling statement: "Since the church receives blessings of the Abrahamic Covenant (Gal 3:14; 4:22–31) by faith without being under or fulfilling that covenant, so the church may receive blessings from the New Covenant without being under of fulfilling that New Covenant."[29]

The problem with this statement is evident from the first passage to which he alludes. Galatians 3:14 addresses the method whereby the Abrahamic Covenant can be fulfilled: ἵνα εἰς τὰ ἔθνη – in order that unto the nations, ἡ εὐλογία τοῦ Ἀβραὰμ γένηται ἐν Χριστῷ Ἰησοῦ – the blessing (singular) of Abraham might come in Christ Jesus. What *singular blessing* promised to Abraham was prophesied to come to the nations or peoples? None from Genesis 12:1–2, but 12:3 speaks of blessing for all the families of the earth. Hence, Galatians 3:14 does not describe the nations as receiving blessings not initially intended for them, but rather it describes the vehicle necessary for fulfillment of God's covenant with Abraham: the death of Christ – and the passage recognizes that the prophesied blessing (from Gen. 12:3) has now been provided for in Christ. In short, the church *is* presently fulfilling at least some aspects of the seventh point of the Abrahamic Covenant. If

---

[26] Pentecost, 124.

[27] Pentecost, 126.

[28] Ibid.

[29] Pentecost, 127.

this is correct, then any connection of the church to NC blessings is, if exegetically unwarranted, theologically unnecessary.

Consider, for example, Pentecost's agreement with the following:

> The New Covenant of Jeremiah 31 necessitated the work of a Mediator and the death of Christ is that which makes a New Covenant possible...All the blessings which come to the church today are based upon the blood of Christ, which was necessarily shed to make possible the New Covenant.[30]

If Pentecost is correct here (and I believe he is), then the church's blessings are based on Christ's blood, and can be understood as deriving from the Abrahamic, rather than the New Covenant. Any connection whatsoever between Israel's covenants and the church is found in this fact: the One who died to ratify the NC did at the same time provide the necessary condition for the fulfillment of Genesis 12:3. In any case, Pentecost, with his *one NC with present blessings for the church view*, differs from Chafer and Walvoord, who hold to two NC's, and seems to represent a separate classification of dispensational thinker in this regard: rather than deliberately accommodating aspects of Covenant theology and working directly in its framework, he simply does not seem to break away from certain traditional aspects of dispensationalism deriving from Covenant theology – even though his observations contain the solution to (what I believe to be) the inconsistency.

Most dispensational thinkers have walked in the two differing sets of footsteps described above (either following the two NC view or alternately the view that there is only one NC and the church presently enjoys its blessings without fulfilling it). For sake of transparency, before I began to argue against it, I

---

[30] Pentecost, 122–123

advocated a position consistent with those held by Pentecost and Scofield (although Scofield does go a bit further than Pentecost in positing that "Christians are now partakers" of the NC[31]). Some years ago I authored a survey of the Bible, and in discussing the NC, I posit,

> There is a sixth element [of the NC] that is not revealed in Jeremiah. This is the fulfillment of the Abrahamic promise that "in you all the nations of the earth shall be blessed." It is the mystery, later to be unveiled, that the Gentiles may participate in the forgiveness element of the New Covenant also (Ephesians 3:1–5). It becomes *the* promise to the church (1 John 2:25).[32]

While I have revisited and edited the statement in a current edition, the initial comment remains a testament to my own evolution on this issue, as ultimately the idea that certain covenant blessings are presently being realized is unavoidably an application of ANY as a hermeneutic device. In short, the inconsistency I am decrying has, in the recent past, been my very own.

PROGRESSIVE DISPENSATIONAL PERSPECTIVES

Nonetheless, for some interlocutors, the two paths more traveled have not offered sufficient exegetical grounding or logical warrant. Founders of Progressive dispensationalism (PD), for example, point to areas such as these when discussing the need for further development in dispensational thought. They

---

[31] C.I. Scofield, *Scofield Bible Correspondence Course Volume I: Introduction to the Scriptures* (Chicago, IL: Moody Bible Institute, 1959), 70.

[32] Christopher Cone, *The Promises of God: A Synthetic Bible Survey*, 3rd Printing (Fort Worth, TX: Exegetica Publishing, 2005), 138.

acknowledge that the hermeneutic devices employed in postulating such positions demand the further revision of the positions. For example, Darrell Bock notes that, "All the covenants of promise are initially realized in the church. This has never been disputed for the Abrahamic covenant in dispensationalism."[33] Bock's comment illustrates a key point in PD thought: since classical dispensational thinkers are willing to accept ANY as a hermeneutic device for understanding the Abrahamic and NC, then there can be no protestation when that same hermeneutic device is applied to the Davidic Covenant.

In applying ANY to the NC, Bock writes of Jeremiah 31:34, "This promise is probably what underlies the earlier eschatological revelation that a day was coming in the midst of restoration when all of the people of God would experience the outpouring of God's Spirit (Joel 2:28–29)."[34] Notice how effortlessly Bock moves past the specific application to Israel and connects the passage to broader prophecy. He continues, "This is what also underwrites Ezekiel's remark about the promise of a new heart and Spirit within them (Ezek 36:26–27)."[35] Bock understands the outpouring of the Holy Spirit on Gentiles in Joel 2 to be a NC event – and one that has present realization.

Of Jeremiah 31:34, Bock explains, "The point here is not that instruction is abolished; rather, it is the loss of a need for any other mediator in conducting the relationship with God."[36] The literal rendering of the text – which would damage the theological point Bock is making – is sacrificed in this case in favor of "the

---

[33] Darrell Bock, "Covenants in Progressive Dispensationalism" in *Three Central Issues in Contemporary Dispensationalism*, Gen. Ed., Herbert W. Bateman IV, (Grand Rapids, MI: Kregel, 1999), 171.

[34] Bock, 191.

[35] Ibid.

[36] Ibid.

point here," which is derived from a nonliteral rendering that accommodates the PD thesis. Bock adds in a later context, "In Jesus, eschatological, regal, messianic promised activity has come to realization in the giving of the Spirit and the granting of a transformed relationship to the Gentiles."[37] If a NC promise is presently being realized in the church (as Bock says it is), and that promise is connected to the Davidic Covenant (as he implies it is by invoking terms such as "regal" and "messianic"), than it should come as no surprise that ANY can be applied to all the covenants of promise, and that the covenants are all being realized (if only initially) at present in the church.

Bruce Ware appeals to Isaiah 55:3–5 as a "new–covenant text,"[38] and asserts that "we see from this text that the New Covenant made with Israel includes a host of Gentile participants, not directly addressed as God's covenant partners."[39] Further, by connecting Joel 2:28–29 with Jeremiah 31:34 (as Bock also does), Ware concludes that the NC "will be an inclusive covenant in which all God's people experience the internalization of the law by the Spirit and so know him in utter faithfulness, with sins forgiven and removed forever and ever."[40] Not only does Ware understand that the NC is inclusive, but he understands it to be realized (though not entirely fulfilled) in the church.

He observes that in order for there to be such a realization there had to be "the internalization of God's law, by the Spirit, in all of God's people."[41] However, "this lack is quickly supplied when

---

[37] Bock, 201.

[38] Bruce Ware, "The New Covenant and the People(s) of God" in *Dispensationalism, Israel and the Church: The Search for Definition*, Craig Blaising and Darrell Bock, eds. (Grand Rapids, MI: Zondervan, 1992), 72.

[39] Ware, 73.

[40] Ware, 83.

[41] Ware, 87.

we turn to Acts and the Epistles...One of the features of the New Covenant is that all those in the community of faith participate in that covenant's eschatological power and blessings, and Acts 2 makes it clear that this feature has now begun to be realized."[42] As for how Ware understands Paul to connect the ministry of the Holy Spirit to the NC, Ware observes, "It seems that Paul has combined in his thinking the new-covenant promise of Jeremiah 31 (see 2 Cor 3:6, where "New Covenant" is used) with the promise of the coming Spirit from Ezekiel 36, for it is clearly the ministry of the Spirit that enlivens and empowers the New Covenant's effectiveness."[43]

As does Bock, Ware combines promises made to Israel with broader promises regarding the pouring out of the Holy Spirit upon Gentiles. Ware attributes such a merge as Pauline, though he hedges somewhat by invoking the word "seems." Still, Ware concludes that there is "One New Covenant, under which differing covenant participants join together, through Christ and the Spirit, as a common people of God – this, then, is the grace and the glory of the marvelous provision of God."[44] Though Ware reckons that the peoples of God are distinct "insofar as God will yet restore Israel as a nation to its land,"[45] one factor that unites them is the present and future NC ministry of the Holy Spirit.

Craig Blaising believes that Paul places the church under the NC as the church obeys Jesus' command to drink the cup of the covenant (1 Cor 11:25-29),[46] despite Paul's explanation that the church simply "proclaims His death until He comes" (v. 26).

---

[42] Ibid.

[43] Ware, 88-89.

[44] Ware, 97.

[45] Ibid.

[46] Craig Blaising and Darrell Bock, *Progressive Dispensationalism* (Grand Rapids, MI: Baker, 1993), 200.

Further, he connects Jeremiah 31:33 with 2 Corinthians 3:3 and Ezekiel 37:14 and 2 Corinthians 3:6.[47] Blaising perhaps goes a bit further than his colleagues when he boldly asserts the certainty of present day realization of the NC in the church:

> It is indisputable that the New Testament views the New Covenant predicted by Jeremiah and Ezekiel as established in the death of Jesus Christ with some of its promised blessings now being granted to Jews and Gentiles who are believers in Jesus. These are not blessings which are like those predicted by Jeremiah and Ezekiel. They are the very same blessings which those prophets predicted. For the New Covenant which is presently in effect through Jesus Christ is not one which is like that predicted by Jeremiah and Ezekiel, but it is that very same covenant which they prophesied which is in effect today.[48]

While Blaising acknowledges there to be still yet unrealized aspects of the NC, he posits that the NC is "the dispensational form in which the Abrahamic blessings are present today."[49] He further suggests that Paul works within NC framework and terminology throughout 2 Corinthians 3 (in connection with Ezekiel 37) and in Romans 11:26–27 (in connection with Isaiah 59:20–21), noting two themes needing further consideration.

First, Blaising argues that Christ's ministry of sending the Holy Spirit is NC related, since "The gift of the Holy Spirit and the cleansing of the heart are again the language of the New Covenant

---

[47] Ibid., 201.

[48] Ibid., 202.

[49] Ibid.

promise."[50] He notes, "the blessing is given to both Jew and Gentile alike."[51] Second, while Blaising asserts the clarity of the NT that "the New Covenant has now been inaugurated, that is that blessings belonging to the New Covenant are now being dispensed to all those who believe in Jesus,"[52] he recognizes that future realizations are expected and will come at the return of Christ. In interpreting these two themes, the weight of Blaising's case is on the similarity of language between NC framework and 2 Corinthians 3 in particular – a similarity not as evident to others as it is apparently to Blaising.

Robert Saucy argues the illegitimacy of the two–NC view, in favor of the perspective that there is one NC and that "both Israel and the church share in this covenant, as in the Abrahamic covenant, for the New Covenant is the realization of the salvation of the Abrahamic promise."[53] Saucy adds, "Although the Old Testament references to the New Covenant were for the nation of Israel, the members of the church also share in its provisions."[54] He uses two devices to connect the church to the NC. First, he notes that since the NC is an amplification of the Abrahamic Covenant, the NC can also be applied to Gentiles.[55] Second, he observes that the "Old Testament prophecies looked forward to the salvation of the New Covenant extending also to the Gentiles."[56] In the first instance, the inclusion of Gentiles as

---

[50] Ibid., 208.

[51] Ibid.

[52] Ibid.

[53] Robert Saucy, *The Church in God's Program* (Chicago,IL: Moody Press, 1972), 78.

[54] Ibid., 80.

[55] Ibid., 80–81.

[56] Ibid., 81.

beneficiaries of the Abrahamic covenant automatically (it seems) qualifies Gentiles for participation in the NC, and in the second, OT references to Gentile salvation are understood by Saucy to be connected ultimately to the NC.

Saucy admits, "the Old Testament did not explicitly predict the coming of the Spirit on the Gentiles,"[57] but notes "it did predict the sharing of the messianic salvation with them."[58] He adds, "Inherent in this New Covenant salvation, as taught in both testaments, is the gift of the Spirit."[59] Based on two premises, Saucy connects the present ministry of the Holy Spirit with the NC:

> P1: Gentile salvation is anticipated as an outworking of the NC.
> P2: NC salvation involves the gift of the Spirit.
> C: Therefore, the present ministry of the Spirit is a NC ministry.

As I have noted previously, the suggestion that Gentile salvation is connected to the NC is neither exegetically warranted nor theologically necessary. Rather Gentile salvation can easily be understood as an outworking of the Abrahamic Covenant, and not in any connection with the NC (other than that it is the same Mediator who makes possible by the same event – His death – the ultimate fulfillment of every aspect of all the covenants of promise).

In summarizing the above PD perspectives on the present ministry of the Holy Spirit in connection with the NC, a few notable factors are evident: (1) broad theological themes are

---

[57] Robert Saucy, *The Case for Progressive Dispensationalism* (Grand Rapids, MI: Zondervan, 1993), 183.

[58] Ibid.

[59] Ibid.

considered more weighty than the fruit of consistently applied grammatical-historical hermeneutics; (2) problem passages are consequently explained away by use of a nonliteral hermeneutic; (3) the application of ANY as a hermeneutic device, employed earlier by Covenant and Classical dispensational theologians, is expanded to include all the unconditional covenants; (4) consequently, the principle of single meaning is de-emphasized; and finally, (5) the methodological lines between Covenant and dispensational theology are broken down to the point that there is no absolute basis for preferring Covenant over dispensational theology. Further, it should be noted that the primary hermeneutic device (ANY) facilitating this breakdown is prominent in Covenant theology, evident in Classical dispensational theology, and utilized not inconsistently by Progressive dispensational theology. Ultimately, by employing ANY as a hermeneutic device, Classical dispensationalism has set the stage for its own demise, and as long as it continues to do appeal to ANY, its criticisms of PD are little more than exercises in hypocrisy.

NEW COVENANT THEOLOGY PERSPECTIVES

Fred G. Zaspel describes New Covenant Theology (NCT) as an attempt to answer the question of relationship between Old and New Testaments, as a movement dissatisfied with elements of the Covenant and dispensational systems, and as one comfortable with the progress represented by PD, for example, to that end.[60] Donald Hochner describes NCT as agreeing with Covenant theology in such areas as five-point Calvinism, the use of figurative hermeneutics, the spiritualization of Israel, and

---

[60] Fred G Zaspel, "A Brief Explanation of New Covenant Theology," http://www.Biblicalstudies.com/bstudy/hermenutics/nct.htm, accessed 7/30/2011.

recognizing many prophesies in the OT of the NT church.[61] Further, Hochner notes that NCT departs from the Covenant system in that NCT does not recognize an OT church (but rather the elect of Israel), but does recognize the beginning of the NT church in Acts 2, and does not agree on the artificial covenants (redemption, works, grace) of the Covenant system, and NCT recognizes that the indwelling of the Holy Spirit in the NT church age differs from His ministry in the NT.[62]

Tom Wells and Fred Zaspel further describes the priority of the NT as a central principle of NCT hermeneutics: "if the New Testament is the apex of God's revelation, then we ought to read the earlier parts of Scripture its light."[63] They emphasize that "NT revelation, due to its finality must be allowed to speak first on every issue that it addresses."[64] In applying this hermeneutic device, Randal Seiver suggests that "We should not expect, based on Jeremiah 31:31–34, a restoration of national Israel, any more than we should expect, based on Jeremiah 30:9; Ezekiel 34:23–24; 37:24–25, a literal restoration of David to the throne of Israel."[65] In this assertion he does not mean that there is no future aspect of NC fulfillment for Israel, but only that any future fulfillment will not be qualitatively different from previous blessings. He clarifies,

---

[61] Donald Hochner, "A Comparison of Three Systems: Dispensationalism – Covenant Theology – and New Covenant Theology," http://www.angelfire.com/ca/DeafPreterist/compare.html, accessed 7/30–2011.

[62] Ibid.

[63] Tom Wells and Fred Zaspel, *New Covenant Theology: Description, Definition, Defense* (Frederick, MD: New Covenant Media, 2002), 1.

[64] Ibid., 7–8.

[65] Randal Seiver, "The New Covenant in Promise and Fulfillment: Jeremiah 31:31–34; Hebrews 8:6–13" http://solochristo.com/theology/nct/ncpromise.htm, accessed 7/30/2011.

There may be a *future restoration* of ethnic Israelites to God's favor through faith in Christ but not a *retrogression* to Judaism. There may be a fuller, future fulfillment of promises that have been, in the higher, New Covenant sense, literally fulfilled already. Yet, in keeping with the nature of typological fulfillment, the future fulfillment must be of the same kind as the fulfillment that has already occurred. Thus, there may be a future restoration of Israel that is fuller *in quantity,* but not different *in quality* from what is now occurring in the conversion of a remnant of ethnic Israelites through gospel preaching.[66]

In short, the NC is presently in force, but that present operative state does not preclude the possibility of more full realization in the future. Seiver appeals to Romans 9:25–26 as evidence that the Gentiles become partakers of NC grace.[67] From there, he claims that Jeremiah 31:34 refers to those in "The Church, God's New Covenant community,"[68] and that "every member of this community, from the least to the greatest, knows the Lord."[69] By reading the NT (Rom 9:25–26) back into the OT (Jer 31:34), Seiver applies a literal hermeneutic to part of the verse (For they shall all know Me...) while ignoring the other (And they shall not teach again...). By this hermeneutic maneuver the NT church is able to receive NC blessings – including the ministry of the Holy Spirit for internalizing the law of the Lord.

NCT is very similar in this respect to PD, underscoring a notable parallel between the founders of each system: PD emerges from dispensationalism and moves toward Covenant

---

[66] Ibid.

[67] Ibid.

[68] Ibid.

[69] Ibid.

theology, while NCT emerges from Covenant theology and moves (at least to some degree) toward dispensationalism. It is fitting, then, that the methodology (application of ANY, primacy of the NT for interpreting the OT, employment of figurative hermeneutics) and conclusions of NCT and PD are largely (though not entirely) compatible in regard to the NC and its applications and fulfillment.

THE IMPORT OF PRESUPPOSITIONS AND METHODOLOGY

Notably, representatives of each perspective – whether Covenant theology, Classical dispensational, Progressive dispensational, or New Covenant Theology – recognize the importance of presuppositions and methodology, and acknowledge the impact of those two factors on the exegetical process. Covenant theology is grounded on the premises of one people of God in covenant relationship, and is governed methodologically by ANY, a hermeneutic device facilitated by the employment of allegorical and spiritualized interpretation. New Covenant Theology varies from this only by degree and specific application of nonliteral hermeneutics, though its founders acknowledge the central role of NT primacy in NCT hermeneutic method – this is a presupposition that sets the course of the hermeneutic methodology. Progressive dispensationalism is premised on "a holistic and unified view of salvation,"[70] and one that is "without distinction."[71]   PD is methodologically grounded in a complementary hermeneutic, which emphasizes NT primacy and welcomes ANY as *the* Scripture–unifying device.[72]

---

[70] Craig Blaising and Darrell Bock, *Progressive Dispensationalism* (Grand Rapids, MI: Baker, 1993), 47.

[71] Ibid.

[72] Ibid., 98.

Classical dispensationalism is usually understood to be grounded upon doxological purpose of God and the distinction between Israel and the church, and governed methodologically by the consistent application of a literal grammatical hermeneutic. Charles Ryrie identifies these three aspects clearly enough – identifying them as the *sine qua non* of dispensationalism.[73] Of the three, perhaps it is best to prioritize the hermeneutic component, since the other two must be derived through the application of the methodology.

If this is the case, then Classical dispensationalism must be – more than any of the other systems discussed here – singularly and completely committed to consistent application of the literal grammatical–historical hermeneutic. In view of our adoption of ANY and our occasional appeal to allegorical and spiritual hermeneutics we have not been faithful to our own system. John Gerstner says as much when he observes,

> Many on both sides think that this minor 'hermeneutical' difference [between the dispensationalist tendency to literalism and the non–dispensational tendency to interpret figuratively] is a more foundational difference than the theological. *We profoundly disagree for we believe that the dispensational literal hermeneutic is driven by an a priori commitment to dispensational theological distinctives* [emphasis and clarification mine].[74]

As Bible students who have historically drawn dispensational conclusions, we must ask ourselves from where those conclusions come – whether they are the fruit of diligent exegesis

---

[73] Charles Ryrie, *Dispensationalism Today* (Chicago, IL: Moody Press, 1965), 44–47.

[74] John Gerstner, *Wrongly Dividing the Word of Truth* (Morgan, PA: Soli Deo Gloria, 1991), 93.

or whether they are merely the working out of a system to which we feel indebted. Perhaps Gerstner is correct in his assertion that our feigned loyalty to the literal grammatical–historical method is mere hypocrisy. Or perhaps, much like Martin Luther – who sensed the need for reform and acted to that end, all the while unable to divorce himself from aspects of the Church he sought to correct – perhaps much like him, our dispensational fathers ran fast and hard to escape the errors they perceived in the Covenant system. Yet they, like Luther, did not perceive the full invasiveness of the bonds that held them fast. And thus, upon making their escape, they understandably failed to recognize that the foundations upon which they began to build were not as purely fashioned as they had intended.

In this present context of the NC and the contemporary ministry of the Holy Spirit, we must examine whether we build on cracked foundation or whether we maintain a fierce loyalty to the authority of God in Scripture by consistently applying the literal grammatical–historical hermeneutic to the text – as our dispensational fathers tried to instruct us, even if their example was imperfect.

SECTION II

EXAMINING RELATED OLD TESTAMENT TEXTS IN CHRONOLOGICAL SEQUENCE

In this section I exegetically consider OT passages that are cited as significant to the positions of the various traditions discussed above. In so doing, I attempt strict adherence to the literal grammatical–historical hermeneutic. The question at stake in this context is whether there is exegetical warrant for understanding these passages as supportive of a present manifestation of the Holy Spirit's NC ministry, or whether His contemporary ministry can be exegetically understood from these passages as disconnected from the NC.

Genesis 12:2–3

2"I will make you into a great nation and I will bless you; I will make your name great, and you will be a blessing. 3 I will bless those who bless you, and whoever curses you I will curse; and all peoples on earth will be blessed through you."[75]

2 וְאֶעֶשְׂךָ לְגוֹי גָּדוֹל וַאֲבָרֶכְךָ וַאֲגַדְּלָה שְׁמֶךָ וֶהְיֵה בְּרָכָה:

3 וַאֲבָרֲכָה מְבָרֲכֶיךָ וּמְקַלֶּלְךָ אָאֹר וְנִבְרְכוּ בְךָ כֹּל מִשְׁפְּחֹת הָאֲדָמָה:

76

[2] καὶ ποιήσω σε εἰς ἔθνος μέγα καὶ εὐλογήσω σε καὶ μεγαλυνῶ τὸ ὄνομά σου, καὶ ἔσῃ εὐλογητός, 3 καὶ εὐλογήσω τοὺς εὐλογοῦντάς σε, καὶ τοὺς καταρωμένους σε καταράσομαι, καὶ ἐνευλογηθήσονται ἐν σοὶ πᾶσαι αἱ φυλαὶ τῆς γῆς.[77]

God makes seven commitments to Abraham in this iteration of the Abrahamic Covenant:

(1) I will make (qal imperfect) you to (or into) a great nation (וְאֶעֶשְׂךָ לְגוֹי גָּדוֹל);

(2) and I will bless you (וַאֲבָרֶכְךָ, piel imperfect);

(3) I will make (piel imperfect) your name great (וַאֲגַדְּלָה שְׁמֶךָ);

(4) and you (or it, as in your name) shall be (qal imperative) a blessing (וֶהְיֵה בְּרָכָה);

(5) and I will bless (piel imperfect) those who bless (piel imperfect) you (וַאֲבָרֲכָה מְבָרֲכֶיךָ);

---

[75] All English Bible references are from *New American Standard Bible: 1995 Update* (LaHabra, CA: The Lockman Foundation, 1995).

[76] All Hebrew references are from *Biblia Hebraica Stuttgartensia: With Westminster Hebrew Morphology.*, electronic ed. (Stuttgart; Glenside PA: German Bible Society; Westminster Seminary, 1996, c1925; morphology c1991).

[77] All LXX references are from *Septuaginta: With Morphology* (Stuttgart: Deutsche Bibelgesellschaft, 1996, c1979).

(6) and whoever is slighting you (וּמְקַלֶּלְךָ, piel participle) I will curse (אָאֹר, qal imperfect);

(7) and they are blessed (וְנִבְרְכוּ, niphal perfect) in you (בְךָ) all (כֹל) families or clans (מִשְׁפְּחֹת) of the ground, or land (הָאֲדָמָה).

The first six pertain directly to Abraham and find fulfillment in his descendants. It might be suggested that this is an instance in which ANY should be applied to the text, but I argue that ANY is not applicable here. Consider, for example, the second commitment God makes to Abraham: "I will bless you." The object (suffix of the verb) is second person singular. God promises here to bless Abraham specifically. That part of that blessing would include his descendants growing into a great nation does not mitigate the personal blessing Abraham would receive. Rather than interpret the second blessing aspect as having more than single meaning, we can understand from other specific promises what some of those blessings would be.

We know that Abraham was blessed in the short term because specific passages indicate that explicitly (14:19; 24:35), and we know that Abraham would still see future blessing because of other specific passages explicitly indicating as much (e.g., 22:17, chronologically after the description of 14:19). Here is an important principle that makes ANY inapplicable to this context: ANY applies double meaning to a specific text (near/far are found in the same pronouncement), while the principle of single meaning requires that if there is to be any kind of near/far aspect those disparate aspects must be exegetically demonstrable from separate references. In short, if single meaning is to be upheld, as the literal grammatical–historical approach warrants, we should not expect near/far referents in the same pronouncement. We should not say that these promises are extended to anyone else – even Isaac, for example – without a specific and explicit pronouncement to that end (as we find inarguably in Genesis 17:21). Without such a specific and explicit statement of expansion or inclusion, we must simply respect the principle of single meaning, and go no further than does the text.

In any case, the first six of these promises are directly for Abraham and are established with his descendants (the children of the promise are those who are descended from Abraham in respect *both* to the flesh and faith [e.g., Jer 31:31–34; Rom 11:5,25]) after him through the line of God's choosing (Rom 9:6–13). The varying use of the qal and piel stems in the Hebrew verbs of these six elements implies different emphases and methods in the fulfillment of these six aspects, perhaps in anticipation of the great many expansions and fulfillments to come within the Land, Davidic, and New Covenants.

The seventh promise, on the other hand, is presented here with the niphal – either as passive or reflexive (here, passive seems the best understanding, though a reflexive meaning does not obviate the point). This seventh element is also distinct from the other six, in that it promises a blessing for those not of Abraham's line according to flesh – all peoples of the earth (πᾶσαι οφυλαὶ τῆς γῆς), as the LXX puts it. This promise is broad enough so as to include every future aspect of blessing for Gentiles (including salvation and the ministry of the Spirit), there is no need to place Gentiles in a covenant relationship to God in order for this aspect to be fulfilled. In fact, that the niphal is used in describing the blessing is an indicator that those peoples who would later experience the promised blessing promised will do so without any relationship even to the Abrahamic covenant. In light of this, it is fair to say that Gentile believers in the church age receive salvation and the ministry of the Spirit, not because God owes it to them (as would be the case if the beneficiaries were in a covenant relationship), but if anything, because God owes it to Abraham – as He obligated Himself by His word (even if only generally so in Genesis 12:3).

Joel 2:28-29 (3:1-2 in BHS and LXX)
28 "It will come about after this That I will pour out My Spirit on
all mankind; And your sons and daughters will prophesy, Your old
men will dream dreams, Your young men will see visions. 29
"Even on the male and female servants I will pour out My Spirit in
those days.

1 וְהָיָ֣ה אַֽחֲרֵי־כֵ֗ן אֶשְׁפּ֤וֹךְ אֶת־רוּחִי֙ עַל־כָּל־בָּשָׂ֔ר וְנִבְּא֖וּ בְּנֵיכֶ֣ם וּבְנֽוֹתֵיכֶ֑ם
זִקְנֵיכֶם֙ חֲלֹמ֣וֹת יַחֲלֹמ֔וּן בַּחוּרֵיכֶ֔ם חֶזְיֹנ֖וֹת יִרְאֽוּ׃
2 וְגַ֤ם עַל־הָֽעֲבָדִים֙ וְעַל־הַשְּׁפָח֔וֹת בַּיָּמִ֖ים הָהֵ֑מָּה אֶשְׁפּ֖וֹךְ אֶת־רוּחִֽי׃

3 Καὶ ἔσται μετὰ ταῦτα καὶ ἐκχεῶ ἀπὸ τοῦ πνεύματός μου ἐπὶ πᾶσαν
σάρκα, καὶ προφητεύσουσιν οἱ υἱοὶ ὑμῶν καὶ αἱ θυγατέρες ὑμῶν, καὶ
οἱ πρεσβύτεροι ὑμῶν ἐνύπνια ἐνυπνιασθήσονται, καὶ οἱ νεανίσκοι
ὑμῶν ὁράσεις ὄψονται, ² καὶ ἐπὶ τοὺς δούλους καὶ ἐπὶ τὰς δούλας ἐν
ταῖς ἡμέραις ἐκείναις ἐκχεῶ ἀπὸ τοῦ πνεύματός μου.

This section follows a pronouncement of future blessing for the
land of Israel (2:18-27). This blessing is directly connected to the
land (e.g., 2:18a), has a perpetual element to it (2:26b, 27b), and
is characterized by the presence of God in the midst of Israel
(2:27a). And it will come about following this (וְהָיָה אַֽחֲרֵי־כֵן) that I
will pour out My Spirit (אֶשְׁפּוֹךְ אֶת־רוּחִי, qal imperfect verb) on all
flesh (עַל־כָּל־בָּשָׂר). The recipient category of the outpouring is all
flesh – not here necessarily restricted to Israel, though the first
four specific recipients are each considered in the second person
plural (your sons בְּנֵיכֶם, your daughters וּבְנוֹתֵיכֶם, will prophesy
וְנִבְּאוּ, your old זִקְנֵיכֶם, your young בַּחוּרֵיכֶם, will see visions חֶזְיֹנוֹת
יִרְאוּ). By inclusion of the male and female servants (v. 29) it is
indicated that there is no discrimination by station in this great
blessing.

It is very possible, if not probable, that all flesh (translated πᾶσαν σάρκα in the LXX) refers to all flesh of Israel for at least two reasons. First, the focus on Israel in the context preceding and following would make a brief insertion of universal reference contextually odd. Second, if all flesh is to be understood in a truly universal sense, then we should not hesitate to include animals in this as well, since they are also described as having flesh (e.g., Genesis 8:17, in which the same terms are used). It is clear that the phrase *all flesh* means to communicate *all of a particular kind of flesh*. If the phrase is necessarily limited rather than universal, in light of the context we should understand it as a universal reference to the nation of Israel. It is also worth noting that even if the universal is meant (as the NASB translates, *all mankind*), this outpouring of the Holy Spirit would not necessarily be a NC blessing, because at the time of Joel's prophecy there was still no such thing as a revealed NC (the NC, proper, was not announced to Jeremiah until more than one hundred years after Joel's writing).

Additionally, considering Peter's appeal to this passage as an explanation for the events of Acts 2:1–13, when the Spirit was poured out on devout Jewish men (Acts 2:5), and considering the surprise of those with Peter when the Spirit was poured out on Gentile believers (Acts 10:45), it seems that Peter and those with him may have understood the Joel prophesy as relating specifically and only to Israel. Further, it is notable that Peter did not claim Joel's prophecy to be fulfilled, rather he said, literally translated, "But this is the having been spoken (ἀλλὰ τοῦτό ἐστιν τὸ εἰρημένον[78]) (Acts 2:16)."

Though Peter does not suggest Joel's prophecy was fulfilled (surely recognizing that all the conditions for fulfillment were not in place, as Israel's land was not revisited for blessing at that time), he does indicate that *this was of the same kind* as that

---

[78] All GNT references in this section are from Barbara. Aland, Kurt. Aland, Matthew. Black et al., *The Greek New Testament, 4th ed.* (Federal Republic of Germany: United Bible Societies, 1993, c1979), 324.

which Joel predicted – this was a manifestation of the outpouring of the Spirit of God on His people. Finally, when God reveals to Peter that the Gentiles had also received the same gift as had the Jews (presumably, the Holy Spirit and repentance, Acts 11:17–18), Peter remembers the words that Christ would baptize in the Holy Spirit (Acts 11:16). When speaking of Jesus' baptizing in the Holy Spirit John did not appeal to Joel's prophecy (John 1:33), nor did Jesus (Acts 1:4–5), and nor does Peter do so in this context.

In short, Peter seemed to understand that the outpouring on the Jews was like that which Joel prophesied, and that the outpouring on Gentiles was a fulfillment of Christ's prophecy and unrelated to the Joel prediction. Based on these factors, I understand the *all flesh* phrasing of Joel to be a universal statement about Israel – that after God restored the land, he would pour out His Spirit upon every Jewish person, as all – calling upon Him – would be saved (Joel 2:32). If this understanding – an attempt to understand the Joel prophecy as Peter understood it – is correct, then the outpouring of the Holy Spirit on the Gentiles may be understood as distinct from the prophecy of Joel – a prophecy consistent with NC conditions as announced especially in Jeremiah 31.

Hosea 1:10 (2:1 in BHS and LXX)

10 Yet the number of the sons of Israel Will be like the sand of the sea, Which cannot be measured or numbered; And in the place Where it is said to them, "You are not My people," It will be said to them, "You are the sons of the living God."

1 ‏וְהָיָה מִסְפַּר בְּנֵי־יִשְׂרָאֵל כְּחוֹל הַיָּם אֲשֶׁר לֹא־יִמַּד וְלֹא יִסָּפֵר וְהָיָה
בִּמְקוֹם אֲשֶׁר־יֵאָמֵר לָהֶם לֹא־עַמִּי אַתֶּם יֵאָמֵר לָהֶם בְּנֵי אֵל־חָי:‏

2 Καὶ ἦν ὁ ἀριθμὸς τῶν υἱῶν Ισραηλ ὡς ἡ ἄμμος τῆς θαλάσσης, ἣ οὐκ ἐκμετρηθήσεται οὐδὲ ἐξαριθμηθήσεται, καὶ ἔσται ἐν τῷ τόπῳ, οὗ

ἐρρέθη αὐτοῖς Οὐ λαός μου ὑμεῖς, ἐκεῖ κληθήσονται υἱοὶ θεοῦ ζῶντος.

In this context of God's judgment on Israel (1:6) and compassion for Judah (1:7) is a prediction of Israel's ultimate restoration. Note that the announcement of separation is said *to them* (לָהֶם, preposition with third person plural pronoun) – to Israel, and that the announcement of sonship is again said to them (לָהֶם). Hosea's prophecy is singularly focused on Israel. In part this is evidenced by the place (בִּמְקוֹם) in which the judgment was pronounced (Jezreel) being that same place where the restoration would take place. If the passage is to be fulfilled literally, a restoration of Israel must take place at Jezreel, in the north of Israel (Hos 1:11). Thus, while at first glance, Paul's use of this passage in Romans 9:25–26 may appear, to include Gentiles in the nation of Israel's restoration, a further examination clarifies that he draws no such application of the Hosea prophecy.

Much like Peter employs Joel 2:28, it seems Paul refers to this passage in Romans 9:25–26 as an illustration of God's working. Paul does not refer to the Hosea passage as being fulfilled, rather he uses comparative language: "As even in the Hosea he says (ὡς καὶ ἐν τῷ Ὡσηὲ λέγει)" (Rom 9:25). Paul compares the present age status of believing Gentiles, who were formerly not God's people and now are called sons of God, to the status of the Jews who stood in judgment during Hosea's day but would later be restored. Paul compares but does not equate – he knows that for the passage to be fulfilled a return in righteousness of national Israel to the land is required, and he elucidates without uncertainty that such is not the case at the time of his writing (note his argument throughout Romans 11 and especially 11:25).

Just as Peter appeals to a prophecy in order to encourage observers not to be disbelieving that the events in question were a manifestation of the Holy Spirit because God had pre-announced that the Holy Spirit would be manifest in such a way, Paul seems to remind His readers that God's calling of former enemies to a relationship of sonship is consistent with His character, and should come as no surprise.

Hosea 2:23 (2:25 in BHS and LXX)
I will sow her for Myself in the land. I will also have compassion on her who had not obtained compassion, And I will say to those who were not My people, 'You are My people!' And they will say, 'You are my God!'"

25 וּזְרַעְתִּיהָ לִּי בָּאָרֶץ וְרִחַמְתִּי אֶת־לֹא רֻחָמָה וְאָמַרְתִּי לְלֹא־עַמִּי עַמִּי־
אַתָּה וְהוּא יֹאמַר אֱלֹהָי:

25 καὶ σπερῶ αὐτὴν ἐμαυτῷ ἐπὶ τῆς γῆς καὶ ἐλεήσω τὴν Οὐκ-ἠλεημένην καὶ ἐρῶ τῷ Οὐ-λαῷ-μου Λαός μου εἶ σύ, καὶ αὐτὸς ἐρεῖ Κύριος ὁ θεός μου εἶ σύ.

That Paul does not apply to Gentiles participation or citizenship in the nation of Israel by his appeal to Hosea 1:10 is even more evident in consideration of the other Hosea passage to which Paul refers. After a precise and terrifying restatement of God's judgment upon Israel (2:1–13), Hosea returns to the theme of restoration for the nation (2:14–23). This proclamation of restoration includes four elements: (1) the people judged will be sown in the land, (2) they will be shown compassion where formerly they were not, (3) they will be called His people when formerly that title was stripped from them, and (4) they will respond in acknowledgment of His relationship to them.

   This first aspect is particularly important in making clear that these restoration promises pertain to a particular people and will take place in a particular location. And I will sow (וּזְרַעְתִּיהָ) her for Me (לִּי) in the land (בָּאָרֶץ, ἐπὶ τῆς γῆς). The antecedent of *her* is Israel (1:5). The *land* is Israel (1:10–11, and probably Jezreel, 2:22). Once again, the restoration of Israel is tied to a specific land. To consider any aspect of these restoration promises as fulfilled – or even expanded for inclusion of others – without recognizing the role of the land is exegetical negligence. Paul, in Romans 9, does not apply this passage to Gentiles, rather he employs it to illustrate the character of God in dealing with those who were formerly far off (as Israel was after her sin).

Isaiah 32:15-18
15 Until the Spirit is poured out upon us from on high, And the wilderness becomes a fertile field, And the fertile field is considered as a forest. 16 Then justice will dwell in the wilderness And righteousness will abide in the fertile field. 17 And the work of righteousness will be peace, And the service of righteousness, quietness and confidence forever.

15 עַד־יֵעָרֶה עָלֵינוּ רוּחַ מִמָּרוֹם וְהָיָה מִדְבָּר לַכַּרְמֶל וְכַרְמֶל לַיַּעַר יֵחָשֵׁב:
16 וְשָׁכַן בַּמִּדְבָּר מִשְׁפָּט וּצְדָקָה בַּכַּרְמֶל תֵּשֵׁב:
17 וְהָיָה מַעֲשֵׂה הַצְּדָקָה שָׁלוֹם וַעֲבֹדַת הַצְּדָקָה הַשְׁקֵט וָבֶטַח עַד־עוֹלָם:
18 וְיָשַׁב עַמִּי בִּנְוֵה שָׁלוֹם וּבְמִשְׁכְּנוֹת מִבְטַחִים וּבִמְנוּחֹת שַׁאֲנַנּוֹת:

15 ἕως ἂν ἐπέλθῃ ἐφ᾽ ὑμᾶς πνεῦμα ἀφ᾽ ὑψηλοῦ. καὶ ἔσται ἔρημος ὁ Χερμελ, καὶ ὁ Χερμελ εἰς δρυμὸν λογισθήσεται. 16 καὶ ἀναπαύσεται ἐν τῇ ἐρήμῳ κρίμα, καὶ δικαιοσύνη ἐν τῷ Καρμήλῳ κατοικήσει, 17 καὶ ἔσται τὰ ἔργα τῆς δικαιοσύνης εἰρήνη, καὶ κρατήσει ἡ δικαιοσύνη ἀνάπαυσιν, καὶ πεποιθότες ἕως τοῦ αἰῶνος,

Isaiah 32 introduces the future reign of a righteous king and just princes (32:1-2), the positive implications on the eyes, the ears, the mind and the tongue (32:3-4), and the implications for fools and rogues – that they will no longer be perceived as noble (32:5-8). Isaiah notes, however, that this prophesied day of justice is not now, and it will not arrive until certain conditions become reality (32:9-14). At least eight, and possibly ten, such conditions are discussed in verses 15-20: (1) the Spirit poured out, (2) wilderness becomes fertile, (3) field considered a forest, (4) justice in the wilderness, (5) righteousness in the field, (6) work of righteousness is peace, (7) service of righteousness is quietness and confidence forever, (8) my people will live in a peaceful habitation, secure and undisturbed, (9) it will hail when the forest comes down, and (10) the city will be utterly laid low.

The ninth and tenth conditions seem decidedly negative, and may not be conditions at all, but may instead represent a return to the theme of present forlornness discussed in verses 9–14. In any case, the first and eighth conditions are especially pertinent to the issue of whether the present ministry of the Holy Spirit is a NC ministry.

The first condition is described in 32:15a: until He (or it) is laid bare or poured out (עַד־יֵעָרֶה, niphal imperfect verb) upon us (עָלֵינוּ) a Spirit (or a spirit) (רוּחַ) from a height (מִמָּרוֹם). This may either reference a spirit (an "it" in the sense of regeneration) or a Spirit ("He" in the sense that the Holy Spirit will have a presence in the people of Israel).

The eighth condition is noted in 32:18: then (or and) they will dwell (וְיָשַׁב, qal imperfect) my people (עַמִּי) in an abode of peace (בִּנְוֵה שָׁלוֹם) and in dwellings of confidence (וּבְמִשְׁכְּנוֹת מִבְטַחִים) and in secure resting places (וּבִמְנוּחֹת שַׁאֲנַנּוֹת). The vav conjunction beginning the verse should not be understood as *then*, meaning the verb following the conjunction chronologically follows the previous conditions identified. Rather, the translators use the word *then* as an interpretive device to separate the modifiers into appropriate categories. Of the ten vav conjunctions in vv. 15–18, only two are translated as *then* by the NASB, one by the ESV (the other is not translated at all), and one by the KJV (with the second instance translated as *and*). It should be understood that these conditions occur concurrently.

This particular outpouring of either a spirit (in terms of collective regeneration) or the Spirit (in terms of His presence within His people) takes place at a time when a king reigns righteously (32:1) and the people of God are living in peaceful dwellings. This is language consistent with the NC, but inconsistent with current conditions. There is no evidence of a king presently reigning – nor any princes. The people of God (whether Israel or any other) are not now dwelling securely or undisturbed.

Isaiah 59:20–21
20 "A Redeemer will come to Zion, And to those who turn from transgression in Jacob," declares the LORD. 21 "As for Me, this is My covenant with them," says the LORD: "My Spirit which is upon you, and My words which I have put in your mouth shall not depart from your mouth, nor from the mouth of your offspring, nor from the mouth of your offspring's offspring," says the LORD, "from now and forever."

20 וּבָא לְצִיּוֹן גּוֹאֵל וּלְשָׁבֵי פֶשַׁע בְּיַעֲקֹב נְאֻם יְהוָה:

21 וַאֲנִי זֹאת בְּרִיתִי אוֹתָם אָמַר יְהוָה רוּחִי אֲשֶׁר עָלֶיךָ וּדְבָרַי אֲשֶׁר־שַׂמְתִּי בְּפִיךָ לֹא־יָמוּשׁוּ מִפִּיךָ וּמִפִּי זַרְעֲךָ וּמִפִּי זֶרַע זַרְעֲךָ אָמַר יְהוָה מֵעַתָּה וְעַד־עוֹלָם:

²⁰ καὶ ἥξει ἕνεκεν Σιων ὁ ῥυόμενος καὶ ἀποστρέψει ἀσεβείας ἀπὸ Ιακωβ. ²¹ καὶ αὕτη αὐτοῖς ἡ παρ ἐμοῦ διαθήκη, εἶπεν κύριος, τὸ πνεῦμα τὸ ἐμόν, ὅ ἐστιν ἐπὶ σοί, καὶ τὰ ῥήματα, ἃ ἔδωκα εἰς τὸ στόμα σου, οὐ μὴ ἐκλίπῃ ἐκ τοῦ στόματός σου καὶ ἐκ τοῦ στόματος τοῦ σπέρματός σου, εἶπεν γὰρ κύριος, ἀπὸ τοῦ νῦν καὶ εἰς τὸν αἰῶνα.

Isaiah 59 includes a pronouncement of the wickedness of the people and their separation from God (59:1–8), a commentary on the implications of their depravity (59:9–15), and a recounting of the intercessory work of the Lord on their behalf (59:16–21). In the latter section is a reference to a particular covenant and two of its major implications (59:21). And I (or, as for me), this is My covenant (וַאֲנִי זֹאת בְּרִיתִי) with them (אוֹתָם) says Yahweh (אָמַר יְהוָה).

In Isaiah it seems there are two (or possibly three if the Noahic Covenant is intended in 54:10) separate covenants referred to be God as *My covenant*. One was operative at the time of Isaiah's writing, was kept by eunuchs who upheld the covenant and the sabbaths (56:4), and was also kept by   foreigners who joined themselves to the Lord (56:6). This seems a direct reference to the Mosaic Covenant, which incidentally, made allowances for those outside the assembly of Israel to participate in some aspects (Lev 19:33–34).

Another, My *covenant of peace* (or more literally, a covenant of My peace וּבְרִית שְׁלוֹמִי), invoked in 54:10, might refer to the Noahic Covenant (in light of the immediate context), to God's covenant with Phinehas (in light of the terminology applied to the covenant in Num 25:10–13 and possibly Mal 2:4–5), or to the covenant promised in Ezekiel (34:25; 37:26) which was still yet future. Since in the language preceding 54:10, Levi and Phinehas are not in view – rather the focus is on Israel as a whole (see 54:4–8), and also in light of the future implication of the reference (note the qal imperfect, תָּמוֹט seems to reference that same covenant considered in Ezekiel. The *My covenant* reference in 59:21 seems also to reference the future covenant considered in Ezekiel. Though the NC title is not applied to this reference or used in its phrasing, it seems that due to its commonalities with the Ezekiel covenant and the Jeremiah 31 NC, that it is appropriate to interpret Isaiah 59:21 as a NC reference.

The Isaiah passage highlights two particular aspects of the covenant. First, My Spirit upon you (רוּחִי אֲשֶׁר עָלֶיךָ). As there is no verb here (literally, no *is*, as the NASB translates), there is no indication of a present tense condition of the Spirit's being upon Israel. Nonetheless, the covenant will include the Spirit of God upon Israel. Regarding the recipient(s), observe the specific reference to redemption arriving at Zion and those who turn from transgression in Jacob (59:20). The second aspect pertains to the word which I have put in your mouth (וּדְבָרַי אֲשֶׁר־שַׂמְתִּי בְּפִיךָ, qal perfect verb in this phrase). That word would not depart from your mouth (לֹא־יָמוֹשׁוּ מִפִּיךָ) the mouth of your seed (וּמִפִּי זַרְעֲךָ) and from the mouth of your seed's seed (וּמִפִּי זֶרַע זַרְעֲךָ). This is threefold, progressively intensifying emphasis. This word will be eternally in the mouth of the seed of Jacob. Observe that this is nation-specific, and that it is into the future eternally. The final key to this passage is the connection with 51:16, which explains that the words God has put in the mouth of Jacob is "you are My people" – an evidence of present and continuing (into perpetuity) status Israel would enjoy before God.

The covenant addressed in Isaiah 59:21, then, does include a pouring out of God's Spirit on Israel, and the context of this inclusion is characterized by future rather than present blessing exclusively for Israel. The present ministry of the Spirit, then, may only be attributed to the Isaiah 59:21 covenant relationship if that significant national element is discarded, and the broader considerations of Isaiah's prophecies are ignored.

Jeremiah 31:31–34 (LXX 38:31–34)
31 "Behold, days are coming," declares the LORD, "when I will make a New Covenant with the house of Israel and with the house of Judah, 32 not like the covenant which I made with their fathers in the day I took them by the hand to bring them out of the land of Egypt, My covenant which they broke, although I was a husband to them," declares the LORD. 33"But this is the covenant which I will make with the house of Israel after those days," declares the LORD, "I will put My law within them and on their heart I will write it; and I will be their God, and they shall be My people. 34 "They will not teach again, each man his neighbor and each man his brother, saying, 'Know the LORD,' for they will all know Me,

from the least of them to the greatest of them," declares the LORD, "for I will forgive their iniquity, and their sin I will remember no more."

31 הִנֵּה יָמִים בָּאִים נְאֻם־יְהוָה וְכָרַתִּי אֶת־בֵּית יִשְׂרָאֵל וְאֶת־בֵּית יְהוּדָה בְּרִית חֲדָשָׁה:

32 לֹא כַבְּרִית אֲשֶׁר כָּרַתִּי אֶת־אֲבוֹתָם בְּיוֹם הֶחֱזִיקִי בְיָדָם לְהוֹצִיאָם מֵאֶרֶץ מִצְרָיִם אֲשֶׁר־הֵמָּה הֵפֵרוּ אֶת־בְּרִיתִי וְאָנֹכִי בָּעַלְתִּי בָם נְאֻם־יְהוָה:

33 כִּי זֹאת הַבְּרִית אֲשֶׁר אֶכְרֹת אֶת־בֵּית יִשְׂרָאֵל אַחֲרֵי הַיָּמִים הָהֵם נְאֻם־ יְהוָה נָתַתִּי אֶת־תּוֹרָתִי בְּקִרְבָּם וְעַל־לִבָּם אֶכְתֲּבֶנָּה וְהָיִיתִי לָהֶם לֵאלֹהִים וְהֵמָּה יִהְיוּ־לִי לְעָם:

34 וְלֹא יְלַמְּדוּ עוֹד אִישׁ אֶת־רֵעֵהוּ וְאִישׁ אֶת־אָחִיו לֵאמֹר דְּעוּ אֶת־יְהוָה כִּי־כוּלָּם יֵדְעוּ אוֹתִי לְמִקְטַנָּם וְעַד־גְּדוֹלָם נְאֻם־יְהוָה כִּי אֶסְלַח לַעֲוֹנָם וּלְחַטָּאתָם לֹא אֶזְכָּר־עוֹד:

³¹ Ἰδοὺ ἡμέραι ἔρχονται, φησὶν κύριος, καὶ διαθήσομαι τῷ οἴκῳ Ισραηλ καὶ τῷ οἴκῳ Ιουδα διαθήκην καινήν, ³² οὐ κατὰ τὴν διαθήκην, ἣν διεθέμην τοῖς πατράσιν αὐτῶν ἐν ἡμέρᾳ ἐπιλαβομένου μου τῆς χειρὸς αὐτῶν ἐξαγαγεῖν αὐτοὺς ἐκ γῆς Αἰγύπτου, ὅτι αὐτοὶ οὐκ ἐνέμειναν ἐν τῇ διαθήκῃ μου, καὶ ἐγὼ ἠμέλησα αὐτῶν, φησὶν κύριος, ³³ ὅτι αὕτη ἡ διαθήκη, ἣν διαθήσομαι τῷ οἴκῳ Ισραηλ μετὰ τὰς ἡμέρας ἐκείνας, φησὶν κύριος Διδοὺς δώσω νόμους μου εἰς τὴν διάνοιαν αὐτῶν καὶ ἐπὶ καρδίας αὐτῶν γράψω αὐτούς, καὶ ἔσομαι αὐτοῖς εἰς θεόν, καὶ αὐτοὶ ἔσονταί μοι εἰς λαόν, ³⁴ καὶ οὐ μὴ διδάξωσιν ἕκαστος τὸν πολίτην αὐτοῦ καὶ ἕκαστος τὸν ἀδελφὸν αὐτοῦ λέγων Γνῶθι τὸν κύριον, ὅτι πάντες εἰδήσουσίν με ἀπὸ μικροῦ αὐτῶν καὶ ἕως μεγάλου αὐτῶν, ὅτι ἵλεως ἔσομαι ταῖς ἀδικίαις αὐτῶν καὶ τῶν ἁμαρτιῶν αὐτῶν οὐ μὴ μνησθῶ ἔτι.

The Abrahamic Covenant included a land aspect that Abraham's descendants would possess a specific land (Gen 15:18–21). The Mosaic (or *old*, as it is called in Jeremiah) Covenant allowed for Israel to live in a portion of that land and to dwell in blessing as long as the nation kept the covenant (Ex 19:5; Deut 28:1–14), but if the nation failed to do so God's judgment would come – a judgment that especially affected Israel's tenure in the land (Deut 28:15–68). Based on an additional covenant discussed in Deuteronomy 29–30 (introduced in 29:1 and 14, and which I generally refer to as the Land Covenant, since it has such a land emphasis), after the curses of the Mosaic Covenant came to pass, God would restore the nation to the land (30:1–5) and would circumcise the heart of the nation in order to create the necessary condition for the people to live (30:6). This provision anticipates the problem illustrated by the Mosaic Covenant: that no people can enjoy eternal covenant blessings of land and nation without a divine provision of God's righteousness – to enjoy eternal blessings required that the recipients must have eternal life. The Land Covenant announces the means whereby Israel would be allowed to enjoy the land into perpetuity: God would work within the hearts of the people to do for them what they were unable to do themselves. Thus, as each covenant is given, it builds on previous ones, and anticipates aspects of the ones to follow.

Jeremiah 31 is the only instance in the OT that a covenant is referred to as *new*, and as such it serves as the primary text for consideration of the NC. In this context God announces, (31:27) with an emphatic *behold* (הִנֵּה), that days are coming (יָמִים בָּאִים). in which three things will take place: (1) Israel and Judah will be repopulated (31:27b), (2) God will watch over them to restore (31:28), and (3) individual responsibility will be emphasized (31:29–30). The introductory phrase is repeated in v. 31 (behold, days are coming, הִנֵּה יָמִים בָּאִים) to introduce days characterized by God's cutting (וְכָרַתִּי) of a New Covenant (בְּרִית חֲדָשָׁה) with the house of Israel (אֶת־בֵּית יִשְׂרָאֵל) and the house of Judah (וְאֶת־בֵּית יְהוּדָה). That this covenant is new, and contrasts the old, (31:32, referring to the Mosaic Covenant with Israel) and that the recipients are identified again in v.32 are key reaffirmations that this New Covenant is made exclusively with that same nation (the dual reference to Israel and Judah accounts for the national division during Jeremiah's time).

As the Land Covenant emphasized that Israel would again dwell in the land (Deut 30:1-5), and briefly anticipated the provision of regeneration (Deut 30:6), this New Covenant is connected with Israel's replanting in the land (Jer 31:27), but its focus is spiritual renewal of the people. The content of the covenant includes five (or seven if the second phrases of the first and fourth aspects are separated from the first phrase of each) elements: (1) God will put His law within them and on their heart He will write it, (2) He will be their God, (3) they shall be His people, (4) they shall not teach any more the knowledge of God, for they shall all know Him, (5) He will forgive their iniquity and remember their sin no more. Notably, any specific reference to the Holy Spirit is absent here, though the connection between the Holy Spirit and the NC is usually made by understanding the event described in Ezekiel 36:27 as hearkening back to Jeremiah 31.

The first of these five is aspects is, in light of Ezekiel 36:27, the one most often associated with the Holy Spirit. God will give His law (נָתַתִּי אֶת־תּוֹרָתִי) in their inward parts (בְּקִרְבָּם). After referring previously to the old covenant (of laws) as being broken (31:32), and because the law referred to here is not articulated (nor is it in the LXX, reading, δώσω νόμους μου), it would not seem to fit the context here to understand this as referencing a return to that former law. Nonetheless, law is emblazoned on the heart of Israel in a manner later described in Ezekiel as involving the Holy Spirit.

As evidenced by this unique internal activity accomplished by God, Israel will acknowledge Him, as He will be their God (וְהָיִיתִי לָהֶם לֵאלֹהִים) (and to them I will be God, καὶ ἔσομαι αὐτοῖς εἰς θεόν), and they will be His people (וְהֵמָּה יִהְיוּ־לִי לְעָם)(and to Me they will be a people, καὶ αὐτοὶ ἔσονταί μοι εἰς λαόν) . That there will be universal acknowledgement of God by the nation of Israel is emphasized in saying that they will not teach each other to know Yahweh (דְעוּ אֶת־יְהוָה). By God's own working the whole (of Israel) will all know Him (כִּי־כוּלָם יֵדְעוּ אוֹתִי). This aspect also has been understood as related to the ministry of the Holy Spirit, but again – He is not mentioned specifically in this context. Still, it is not unreasonable to understand that, as in Ezekiel 36:27, the Holy Spirit may be directly involved in this universal (for Israel) awareness of God.

There are, however, problems in linking the present ministry of the Holy Spirit to His role anticipated in Jeremiah 31:31–34. This passage describes with great specificity the recipients of the covenant and its blessings. If there is to be understood from NT passages (such as 2 Cor 3:3–6) an inclusion of the church into the NC ministry of the Spirit, those passages should be very explicit in stating such expansion. Further, those passages would need to also explain the scope of those expanded blessings. For example, do the Gentiles participate in all NC blessings or just the spiritual ones? If throughout OT prophecy Israel's physical restoration to the land is linked with a spiritual renewal, it seems very arbitrary and exegetically unfair to impart those spiritual blessings to the church but hold back the physical ones. Unless there is explicit expansion in the NT, the principle of single meaning requires that we understand the NC ministry of the Holy Spirit as for Israel exclusively.

To suggest that 2 Corinthians 3, for example, contains NC language (as does Blaising) is not sufficient exegetical warrant – even if true – to expand the NC blessings to include the church. Yes, Paul does contrast tablets of stone with the human hearts (2 Cor 3:3, οὐκ ἐν πλαξὶν λιθίναις ἀλλ' ἐν πλαξὶν καρδίαις σαρκίναις). Yes, Paul contrasts that which is written with the Spirit (2 Cor 3:6, οὐ γράμματος ἀλλὰ πνεύματος· τὸ γὰρ γράμμα ἀποκτέννει, τὸ δὲ πνεῦμα ζῳοποιεῖ). But does Paul's invoking of these contrasts imply an expansion of NC blessings to include the church?

Some say *yes*, based on Paul's statement that He made us servants of a New Covenant (2 Cor 3:6, ἡμᾶς διακόνους καινῆς διαθήκης). But this conclusion is not exegetically necessary and is perhaps even contrary to the text. The second person plural (you) is contrasted with the first person plural (we) in 3:1–2. The antecedent of the second person plural is the church of God with all the saints who are throughout Achaia (1:1), while the antecedent of the first person plural is Paul and Timothy (1:1). Paul distinguishes the *us* from the *you*, and in so doing does not identify his audience as servants of a New Covenant, but rather him and Timothy. In what way then do they serve the NC? The answer is not obvious from 2 Corinthians 3, however, I argue that he makes the answer clear later when he describes his ministry to the Gentiles as facilitating the salvation of Israel (Rom 11:11–15).

In understanding Paul to include the church in NC blessings, some point to Paul's restatement of Christ's words in 1 Corinthians 11:24–25 (Paul quotes part of Luke 22:20). Importantly, though, Paul does not apply the covenant to the church. The purpose he gives for the church's participation in the bread and the cup is simply to proclaim the Lord's death until He comes (11:26). There is no exegetical warrant in this passage for including the church in NC blessings, other than to understand that all the blessings of the church come from One who mediated the NC for Israel by His death, thereby providing for the fulfillment of the first six aspects of the Abrahamic Covenant, and who also by His death provided for the fulfillment of the seventh aspect (Gen 12:3).

The only other NT references to the NC of Jeremiah 31, besides the one by Jesus (Luke 22:20), and the two by Paul (1 Cor 11:25; 2 Cor 3:6) are found in Hebrews. The first is in 8:8 and 13, a context which quotes nearly verbatim the LXX translation of Jeremiah's NC, and a context in which old and new are contrasted – with new shown to be superior. The thrust of this context is that Christ is a superior mediator to Moses, since He mediates a better covenant (8:6). There is no explicit or implicit connection of the NC to the church. Yes, the NC is described in 8:6 as *lawgiven* (or enacted, as the NASB translates the verb, νενομοθέτηται – a perfect passive indicative), but no indication therein is evident that NC blessings are being enjoyed at present by anyone. The focus is the Mediator – the covenant is only discussed to illustrate the truth about the Mediator.

The next reference is in 9:15, another context emphasizing the superiority of the Mediator, with no direct connection between the NC and the church, and one in which old and new are contrasted (the church was never party to the old, so any attempt at connecting the church to the new must also admit some connection to the old – a maneuver Covenant theology is happy to oblige). The final reference is in 12:24, which simply identifies Christ as the mediator of a New Covenant, and cites the superiority of His sprinkled blood over the blood of Abel. Again, no application of the covenant to the church, neither explicit nor implicit.

In short, there are a total of seven references to the NC from the Gospels on, and not one of them makes any explicit claim of application to the church, nor is there any exegetical necessity that they be understood as doing so implicitly. If the texts – both OT and NT – *can* be understood to show no connection between the present ministry of the Holy Spirit and the NC, then what is the motivation to force such a connection?

Ezekiel 11:17–20

17 "Therefore say, 'Thus says the Lord GOD, "I will gather you from the peoples and assemble you out of the countries among which you have been scattered, and I will give you the land of Israel.'" 18 "When they come there, they will remove all its detestable things and all its abominations from it. 19 "And I will give them one heart, and put a new spirit within them. And I will take the heart of stone out of their flesh and give them a heart of flesh, 20 that they may walk in My statutes and keep My

ordinances and do them. Then they will be My people, and I shall be their God

17 לָכֵן אֱמֹר כֹּה־אָמַר אֲדֹנָי יְהוִה וְקִבַּצְתִּי אֶתְכֶם מִן־הָעַמִּים וְאָסַפְתִּי אֶתְכֶם מִן־הָאֲרָצוֹת אֲשֶׁר נְפֹצוֹתֶם בָּהֶם וְנָתַתִּי לָכֶם אֶת־אַדְמַת יִשְׂרָאֵל: 18 וּבָאוּ־שָׁמָּה וְהֵסִירוּ אֶת־כָּל־שִׁקּוּצֶיהָ וְאֶת־כָּל־תּוֹעֲבוֹתֶיהָ מִמֶּנָּה: 19 וְנָתַתִּי לָהֶם לֵב אֶחָד וְרוּחַ חֲדָשָׁה אֶתֵּן בְּקִרְבְּכֶם וַהֲסִרֹתִי לֵב הָאֶבֶן מִבְּשָׂרָם וְנָתַתִּי לָהֶם לֵב בָּשָׂר: 20 לְמַעַן בְּחֻקֹּתַי יֵלֵכוּ וְאֶת־מִשְׁפָּטַי יִשְׁמְרוּ וְעָשׂוּ אֹתָם וְהָיוּ־לִי לְעָם וַאֲנִי אֶהְיֶה לָהֶם לֵאלֹהִים:

¹⁷ διὰ τοῦτο εἰπόν Τάδε λέγει κύριος Καὶ εἰσδέξομαι αὐτοὺς ἐκ τῶν ἐθνῶν καὶ συνάξω αὐτοὺς ἐκ τῶν χωρῶν, οὗ διέσπειρα αὐτοὺς ἐν αὐταῖς, καὶ δώσω αὐτοῖς τὴν γῆν τοῦ Ισραηλ. ¹⁸ καὶ εἰσελεύσονται ἐκεῖ καὶ ἐξαροῦσιν πάντα τὰ βδελύγματα αὐτῆς καὶ πάσας τὰς ἀνομίας αὐτῆς ἐξ αὐτῆς. ¹⁹ καὶ δώσω αὐτοῖς καρδίαν ἑτέραν καὶ πνεῦμα καινὸν δώσω ἐν αὐτοῖς καὶ ἐκσπάσω τὴν καρδίαν τὴν λιθίνην ἐκ τῆς σαρκὸς αὐτῶν καὶ δώσω αὐτοῖς καρδίαν σαρκίνην, ²⁰ ὅπως ἐν τοῖς προστάγμασίν μου πορεύωνται καὶ τὰ δικαιώματά μου φυλάσσωνται καὶ ποιῶσιν αὐτά, καὶ ἔσονταί μοι εἰς λαόν, καὶ ἐγὼ ἔσομαι αὐτοῖς εἰς θεόν.

Ezekiel is commissioned to speak to Israel (11:14–16) about a future ingathering and restoration to the land of Israel (11:17). The return to the land will accompany a turn to righteousness (11:18) and a regeneration (11:19). God will give them one heart (וְנָתַתִּי לָהֶם לֵב אֶחָד). The LXX reads *another* heart (καρδίαν ἑτέραν). He will put a new spirit in their inward parts (וְרוּחַ חֲדָשָׁה אֶתֵּן בְּקִרְבְּכֶם). This phrase especially seems to refer to   regeneration, and may anticipate an Ezekiel 36:27 reference to the Holy Spirit. The reason for this new life is for the purpose that (לְמַעַן or ὅπως) they will walk in His statutes and ordinances and do them. Once again, the regenerative aspect is accompanied by a return to the land, and an empowerment for obedience in contrast to the feebleness of their fleshly heart (11:19). The new allows them to overcome their deficiencies that were exposed by the old. And while there is certainly a parallel between what Ezekiel describes here and how the Holy Spirit in the present age allows the believer to be freed from sin (Rom 6:1–11) and how He enables obedience to God's commandments (Rom 6:15–23), except for engaging in the logical fallacy of guilt by association, there is no warrant for connecting the ministry of the Holy Spirit in Israel's restoration, as described here, with His present ministry in the church age.

Ezekiel 36:25–30
25 "Then I will sprinkle clean water on you, and you will be clean; I will cleanse you from all your filthiness and from all your idols. 26 "Moreover, I will give you a new heart and put a new spirit within you; and I will remove the heart of stone from your flesh and give you a heart of flesh. 27 "I will put My Spirit within you and cause you to walk in My statutes, and you will be careful to observe My ordinances. 28 "You will live in the land that I gave to your forefathers; so you will be My people, and I will be your God. 29 "Moreover, I will save you from all your uncleanness; and I will call for the grain and multiply it, and I will not bring a famine on you. 30 "I will multiply the fruit of the tree and the produce of the field, so that you will not receive again the disgrace of famine among the nations.

25 וְזָרַקְתִּי עֲלֵיכֶם מַיִם טְהוֹרִים וּטְהַרְתֶּם מִכֹּל טֻמְאוֹתֵיכֶם וּמִכָּל־גִּלּוּלֵיכֶם
אֲטַהֵר אֶתְכֶם:
26 וְנָתַתִּי לָכֶם לֵב חָדָשׁ וְרוּחַ חֲדָשָׁה אֶתֵּן בְּקִרְבְּכֶם וַהֲסִרֹתִי אֶת־לֵב הָאֶבֶן
מִבְּשַׂרְכֶם וְנָתַתִּי לָכֶם לֵב בָּשָׂר:

27 וְאֶת־רוּחִי אֶתֵּן בְּקִרְבְּכֶם וְעָשִׂיתִי אֵת אֲשֶׁר־בְּחֻקַּי תֵּלֵכוּ וּמִשְׁפָּטַי תִּשְׁמְרוּ וַעֲשִׂיתֶם:

28 וִישַׁבְתֶּם בָּאָרֶץ אֲשֶׁר נָתַתִּי לַאֲבֹתֵיכֶם וִהְיִיתֶם לִי לְעָם וְאָנֹכִי אֶהְיֶה לָכֶם לֵאלֹהִים:

29 וְהוֹשַׁעְתִּי אֶתְכֶם מִכֹּל טֻמְאוֹתֵיכֶם וְקָרָאתִי אֶל־הַדָּגָן וְהִרְבֵּיתִי אֹתוֹ וְלֹא־אֶתֵּן עֲלֵיכֶם רָעָב:

30 וְהִרְבֵּיתִי אֶת־פְּרִי הָעֵץ וּתְנוּבַת הַשָּׂדֶה לְמַעַן אֲשֶׁר לֹא תִקְחוּ עוֹד חֶרְפַּת רָעָב בַּגּוֹיִם:

[25] καὶ ῥανῶ ἐφ᾽ ὑμᾶς ὕδωρ καθαρόν, καὶ καθαρισθήσεσθε ἀπὸ πασῶν τῶν ἀκαθαρσιῶν ὑμῶν καὶ ἀπὸ πάντων τῶν εἰδώλων ὑμῶν, καὶ καθαριῶ ὑμᾶς. [26] καὶ δώσω ὑμῖν καρδίαν καινὴν καὶ πνεῦμα καινὸν δώσω ἐν ὑμῖν καὶ ἀφελῶ τὴν καρδίαν τὴν λιθίνην ἐκ τῆς σαρκὸς ὑμῶν καὶ δώσω ὑμῖν καρδίαν σαρκίνην. [27] καὶ τὸ πνεῦμά μου δώσω ἐν ὑμῖν καὶ ποιήσω ἵνα ἐν τοῖς δικαιώμασίν μου πορεύησθε καὶ τὰ κρίματά μου φυλάξησθε καὶ ποιήσητε. [28] καὶ κατοικήσετε ἐπὶ τῆς γῆς, ἧς ἔδωκα τοῖς πατράσιν ὑμῶν, καὶ ἔσεσθέ μοι εἰς λαόν, κἀγὼ ἔσομαι ὑμῖν εἰς θεόν. [29] καὶ σώσω ὑμᾶς ἐκ πασῶν τῶν ἀκαθαρσιῶν ὑμῶν καὶ καλέσω τὸν σῖτον καὶ πληθυνῶ αὐτὸν καὶ οὐ δώσω ἐφ᾽ ὑμᾶς λιμόν, [30] καὶ πληθυνῶ τὸν καρπὸν τοῦ ξύλου καὶ τὰ γενήματα τοῦ ἀγροῦ, ὅπως μὴ λάβητε ὀνειδισμὸν λιμοῦ ἐν τοῖς ἔθνεσιν.

In this context, God announces His purpose in the coming restoration of Israel – for His name's sake (36:22). He reiterates that Israel will return to her land (36:24), and then in nearly identical language to the pronouncement in Ezekiel 11:18–20, He describes His future cleansing of Israel (36:25), giving Israel a new heart and spirit (36:26), putting His Spirit within them (36:27a) and causing them to obey His statutes and ordinances (36:27b). This regenerative aspect is accompanied by a return to the promised land (36:24 and 28) and a forgiveness of sin (36:29a) that will reverse previous curses on the land itself (36:29b–30). Once again, nothing in these OT passages indicates that the aspect of regenerative blessing should be segregated from the land and forgiveness blessings. And again, if such a maneuver is made to parse the blessings, the question is begged as to how one should decide which blessings may be claimed by the church and which may not – since there is no NT commentary on such parsing.

Ezekiel 37:14
"I will put My Spirit within you and you will come to life, and I will place you on your own land. Then you will know that I, the LORD, have spoken and done it," declares the LORD.'"

14 וְנָתַתִּי רוּחִי בָכֶם וִחְיִיתֶם וְהִנַּחְתִּי אֶתְכֶם עַל־אַדְמַתְכֶם וִידַעְתֶּם כִּי־אֲנִי יְהוָה דִּבַּרְתִּי וְעָשִׂיתִי נְאֻם־יְהוָה:

[14] καὶ δώσω τὸ πνεῦμά μου εἰς ὑμᾶς, καὶ ζήσεσθε, καὶ θήσομαι ὑμᾶς ἐπὶ τὴν γῆν ὑμῶν, καὶ γνώσεσθε ὅτι ἐγὼ κύριος λελάληκα καὶ ποιήσω, λέγει κύριος.

Once again, the working of the Spirit in Israel's restoration is directly associated with a return to the land, but this time it involves resurrection, and not simply an ingathering from the nations (37:12–13). It should be noted that in every OT instance discussing a regenerative aspect for Israel, a physical return to the land of Israel – for the people of Israel – is always in view. In this passage God's part is to give His Spirit (וְנָתַתִּי רוּחִי) in you (בָכֶם, preposition with second person plural suffix). The referent is them (37:12) who are the whole house of Israel (כָּל־בֵּית יִשְׂרָאֵל). The result of this divine action is that Israel would live (וִחְיִיתֶם, in the LXX, καὶ ζήσεσθε – you will live), and God would cause them to rest (וְהִנַּחְתִּי אֶתְכֶם, hiphil [causative], you will rest) on their own land (עַל־אַדְמַתְכֶם, upon your land). Notice here that the regenerative aspect of blessing is inseparable from the land element. They are not independent aspects, but rather are interconnected and mutually necessary. There seems no room here for considering one aspect of blessing to be applied without the other.

CONCLUSION

Each of the theological systems considered above have, in varying degrees, and to the detriment of the text, separated the regenerative blessing of Israel from her land blessing, in order to show some present application or fulfillment in the present church age. Specifically, each asserts that the contemporary ministry of the Holy Spirit is a NC blessing having some realization in the church today – whether in full or in part. I have suggested that these assertions stem from a theological necessity within Covenant theology, and that they are incompatible with the literal grammatical–historical hermeneutic applied to the passages discussed above. I have further suggested that the adoption of these ideas within Classical dispensationalism represents a gaping departure from its own distinctive methodology, in favor of ANY as a hermeneutic device, and that such a departure is an inconsistency upon which Progressive dispensationalism has pounced in justification of its own inconsistent hermeneutic applications of ANY. Finally, I argued exegetically that if one applies literal grammatical–historical methodology to the passages cited, one will discover no exegetical nor theological necessity to place the church in any connection to the NC – besides that the church and Israel will enjoy relationships with Jesus Christ, Mediator of the NC, and the Mediator between God and man.

5

THE LORD'S SUPPER
AND THE NEW COVENANT

George Gunn

The significance of the Church's relationship to the New Covenant vis-à-vis Pretribulationism was recently highlighted in a discussion of the futurist interpretation of Revelation. In their recent book on *Biblical Interpretation,* Köstenberger and Patterson defend a posttribulation rapture approach to the Book of Revelation in the following words:

> ... modified futurists affirm *only one* return of Christ to earth allowing the church to persevere through the tribulation. This is largely due to the inauguration of the New Covenant making all believers in Jesus the spiritual descendants of Abraham and therefore covenant members of the people of God – true Israel.[1]

While this chapter does not address the Book of Revelation directly, the question of whether or not the New Covenant has been "inaugurated," must address the references to the New Covenant in the Lord's Supper. All three synoptic Gospels and the apostle Paul agree that Jesus referred to the New Covenant in

---

[1] Andreas Köstenberger and Richard D. Patterson, *Invitation to Biblical Interpretation* (Grand Rapids: Kregel, 2011), 525.

establishing the Lord's Supper. This observation, perhaps more than any other, has led many believers to assume that the Church has some connection to the New Covenant and is in some way either fulfilling or participating in the New Covenant. This chapter will examine the historical background, contextual setting and significant terminology used in these Scriptural references to develop an understanding of just how, if at all, the Church may be related to the New Covenant.

The Lord's Supper is one of the two fundamental institutions given by Christ to the Church. Assuming that the "New Covenant" to which Jesus referred in the Upper Room was the same as the "New Covenant" of Jeremiah 31, many interpreters have concluded that the Church must therefore be participating in some way in this New Covenant. This, however, poses significant questions both hermeneutically and theologically. Hermeneutically, it is clear from Jeremiah 31:31 that the human parties to this covenant are "the house of Israel" and "the house of Judah." In what sense can this language be understood to include others who are *not* of "the house of Israel" or "the house of Judah"? Theologically, if God fulfills His covenant promises to Israel by carrying out either all or some of those promises on behalf of the Church, is there then some degree of continuity between Israel and the Church whereby the Church is not a distinct people, separate from Israel? In other words, does not the assumed participation of the Church in Israel's covenant strike at the very foundation of dispensational distinctions? What are the implications for such an important dispensational doctrine as the Pretribulational Rapture? This chapter will put forth the position that the "New Covenant" of the Upper Room Discourse is indeed the same as the "New Covenant" of Jeremiah 31, but that the New Covenant has not yet been enacted, nor is the Church a participant in the New Covenant.

The relevant texts relating the New Covenant to the Lord's Supper are the following:

Matthew 26:27–29	Mark 14:23–25	Luke 22:20	1 Corinthians 11:25
And when He had taken a cup and given thanks, He gave it to them, saying, "Drink from it, all of you; 28 for *this is My blood of the covenant, which is poured out for many for forgive-ness of sins. 29 "But I say to you, I will not drink of this fruit of the vine from now on until that day when I drink it new with you in My Father's kingdom."	And when He had taken a cup and given thanks, He gave it to them, and they all drank from it. 24 And He said to them, "This is My *blood of the coven-ant, which is poured out for many. 25 "Truly I say to you, I will never again drink of the fruit of the vine until that day when I drink it new in the kingdom of God."	And in the same way He took the cup after they had eaten, saying, *"This cup which is poured out for you is the New Covenant in My blood.*	In the same way He took the cup also after supper, saying, *"This cup is the New Covenant in My blood*; do this, as often as you drink it, in remembrance of Me."

WHICH NEW COVENANT?

Some early dispensational writers, in an effort to distance the church from Israel's covenant, espoused the theory that there were two "New Covenants" – one for Israel and another for the Church.[2] This view held that the "New Covenant" to which Jesus referred in the upper room was the Church's New Covenant, not Israel's. This view has since been abandoned by most

---

[2] Lewis Sperry Chafer, *Systematic Theology* Dallas: Dallas Seminary Press, 1948), VII:98–99; Charles C. Ryrie, *The Basis of the Premillennial Faith* (Neptune, NJ: Loizeaux Brothers, 1953), 117; John F. Walvoord, *Millennial Kingdom,* 218–219.

dispensational writers.[3] Today, it is the near unanimous position among dispensationalists that the New Covenant to which Jesus referred was the same as that revealed in Jeremiah 31. This appears to be an inescapable conclusion.

Covenant Terminology

Some confusion surrounding discussions of the New Covenant involves the problem of definition of terms. Legal terminology pertaining to covenants, contracts and testaments is highly developed in modern jurisprudence, and terms have specific meanings that have developed over the course of many centuries of legal history. Thus, when one says that the New Covenant has been "ratified," "inaugurated," or "enacted," one might come to certain conclusions about the status of the New Covenant based on how these terms are understood in contemporary parlance. But such terminology belongs to our modern world, not to the world of the Bible. There is one Biblical term that was used in reference to putting a covenant into force, namely the term "cut" (Heb. כָּרַת *karat*). Once a covenant was cut, it was in full legal force, and its parties were bound to its terms. There was no concept known in Biblical times of a covenant that was partially in force, or of one that was put in force with different parties than the signatories.

The term "inaugurate" has come into recent use by some to connote the idea that the New Covenant is somehow currently in partial force, but that its full force awaits a future day. Thus, Bruce Ware writes that the New Covenant "is inaugurated

[3] Charles C. Ryrie *Dispensationalism*, rev. ed. (Chicago: Moody Press, 1995), 170–174; John F. Walvoord, "Does the Church Fulfill Israel's Program?" Part 3, *Bibliotheca Sacra* 137/547 (July–Sept 1980): 220.

partially first and fulfilled in its entirety later."[4] Ladd introduced the term "inaugurate" into the jargon of New Testament theology in the sense of "Inaugurated Eschatology." He explained the present church age as being, "that of inaugurating a time of fulfillment in advance of an eschatological consummation, and ... in a real sense the Kingdom of God in his mission invaded history ...."[5] Whether or not one subscribes to Ladd's version of realized eschatology, one must wonder whether such a notion can legitimately be applied to the enactment of covenants. It is not clear why Ladd chose the term "inaugurate" to describe his view. Perhaps it was due to the practice in America of *inaugurating* a president before he actually begins *executing* his office,[6] but that is clearly a connotation that is entirely contemporary and is found neither in Biblical contexts involving the enactment of covenants, nor in any extant literature from the Ancient Near East. Were it not for Ladd's use of the term "inaugurate" to connote a realized eschatology, no one would have thought that the term could

---

[4] Bruce A. Ware, "The New Covenant and the People(s) of God," in *Dispensationalism, Israel and the Church: The Search for Definition*, ed. Craig A. Blaising and Darrell L. Bock (Grand Rapids: Zondervan, 1992), 96.

[5] George Eldon Ladd, *A Theology of the New Testament* (Grand Rapids: Eerdmans, 1974), 106. A more recent proponent of inaugurated eschatology is D. A. Carson, *The Gospel According to John* (Grand Rapids: Eerdmans, 1991), 256.

[6] Article II, section 1 of the U.S. Constitution actually only prescribes that "before he enter on the Execution of his Office, he [the President] shall take the following Oath or Affirmation." In actual practice inaugural celebrations usually last ten days, from five days before the inauguration to five days after.

denote a partial enactment of a covenant.[7] Those who do so impose a false dichotomy on the terms of the New Covenant by insisting that only the "spiritual" terms of the covenant are in force today.[8] But this is to impose a distinction that is not warranted in the text. The text of Jeremiah 31 does not suggest a distinction between "spiritual" terms versus "temporal" terms. The attempt to distinguish between spiritual and temporal terms in the New Covenant is analogous to attempts to distinguish between "civil," "ceremonial," and "moral" terms of the Mosaic Covenant. Such distinctions cannot be made exegetically. When the covenant is enacted (i.e. "cut"), it is enacted fully and is enacted with the contracted parties.

The Blood of the Covenant

A. The Relationship of the Blood to the Cutting of the Covenant

What did Jesus mean when He referred to the "blood of the covenant"? What relationship does this blood have to the cutting of the New Covenant? Fairly typical among Christian commentators is the view of Charles Hodge:

> "The blood of the covenant" means here [in 1 Cor. 11:25], as in Ex. 24, 8, the blood by which the covenant was ratified and its blessings secured. The passage referred to in Exodus shows the manner in which covenants were anciently ratified in the East. A victim was slain and the

---

[7] The term "inaugurate" simply means "to induct into an office with suitable ceremonies," "to bring about the beginning of." Etymologically, it comes from the Latin *inauguratus/inaugurare* "to practice augury" (*Webster's Ninth New Collegiate Dictionary* [Springfield, MA: Merriam–Webster, 1983], 608).

[8] Robert L. Saucy, *The Case for Progressive Dispensationalism* (Grand Rapids: Zondervan, 1993), 134.

blood sprinkled upon the contracting parties, by which they were solemnly bound to their mutual engagements... This covenant is called *new* in reference to the Mosaic covenant. The latter was ratified by the blood of animals; the new, by the blood of the eternal Son of God.[9]

A major assumption in the argument for the church's participation in the New Covenant is that the shedding of the blood of the covenant on the cross was the vehicle for enacting the covenant. However, based on both a survey of Biblical covenants, and on what is known of Ancient Near Eastern covenants, such would not be the assumption of one who lived in the Ancient Near East. Rather, the vehicle of covenant enactment ("cutting") was the swearing of the oath; the blood served a different purpose. The function of oath swearing as the means for covenant enactment is clearly seen in the Old Testament both in Ezekiel 17:13 and in Hosea 10:4.

Ezekiel 17:11–24 discusses the appointment of Zedekiah to the position of governorship in Jerusalem by Nebuchadnezzar. This appointment was made according to the established conventions of Ancient Near Eastern covenants. Verse 13 states that Nebuchadnezzar "made a covenant with him [Zedekiah], putting him under oath." The expression "putting him under oath" (בְּאָלָה) renders the Hebrew preposition בְּ, used here to express the instrument[10] of the covenant enactment. There is no indication that any sacrifice accompanied this covenant enactment, and there is no reason to suspect that such was the case.

---

[9] Charles Hodge, *An Exposition of the First Epistle to the Corinthians*, (Grand Rapids: Eerdmans, 1980 reprint), 227.

[10] For the instrumental use of בְּ, see Ronald J. Williams, *Williams' Hebrew Syntax* 3rd edition (Toronto: University of Toronto Press, 2007), 98.

Hosea 10:4 describes the unfaithful northern kingdom of Israel who "with worthless oaths make covenants," a reference to agreements into which Israel entered with the surrounding nations. The expression "with worthless oaths" translates the infinitive absolute (אָלוֹת) used to express the manner in which these covenants were enacted.[11] Blood sacrifices may or may not have been ancillary parts of the covenant enactment ceremonies, but the instrument of enactment was considered to be the swearing of the oath.

The supposition that it was the shedding of blood that enacted the covenant is sometimes based on the proposed etymology of "cut" as coming from the act of dividing animal carcasses for the covenant ceremony, as in Genesis 15.[12] This etymology, however, is not certain, and clearly, there were covenants both in the Bible (e.g. the Davidic Covenant and the "Land" Covenant of Deut 29–30, as well as covenants between people such as Jacob and Laban, Gen 31:44) and elsewhere in the Ancient Near East[13] that were "cut" without the attendant shedding of blood. Weinfeld discusses this etymology, and, while admitting its possibility, states "it is equally possible that 'to cut' is figurative for 'decide, decree,' as in Akk[adian] *parāsu*, 'to decide,'

---

[11] For the infinitive absolute of manner, see Williams, 84.

[12] Andy Woods, "What is the Relationship of the Church to the New Covenant," http://www.spiritandtruth.org/teaching/documents/articles/12/12.htm (accessed 1/7/2012).

[13] M. Weinfeld, "בְּרִית *berith*" in G. Johannes Botterweck and Helmer Ringgren, *Theological Dictionary of the Old Testament* (Grand Rapids: Eerdmans), II:259–63.

Aram[aic] *gzr*, Lat. *decider*, German *entscheiden*, etc."[14] This latter etymology is a better explanation in light of those attested covenants that were "cut" without the shedding of blood.

The closest OT parallel to the expression "blood of the covenant" occurs in Exodus 24:8, "Behold the blood of the covenant, which the LORD has made ("cut" כָּרַת) with you in accordance with all these words." This text needs to be examined carefully. After the recording of the Ten Commandments (20:1–17), instructions were given for an earthen or uncut stone altar (20:24–26), then various laws (21:1 – 23:13), and finally the three national feasts (23:14–19). The substance of the Sinai covenant was contained in Exodus chapters 20–23. Then, in chapter 24 the covenant was "cut" (i.e. enacted or put into force). The cutting of the covenant was accompanied by two actions: (1) the application of blood (verses 6, 8), and (2) the swearing of the oath (verse 7). But the application of the blood took place in two phases. In the first phase (verse 6) the altar was sprinkled with blood; in the second phase (verse 8) the people were sprinkled with blood. It was between these two applications of blood that the covenant was cut by the swearing of the oath.

> Exodus 24:7 Then he took the book of the covenant and read *it* in the hearing of the people; and they said, "All that the LORD has spoken we will do, and we will be obedient!"

When the blood was afterward applied to the people in verse 8, it is apparent that the covenant was already cut.

---

[14] Weinfeld, II:259. See also Ludwig Koehler, Walter Baumgartner, M. E. J. Richardson and Johann Jakob Stamm. *The Hebrew and Aramaic Lexicon of the Old Testament*, (Leiden; New York: E.J. Brill, 1999), 500. Another possible etymology is that the terms of the covenant were literally "cut" into the stone tablets in the engraving process.

> Exodus 24:8 So Moses took the blood and sprinkled *it* on the people, and said, "Behold the blood of the covenant, which the LORD has made (כָּרַת) with you in accordance with all these words."

This observation makes it clear that, while the blood clearly had some relationship to the covenant, it was the swearing of the oath that actually resulted in the cutting of the covenant. This corresponds exactly with what is known about Ancient Near Eastern covenants. According to Weinfeld it was the swearing of the oath that enacted the covenant.[15] Beacham is quite clear on this point:

> That which immediately and legally placed a covenant in force was the oath.   Although various symbolic conventions might attend ANE ratification ceremonies, the one component essential to all covenants was the swearing of the oath.   Only by this means was the covenant formally actuated, enacted, or ratified ("cut" כָּרַת). A covenant ceremony might include a meal. It could incorporate some form of sacrifice. A token might be assigned, a libation or some other physical act performed. Nevertheless, there was no legal contract, no implementation of terms or benefits in part or in whole, and no obligatory force or factual realization until the moment

---

when the party (unilateral) or parties (bilateral) officially swore to the terms of record.[16]

In fact, the terms "covenant" (בְּרִית) and "oath" (אָלָה) are so closely related conceptually that they were used both in the Old Testament and in other Ancient Near Eastern literature as synonyms.[17]

 If the function of the blood was not to cut the covenant, then what was the purpose of the blood? Since the blood of the Sinaitic Covenant was applied both to the altar (Ex 24:6) and to the people (Ex 24:8) it would appear that the blood's purpose was to sanctify the people (and the altar). Clearly, blood is not necessary for the cutting of a covenant. A number of OT covenants were cut without the shedding of blood (the Davidic Covenant, the "Land" Covenant of Deuteronomy 29–30, and likely the Noahic Covenant[18]). Beacham describes a number of features that could

---

[16] Roy E. Beacham, "The Church Has No Legal Relationship to or Participation in the New Covenant," unpublished chapter in a book on the New Covenant scheduled to be published, 13; quotation used by permission of the author. Dr. Beacham presented the substance of this chapter at the Council on Dispensational Hermeneutics, September 23, 2009, Baptist Bible Seminary, Clarks Summit, PA, under the title, "The New Covenant of Scripture in ANE Covenant Context: A Preliminary Paper" (http://www.bbc.edu/council/documents/Roy_Beacham_ANE-Covenants-and-NC.pdf), 12.

[17] Other synonyms include *dabhar,* "word, promise," and *'amanah,* "firm covenant." In OT language one may "cut" a *dabhar* (Hag. 2:5), cut an *'alah* (Dt. 29:13[14]), or cut an *'amanah* (Neh. 10:1 [9:38]), Weinfeld, 260.

[18] Gen. 8:20, Noah's offering is described as a "burnt offering" (עֹלָה) with a sweet smelling savor that arose to God. This appears to be different from the blood offerings that were associated with covenants. Even with the sacrifices of the Abrahamic Covenant (Gen. 15:9–10), it appears that the significance of these had to do more with the death of these animals than with the application of their blood.

accompany Ancient Near Eastern covenants. These ancillary features, sacrifices among them, he terms "Covenant Complements:"

> In the ANE the term "cutting" a covenant referred to the formal act of ratification which occurred when the parties swore to the terms of the instrument. Numerous attendant ceremonial features or symbolic acts might accompany or complement the formal ratification of ANE covenants. Such complementary elements were optional for inclusion or non-inclusion in the ceremony. All of these features, despite their optional inclusion, were highly emblematic. None of them, however, were essential to covenant making or officially enacted the contract.[19]

Beacham continues, regarding the significance of sacrifices to Ancient Near Eastern covenants, as follows:

> If a covenant ceremony did include a sacrifice, the sacrifice was ancillary to formal ratification. It made the parties fit for covenant relationship and symbolized their commit[ment] to covenant fulfillment, all in guarantee that the covenant could and would be actuated. The sacrifice and the sacrificial animals were, nonetheless, "subordinate to a fixed ritual procedure." Covenants could be made without a sacrifice. Even when included, the sacrifice itself, like other covenant complements, did not constitute enactment or ratification of the covenant.[20]

---

[19] Beacham, 13.

[20] Ibid. 14. See also Weinfeld, 262.

In defense of the notion that blood sacrifice might be the instrument by which a covenant was enacted, appeal might be made to Psalm 50:5 which refers to "those who have made [lit. "cut"] a covenant with Me by sacrifice." The verse appears to suggest that sacrifice was the instrument by which the covenant was cut; however, this notion is based on the way the Hebrew has been translated (or mistranslated). The English "by" translates the Hebrew preposition עַל. While in English, "by" may carry an instrumental sense; this is not a legitimate sense for עַל. The preposition עַל is probably used here in the sense of association.[21] Thus Psalm 50:5 may be understood as, "they made with me a covenant accompanied by sacrifice." The *Hebrew Aramaic Lexicon of the Old Testament* also translates "by sacrifice," but it does not intend to convey the idea of instrument; the translation falls under the category of uses that mean "on the side of."[22] By this reckoning, Psalm 50:5 means "they made a covenant with me along side of the sacrifice." In other words, the sacrifice to which Psalm 50:5 refers was ancillary to, and accompanied, the cutting of the covenant.

Thus, though Jesus' blood shed at Calvary bears a definite relationship to the New Covenant, its shedding was not the event that "cut," or enacted, the New Covenant. The shedding of Jesus' blood was ancillary to the covenant and makes the cutting of the covenant possible, since by it, Israel must be sanctified and made suitable for entrance into the covenant. But the actual cutting of the covenant awaits the swearing of the oath by Israel, an event that will accompany the Second Coming of Christ.

---

[21] Williams, *Hebrew Syntax*, §293.

[22] Ludwig Koehler, Walter Baumgartner, M. E. J. Richardson and Johann Jakob Stamm. *The Hebrew and Aramaic Lexicon of the Old Testament* (Leiden; New York: E.J. Brill, 1999), 826.

B. The Use of Blood Terminology

It is sometimes argued that Jesus' reference to the "blood of the covenant" at the institution of the Lord's Supper (Matt 26:28; Mark 14:24) as a description of His death on the cross must mean that the covenant was, in fact, enacted at the cross. If the covenant was not cut by shedding His blood on the cross, then why would Jesus refer to it as the "blood of the covenant"? Why refer at all to the "covenant" if it was not to be cut at the cross? On the face of it, this appears to be a forceful argument, at least from the contemporary believer's perspective. But care must be taken not to read back into these words meaning that can only come from later revelation. Jesus' words must be viewed from the perspective of what the disciples knew on the eve of Jesus' crucifixion. The issue here is one of semantic reference. The believer of the twenty–first century is well aware of the fact that Israel has not come into the New Covenant. But the disciples on the eve of Jesus' crucifixion could not have known, or even suspected, that Israel might be two thousand years away from entering into the covenant.

What language might Jesus have used to convey to His disciples the significance of the blood He would shed the following day? On the basis of their knowledge of the Old Testament Scriptures, the choices were somewhat limited. If one were living in first century Judea before the cross, and one wished to speak of the forgiveness of sins, a regenerated life, and the power of the Holy Spirit, to what Old Testament passage would he refer? Since the Church was an unrevealed mystery in the Old Testament, one's choice of language to refer to redemption was necessarily limited. In fact, the only language in the Old Testament Scriptures that encompasses all the ideas of forgiveness of sins, a regenerated life, and the power of the Holy Spirit, is language that describes the New Covenant. For Jesus to say that the blood of His cross was the blood of the covenant was true, but it does not require that His reference be restricted to the New Covenant only. For the disciples it was a meaningful reference. For the twenty–

first century believer one might use different terminology to refer to the same blood. The New Testament Epistles and Revelation speak of Christ's blood in relation to redemption, propitiation, justification, reconciliation, forgiveness and sanctification. One might legitimately refer to Jesus' blood shed on the cross as the "blood of redemption" (Acts 20:28; Eph 1:7; 1Pet 1:19; Rev 5:9), the "blood of propitiation" (Rom 3:15), the "blood of justification" (Rom 3:25; 5:9), the "blood of reconciliation" (Col 1:20), the "blood of forgiveness" (Heb 9:22), or the "blood of sanctification" (Heb 13:12; 1 John 1:7).

Any of these terms could make legitimate semantic reference to the blood that Jesus shed on the cross. For that matter, even speaking proleptically any time after Genesis 3:15, one might have referred to the "blood of the woman's seed," or after Isaiah 52–53 to the "blood of Yahweh's Servant." For Jesus to refer in the upper room to His cross work as the "blood of the New Covenant" was a meaningful semantic reference for the disciples at that time and at that stage of their understanding of God's program. But it did not necessarily mean that the New Covenant was to be cut at the cross. Redemption was paid for by that blood, and thereby the cutting of the covenant made possible.

Paul's Reference to a Largely Gentile Church

It is one thing for the Lord to use New Covenant language from the Old Testament with His pre–Pentecost Jewish disciples to describe His blood of redemption, but what about Paul's language addressed to a largely Gentile church many years after Pentecost? While the institution of the Lord's Supper preceded the beginning of the Church at Pentecost, it might be argued that Paul's use of the same New Covenant language in 1 Corinthians 11:25 leads inevitably to the conclusion that the Church participates in the New Covenant.[23]

---

[23] Decker, 449–50; Woods, 8–9.

> The Lord Jesus in the night in which He was betrayed took bread; and when He had given thanks, He broke it and said, "This is My body, which is for you; do this in remembrance of Me." In the same way *He took* the cup also after supper, saying, 'This cup is the New Covenant in My blood; do this, as often as you drink *it*, in remembrance of Me.' For as often as you eat this bread and drink the cup, you proclaim the Lord's death until He comes." (1 Cor. 11:25-26)

Why should Jesus refer to the cup as "the New Covenant in My blood" if the church was not in some way participating in the New Covenant? In answering this question, it is important to recognize that the Lord's Supper has both past, present, and future orientations.

- Past – "My body," "My blood," "the Lord's death," "in remembrance of Me"
- Present – "do this," "as often as you drink it," "you proclaim"
- Future – "the New Covenant," "until He comes"

There is a significant distinction in the text in that, while the "body" of Christ (μού ... σῶμα) is said to be for the believers (ὑπὲρ ὑμῶν), the New Covenant is not said to be ὑπὲρ ὑμῶν. Apart from this omission, Paul's language is almost identical to Luke's (Luke 22:20).[24] But whereas Luke was describing Jesus' words to His pre–Pentecost Jewish disciples, Paul has omitted a reference to

---

[24] Marshall argues for Luke's text being more primitive than Paul's, and thus Paul is likely dependent on Luke; see I. Howard Marshall, *The Gospel of Luke* (NIGTC) (Grand Rapids: Eerdmans, 1978), 800, 803. This would make Paul's omission even more significant.

the direct application of the covenant to believers of the Church Age.

That the cup should be given a separate focus from the bread is in keeping with the way the Supper was originally instituted. Lane notes, "Jesus' word and action with the bread was independent from the word spoken over the cup. The two sayings were originally separated from each other by the sharing of the main body of the meal, and they must be expounded separately."[25] He further explains:

> Following the main meal (cf. I Cor. 11:25)... the third cup of red wine mixed with water, and with his eyes on the cup pronounced the prayer of thanksgiving on behalf of all, with the concluding words: "May the All-merciful One make us worthy of the days of the Messiah and of the life of the world to come. He brings the salvation of his king. He shows covenant-faithfulness to his Anointed, to David and to his seed forever. He makes peace in his heavenly places. May he secure peace for us and for all Israel. And say you, Amen."[26]

Thus, there appears to be a two-fold significance in the elements, one looking back (the body representing His death, looking back to the cross work), the other looking to the future (the blood representing His return to fulfill the New Covenant).[27] The bread has a definite historical reference, the cross; the cup

---

[25] William L. Lane, *The Gospel According to Mark* (NICNT) Grand Rapids: Eerdmans, 1974), 506. See also Marshall, 805.

[26] Ibid.

[27] John Master, "The New Covenant" in Wesley R. Willis and John R. Master, *Issues in Dispensationalism* (Chicago: Moody Press, 1994), 99–100.

apparently has a futuristic reference, the fulfillment of the New Covenant in the kingdom. This two-fold temporal reference in the elements is consistent with what Jesus had said to His disciples in the upper room. Jesus had spoken of His next partaking of the cup "in the kingdom of God" (Mark 14:25) and had concluded the supper with the singing of the eschatological Psalm 118 (Mark 14:26). Similarly, in 1 Corinthians 11 there is both the historical reference ("you proclaim the death of the Lord") and the future reference ("until He come," verse 26). Believers of the Church Age, while remembering the cross, must not forget that Jesus is coming again.

> Foreswearing feasting and wine, Jesus dedicated himself with a resolute will to accept the bitter cup of wrath offered to him by the Father. Yet there is here a clear anticipation of the messianic banquet when the Passover fellowship with his followers will be renewed in the Kingdom of God.... The reference to "that day" envisions the parousia and the triumph of the Son of Man.... The cup from which Jesus abstained was the fourth, which ordinarily concluded the Passover fellowship.... The cup which he refused was the cup of consummation, associated with the promise that God will take his people to be with him. This is the cup which Jesus will drink with his own in the messianic banquet which inaugurates the saving age to come.[28]

Thus, Paul's future pointing reference to the New Covenant meant neither that the covenant had been cut, nor that the church was participating in that covenant. The blood of that covenant had been shed, making possible its future enactment. In

---

[28] Lane, 508–509.

the meantime, that same blood, the blood of the New Covenant, was also the blood of redemption for the church.

The Early Church's View of Their Relationship to Israel's Covenants
Early church history suggests that there may have been a conscious effort to disassociate the church from Israel's covenants in the observance of the Lord's Supper. One of the contentious issues that separated the eastern Byzantine church from the western Roman church concerned whether leavened or unleavened bread should be used in the Lord's Supper. Clearly, when Jesus instituted the Lord's Supper, it was at a Passover meal using unleavened bread. It appears, however, that prior to the seventh century, with the exception of the Ebionites, the common elements in the Lord's Supper were *leavened* bread and wine mingled with water.[29]

Some time subsequent to the seventh century, it became customary in the western church to use unleavened bread.[30] By the eleventh century the controversy between east and west over leavened versus unleavened bread became quite heated, and in 1053 Cerularius, along with Leo of Achrida, wrote to John, bishop of Trani, that the churches of the west were "following the practice of the Jews ... contrary to the usage of Christ [in that] they employ in the eucharist unleavened bread; that they fast on Saturday in Lent; that they eat blood and things strangled in violation of the decree of the Council of Jerusalem; and that during the fast they do not sing the hallelujah."[31] This letter is

---

[29] Philip Schaff and David Schley Schaff, *History of the Christian Church* (Oak Harbor, WA: Logos Research Systems, Inc., 1997), Vol 2, §68.

[30] F. L. Cross and Elizabeth A. Livingstone, *The Oxford Dictionary of the Christian Church*, 3rd ed. rev. (Oxford; New York: Oxford University Press, 2005), 235. Among the earliest undisputed witnesses for unleavened bread are Alcuin (*ep.* 90, ad fratres Lugdunenses, AD 798; *PL* 100. 289) and his pupil, Rabanus Maurus (*Instit. Cler.* 1. 31).

[31] Schaff, §68.

quite interesting because it does not appear to be motivated by any kind of anti-Semitic attitude. The positive references both to the Jerusalem Council of Acts 15 and to the singing of the hallelujah – the *Hallel* (Psalms 113-118) sung at the Passover meal – show that there is no bias against the Jews *per se.* Nevertheless, the criticism for using unleavened bread as something that was "contrary to the usage of Christ" is suggestive. It appears to have been quite important to Cerularius that the Lord's Supper be disassociated from its connection to the Passover. Indeed, his criticism of the western church in this matter led him to coin a new term, *Azymites*, to describe those involved in the heresy of using unleavened bread (*azyma* from α ΄ζυμος, "unleavened") instead of common bread.[32]   Schaff explains, "The Greeks insist that our Lord in instituting the eucharist after the passover-meal used true, nourishing bread (α ΄ρτος from αι ΄ρω), as the sign of the new dispensation of joy and gladness; while the lifeless, unleavened bread (ἄζυμον) belongs to the Jewish dispensation."[33]

What does all this mean relative to the Church's participation or non-participation in the New Covenant? It may mean nothing at all. Like many issues in history it can be difficult to assign motives to the actions of men. But this controversy does suggest that the early church, by its use of leavened bread, sought to disassociate the Lord's Supper from the covenants of Israel. And, if that is the case, then it is likely that the early church did not view the cup of the Lord's Supper as signifying the Church's participation in Israel's New Covenant.

---

[32] Ibid. In response, the Latins called the Greeks *Fermentarei!*

[33] Ibid.

CONCLUSION

Both in the institution of the Lord's Supper and in Paul's reference to Christ's words in his instructions to the Corinthian church about the Lord's Supper, reference is made to the New Covenant. This has led many believers to conclude that the church is in some way participating in the New Covenant. This appears to be a problem in that God clearly stated through the prophet Jeremiah that the New Covenant was to be made with "the house of Israel and the house of Judah." This chapter has sought to show how the language used by Christ and Paul in reference to the New Covenant in the Lord's Supper does not require participation of the Church in Israel's New Covenant.

First, it was established that the reference to the "New Covenant" in the Lord's Supper was to the same covenant as that to which Jeremiah 31 refers.

Second, attention was given to the matter of definition of terms. In particular, focus was placed on the Biblical term "to cut" (כָּרַת) which means to enact and to place fully in force the terms of a covenant. Problems introduced by added semantic baggage attached to the term "inaugurate" were evaluated as to their impact on this discussion.

Third, the role of Christ's blood in relation to the "cutting" of the New Covenant was explored. It was established that the shedding of Christ's blood was not the instrument by which the covenant was cut; rather, the cutting of the covenant will be effected by the swearing of the oath of the covenant by Israel at Christ's Second Coming. The blood, on the other hand, makes the future cutting of the covenant a possibility, and the expression "blood of the covenant" is a reasonable and adequate reference to Christ's blood of redemption, when used in a pre–Pentecost setting among Jewish disciples.

Fourth, Paul's use of New Covenant language when addressing the Corinthian church was examined. It was seen that Paul's omission of the phrase "for you" in connection to the cup made a separation between the church and the New Covenant; furthermore, the two-fold temporal reference in the two elements of the Lord's Supper (the bread looking back in time to Christ's death, the cup looking forward in time to Christ's Second Coming) argues for a non-involvement by the Church in the New Covenant.

Finally, the controversy in the early church over whether leavened or unleavened bread should be used in the Lord's Supper was examined, and the hypothesis was hazarded that the early church's use of leavened bread may be due to their unwillingness to be associated with Israel's covenants.

6

ROMANS 11:17 AND THE NEW COVENANT

George Gunn

One argument sometimes put forth to support the notion that the church is currently participating in the New Covenant stems from Romans 11:17,

> But ... some of the branches were broken off, and you, being a wild olive, were grafted in among them and became a partaker of the root and fatness of the olive tree.

On the basis of this verse it is argued that the church has either been grafted into Israel or grafted into Israel's covenants.[1] This interpretation, however, cannot be supported from the context. This chapter will argue that the tree into which Gentiles have been grafted represents neither Israel nor Israel's covenants. Instead, the tree represents the place of mediatorial administrative responsibility in the carrying out of God's dispensational program.

---

[1] Carson and Moo, for example, while still holding to a future for Israel, nevertheless refer to a "transfer of covenant privileges from Israel to the church," D. A. Carson and Douglas J. Moo, An Introduction to the New Testament, Second Edition (Grand Rapids: Zondervan, 2005), 392.

THE CONTEXT SURROUNDING VERSE 17

The entire passage, Romans 11:11–24, has suffered from gross misinterpretation due to its being viewed from a non-dispensational perspective. Covenant theologians, with their supercessionist presuppositions, have imported a soteriological theme to this passage that is foreign to the context. This presupposition has led some to derive from this passage views of the relationship between Israel and the church that are faulty. A common misunderstanding views the church as having been grafted into Israel. For example, Craig Keener writes, "Gentile Christians must remember that they are grafted into a Jewish faith, and that when they are grafted into the Old Testament people of God, they accept not only Israel's spiritual history as their own but also Jews as in some sense their siblings...."[2] Such a view is not only theologically unsound, but exegetically irresponsible. Paul was discussing a primarily dispensational theme throughout chapters 9–11, not a primarily soteriological one.[3] Though soteriology figures significantly in a secondary way in the development of Paul's argument, the main theme has to do with how God administers His affairs in the world and the role that national Israel plays in this administration.

Problems in interpreting the significance of the "root" emerge from viewing this passage from a soteriological perspective. It is tempting to view this passage as soteriological, since so much of the book of Romans focuses on soteriology.

---

[2] Craig S. Keener and InterVarsity Press, The IVP Bible Background Commentary: New Testament (Downers Grove, Ill.: InterVarsity Press, 1993), Rom 11:9.

[3] Moo comes close to seeing this when he observes, "Paul is thinking mainly in terms of corporate bodies, not in terms of individuals within those bodies." Douglas Moo, The Epistle to the Romans, New International Commentary on the New Testament (Grand Rapids: Eerdmans, 1996), 686.

However, one should recognize that the context of chapters 9–11 is quite different from that of chapters 3–8. While chapters 3–8 do indeed focus on soteriology, chapters 9–11 resume a theme that had been introduced at 3:1-2. Romans 11:17 occurs near the end of an extended section of Romans dealing with God's plan for Israel. Chapters 9–11 actually constitute a resumption of a subject that had been introduced at the beginning of chapter 3. Having established the equal guilt of both Jews and Gentiles in chapters 1 and 2, Paul asked the question, "What, then, is the advantage of the Jew, or what is the profit of circumcision?" (Rom 3:1). Paul began to answer this question by enumerating a list in Romans 3:2, "First, the oracles of God were entrusted to them."[4] But right away this list is interrupted by a discussion of righteousness by faith.

This "digression" continues for the next six chapters. Chapter 9 opens with a resumption of the enumerated list in verse 4 as follows: "Whose are the adoption, and the glory, and the covenants, and the giving of the law, and the temple service, and the promises, from whom came the fathers, and from whom came the Messiah according to the flesh." Thus, in all (including Rom. 3:2), Paul enumerated 9 items which describe "the advantage of the Jew." In reply to the question, "What, then, is the advantage of the Jew, or what is the profit of circumcision?" Paul began to enumerate a list of advantages held by the Jew. The first item is named in 3:2. Beginning the list with the ordinal numeral "first" (πρω τον), the first item named is: "They were entrusted with the divine writings of God." God committed to national Israel the responsibility of guarding and transmitting the Scriptures. This responsibility is independent of national Israel's salvation; it

---

[4] The ordinal numeral πρω τος assumes that it will be followed by at least one more item. There is no second item listed in chapter 9. The remaining items are not mentioned until chapter 11. Chapter 11 is further tied together with this verse by the repetition of the term α πιστία which occurs both in 3:3 and in 11:20, 23.

is not a soteriological issue. It is, instead, a dispensational matter. The list of advantages to the Jew is resumed in 9:4–5. Combining these two segments, the following list of advantages is seen:

1. They were entrusted with guarding and transmitting the Scriptures.
2. "The adoption" belongs to them. That is, of all the nations represented in humanity, only Israel can lay claim to being adopted as God's unique "child."
3. The glory belongs to them. That is, God's Shekinah glory dwelt only in the midst of Israel, never in any of the Gentile nations.
4. The covenants belong to them. Specifically, the Abrahamic, Davidic, and New Covenants.[5]
5. The giving of the law (νομοθεσία) belongs to them. God had given His law, contained in the Mosaic Covenant, only to the nation of Israel, and to no other nation.
6. The temple service (λατρεία) belongs to them. The unique administration of the tabernacle/temple, also contained in the Mosaic Covenant, was given only to Israel.
7. The promises were given to them. While there may be general promises made to the Gentile nations, they are all comprehended as deriving from the blessings of the Abrahamic Covenant. Thus, the promises are uniquely given to Israel.
8. They are the source of the forefathers (Abraham, Isaac, and Jacob).
9. They constitute the human lineage of the Messiah.

---

[5] Possibly, the Mosaic could be included here; however, that is probably to be understood under the next item, the νομοθεσία. The Noahic covenant, of course, was not uniquely Jewish, but neither was it uniquely the possession of any other nation. The Noahic covenant is universal, covering all of mankind. Paul's point in saying that the covenants belong to Israel is simply that there is no other nation to whom God has given His covenants.

This list of nine advantages for national Israel sets the stage for understanding chapters 9–11. The context is not specifically soteriological, though it is related to salvation; it is primarily dispensational. These nine advantages spell out the administrative responsibilities that were entrusted to national Israel. In chapters 9–11, Paul spells out both why and how Israel's responsibility as God's administrative mediator in the world has been suspended during the church age. He also describes how they will be restored ultimately to that position of mediatorial administrative responsibility. This contextual background plays an important role in understanding what the "root" of the olive tree represents.

In light of this exalted and privileged position of Israel, it seems an enigma that the Jews had rejected the Messiah at His first advent. Chapters 9–11 offer an explanation to this enigma. Chapter 9 explains that God's election of Israel guarantees that they will eventually acknowledge that Jesus is their Messiah. Chapter 10 explains the means by which elect Israel will come to acknowledge that Jesus is their Messiah, namely through the preaching of the Gospel. Chapter 11 explains how present day Israel's unbelief relates to the present age and what the believing Gentiles' attitude toward national Israel should be.

Chapter 11 begins by discussing the doctrine of the remnant. Though Israel has often known periods in her history that were dominated by unbelief, there have always been, and will always be, some individual Israelites who will walk by faith in Yahweh (vv. 1–10). The existence of such a believing remnant is evidence that the entire nation will one day be brought to faith. That being the case, how should present day Gentile believers view national Israel in their time of unbelief? This is the primary question addressed in Romans 11:11–24. The chapter concludes (vv. 25–36) with a description of the restoration of Israel at the Messiah's Second Advent (when "The deliverer will come out of Zion and will turn away ungodliness out of Yakov," v. 26) and the bringing of Israel into the New Covenant ("And this is my covenant with them, when I forgive their sins," v. 27). As Stifler noted, "When God's purpose in breaking them off is served their blindness will be removed (II Cor. 3:14–16), and they will come into the blessed 'advantage' mentioned in 3:2."[6]

THE ARGUMENT OF VERSES 11–24

The church at Rome consisted of both believing Jews and believing Gentiles. These two groups, formerly hostile toward each other, were now brought together in Christ. Ideally, they were united in Christ, but experientially, former hostilities may have persisted. Some degree of anti–Semitism appears to have existed among believing Gentiles – if not toward believing Jews, certainly toward the bulk of Jews who remained in unbelief. In this passage, Paul exhorted the believing Gentiles not to harbor anti–Semitic attitudes towards unbelieving national Israel (Rom. 11:18). Instead, believing Gentiles were to view national Israel as God's sanctified people who were serving an important role in the outworking of God's purposes in the world. Paul developed this exhortation by pursuing two lines of argumentation: (1) Israel's unbelief was a temporary stumble that resulted in great blessing for the Gentile world, but national Israel will eventually recover from their stumble and will yet receive the fulfillment of God's covenants and promises that were made to the forefathers, verses 11–12; (2) Israel was, and will remain, a holy nation, a remnant of which will always believe, and ultimately, the entire nation will be saved, verses 13–24.

As Paul developed the first part of his argument (vv. 11–12), he explained first, that two positive things resulted from Israel's "stumble": (1) salvation has come to the Gentiles, verse 11a. (2) Israel itself will be provoked to jealousy over the Gentiles' receiving of such blessing, verse 11b. This provoking to jealousy

---

[6] James M. Stifler, The Epistle to the Romans (Chicago: Moody Press, 1960), 193.

will eventually lead to national Israel's fulfilling of the covenants and promises made to the forefathers, verse 12.

Paul then directly addressed the anti-Semitic attitude of the Gentile believers as he spoke to them directly in verse 13 ("But I say to you Gentiles..."). A substantial part of the motivation for Paul's ministry to the Gentiles was that by his Gentile outreach, he may in fact move Israel to the point of jealousy, so that some of them may be saved, verse 14.

Beginning in verse 15, Paul employed three illustrations of how all of national Israel will eventually come to faith. The first of these illustrations came from Ezekiel's vision of the valley of dry bones (Ezek 37:1-14). Paul referred to this prophecy by the succinct expression "life from the dead" (v. 15). What Ezekiel foresaw will yet come to pass; spiritually dead Israel will one day have the breath of God breathed into it, and all Israel will be saved.

The second illustration was put forth in verse 16a. The illustration is from the Pentecost loaves presented to the priests in the temple (Num 15:17-21). At Pentecost (*Shavu'ot*) a small portion of a lump of wheat dough was pinched off, formed into a loaf, baked and presented to the priests. This "first fruit" offering sanctified the entire lump of dough. Likewise, Paul argued, the remnant of Jews who were coming to faith was evidence that national Israel in its entirety was sanctified.

The third illustration received the most attention of the three and encompassed verses 16b-24. This was an illustration involving an olive tree. Three parts of this olive tree are distinguished from each other: the branches, representing national Israel; olive shoots grafted in from a wild tree, representing believing Gentiles; the root or lower portion of the tree, representing the position of privilege and administrative responsibility into which God places his mediatorial representatives on the earth. Unbelieving national Israel was described as branches that had been broken off (vv. 17-18). God had removed national Israel from the privileged place of being used as God's mediatorial agent in the world. Some of the original branches, however, remained; these were the remnant of Jews who believed in the Messiah and were subsequently incorporated into the church. Where national Israel was once in the place of mediatorial responsibility, God had now placed believing Gentiles. These believing Gentiles, along with the remaining original branches, were also incorporated into the church. While national Israel had been removed from the place of mediatorial responsibility, the church (composed of believing Jews and Gentiles) was now occupying that place.

This privileged position for believing Gentiles was not to become a cause of arrogance (vv. 18–22), for they had achieved this position, not by their own efforts or good works; rather, they stood by faith (v. 20). In fact, Gentiles would not hold this position in perpetuity; rather, God will one day remove the Gentiles from the position of mediatorial responsibility (vv. 21, 22) and place national Israel back into that position (v. 23–24).

IDENTITY OF THE ROOT

Paul speaks of a "root" in which the engrafted branches partake of nourishing fatness. It is ultimately the identification of this "root" that constitutes the primary difficulty in interpreting this passage. The word "root" (ῥίζα) is found in Greek from the time of Homer (VIII BC) and refers literally to the root of a tree or plant. While it may refer to the portion of the tree or plant that remains underground, it may also refer to "that which grows from a root,"[7] the portion of the tree or plant that is nearest the ground (lower trunk), that into which a grafting may be placed. For example Isaiah 53:2 refers to a "root out of dry ground" (שֹׁרֶשׁ מֵאֶרֶץ צִיָּה) for which the LXX translators put ῥίζα ἐν γῇ διψώσῃ ("a root in a thirsty ground"). In Isaiah's figure, this ῥίζα refers to "the

---

[7] BDAG, 906.

suckling, i.e., (in a horticultural sense) the tender twig which sucks up its nourishment from the root and stem."[8] In Romans 11:16–17, it clearly refers to the lower portion of the tree, that is, the trunk from which branches grow and into which shoots maybe grafted.

1. The root probably does not represent the Patriarchs,[9] for Israel has not been broken off from the Patriarchs, as Romans 9:5 makes clear. Furthermore, while it may be admitted that believing Gentiles are "sons of Abraham" (Gal 3:7), they are not similarly related to Isaac and Jacob.[10]

2. The root probably does not represent the covenants, for Paul has before established that the covenants are Israel's (Rom. 9:4). It is inconceivable that Paul would here state that Israel had been cut off from the covenants.

3. The root probably does not represent salvation, for national Israel was connected with the root prior to Christ's first advent, yet clearly Israel was not yet saved.

4. The root probably does not represent "Israel," for Israel has been broken off from the root.

5. The root probably does not represent "Christ," since Israel was connected with the root prior to Christ's first advent, yet national Israel throughout the Law dispensation could hardly be described as being "in Christ."

---

[8] Carl Friedrich Keil and Franz Delitzsch, Commentary on the Old Testament. (Peabody, MA: Hendrickson, 2002), Is 53:2.

[9] According to Cranfield this is the majority opinion (p. 565).

[10] Morris appears to have seen this weakness in the argument, so he adds the parenthetical remark, "perhaps he means only Abraham" (p. 411). But it is still true that Paul, according to Romans 9:5, did not regard Israel as broken off from Abraham.

There is a relationship between the salvation of Israel and their being grafted back into the position of mediatorial administrative responsibility. National salvation by means of the New Covenant is a prerequisite to Israel's engrafting (Jer 31:33–34), but the soteriological theme is secondary to the dispensational theme in this passage. The "root," then, is best seen as representing the place of mediatorial administrative responsibility. Under Israelite dispensations (Promise, Law, Kingdom) this place of responsibility is administered via the covenants. But under non-Israelite dispensations (Innocence, Conscience, Human Govern-ment, Grace) mediatorial responsibility is unrelated to Israel's covenants (including the New Covenant). National Israel occupied that place of mediatorial responsibility before the first advent. At their rejection of Jesus, the nation was broken off from that position, and in their place, Gentiles of the church have been grafted in, alongside of those remnant Jews (the branches that were not broken off) who believe in Jesus and are thus incorporated into the church.

THE "BREAKING OFF" OF THE NATURAL BRANCHES

This "breaking off" is different from the "cutting off" (ε κκόπτω) of Gentiles mentioned in lines 45 and 50, a distinction noted in nearly every major English translation.[11] Israel was broken off violently as a result of their unbelief. Paul may have had in mind Jeremiah 11:16 which uses the figure of breaking off[12] olive

---

[11] The one exception is American Bible Society's *Good New Translation,* which translates both as "break."

[12]   The Hebrew root may represent either of two separate linguistic roots, meaning "to smash, shatter, break," or meaning "to be bad, spoiled." Translations and expositors differ as to which is meant in Jeremiah 16:11, but "break" collocates well with "branches," and may be the better choice. If so then this provides a suitable OT reference for Paul's figure.

branches as a symbol for God's judgment against Israel.[13] This violent breaking off may even be somewhat prophetic of the future woes to be experienced by Israel in the destruction of the temple and subsequent scattering of Israel and generations of turmoil and persecution. It is not certain that Paul had these things in mind, but he certainly may have understood these things based on Moses' prediction of Deuteronomy 28–29 and on Jesus' Olivet Discourse in Luke 21. Moo fails to grasp the significance of the difference between ἐκκλάω and ε κκόπτω when he refers to Israel's having been "cut off."[14] That this breaking off is temporary is clearly spelled out in verse 23 (lines 46–48) making Moo's following statement perplexing: "... branches, whether Jewish or Gentile, that do not remain attached to that tree are doomed to wither and die."[15] If it is argued that Israel now "dead" will be raised to life (as in v. 15), then what of verse 22 which speaks of a future cutting off of the Gentiles? The attempt to understand this metaphor from a soteriological (i.e., Covenant Theology) perspective leads to great difficulty and probable Arminian implications.

Paul highlights the difference between Jew and Gentile by portraying them in his metaphor as branches that are "according to nature" (κατὰ φύσιν), verses 21, 24, and "contrary to nature" (παρὰ φύσιν), verse 24. The preposition κατά ("according to"), when used with an accusative object, occurs 399 times in the New Testament. It frequently has either a spatial reference ("along, over, through, in, upon," etc.) or temporal reference ("at, on, during"). Here, it has neither spatial nor temporal reference

---

[13] Joseph Shulam and Hilary Le Cornu, *A Commentary on the Jewish Roots of Romans* (Baltimore: Messianic Jewish Publishers, 1997), 372.

[14] Moo, *The Epistle to the Romans,* 701. Even the TNIV, of whose translation committee Moo was a member, preserves the distinction between "break" and "cut."

[15] Ibid. 704.

but signifies a relationship ("with respect to, in relation to, according to") similar to its use in the phrase "according to the flesh" in Romans 1:3; 4:1; 9:3, 5. BDAG suggests that here in Romans 11:21 translating the phrase as "in line with," or "in accordance with" would sound somehow "cumbersome" and that a better translation would be to render it as an adjective, "the natural branches."[16] This, however, misses the point. To be sure, in Paul's figure they are natural branches, but so are the wild olive shoots that are grafted into the tree. Paul's point is that these branches that were broken off are of a different nature than the wild olive shoots. To say that these branches are "according to nature" (κατὰ φύσιν) signifies that they correspond to the nature of the cultivated olive tree. The term "nature" (φύσις) is attested in Greek from the time of Homer (VIII BC). In classical Greek this term had reference to the "natural qualities, powers, constitution, condition, of a person or thing."[17]

To translate this merely as "nature" in English may produce an erroneous connotation, unless it is coupled with a limiting phrase such as "nature *of the cultivated olive tree.*" It is not "natural" as opposed to "synthetic," neither is it "nature" as opposed to an urban setting." Rather, it has reference here to the innate qualities of the cultivated olive tree. This is not quite the same as saying that they are "natural branches." The point is that national Israel has been constituted by God in such a way as to make them better suited to function as His mediatorial representatives than the Gentiles are. This notion goes back to Paul's nine-fold list of advantages to the Jew in 3:2; 9:4-5.

This preposition   παρά ("contrary to") is used with all three oblique cases and has a very wide semantic range in all three of these cases. When used with an accusative object, παρά

---

[16] BDAG, 513.

[17] H.G. Liddell, *A Lexicon: Abridged from Liddell and Scott's Greek-English Lexicon* (Oak Harbor, WA: Logos Research Systems, Inc., 1996), 876.

may refer to (1) a physical position "by, along, at the edge of, by the side of, near, on;" (2) time "during, from;" (3) comparative advantage "in comparison to, more than, beyond;" (4) degree that falls short in comparison "except for, almost;" (5) causality "because of;" (6) that which does not correspond to what is expected "against, contrary to;" (7) that which is less "less." Here in Romans 11:24 it used in the sixth meaning above, "against, contrary to," as also in the following:

- Romans 1:26 παρὰ φύσιν "contrary to nature"
- Romans 4:18 παρ' ἐλπίδα "contrary to hope"
- Romans 6:17 παρὰ τὴν διδαχήν "contrary to the teaching"
- Acts 18:13 παρὰ τὸν νόμον "contrary to the law"
- Gal 1:8 παρ' ὃ εὐηγγελισάμεθα ὑμῖν "contrary to what we preached to you"

The contrast between παρά and κατά is an intended word–play to show the inherent suitability of the Jews for the position in the world as God's mediators. Though broken off for now, they must one day be grafted back in to the place of administrative responsibility for which they are well suited.

THE ENGRAFTING OF THE WILD BRANCHES

"Wild olive branches" (ἀγριέλαιος) may be either an adjective or a noun. Both are attested from the fourth to third centuries BC (the adjective in Theocritos, the noun in Theophrastos). As a noun it refers to the wild olive tree, a compound of ἄγριος "wild," "uncontrolled," "growing in the open field" (cp. α γρός "field," "countryside") and ἐλαία "an olive tree." Here it appears to be used as an adjective. In the New Testament the term occurs only in this passage (vv. 17, 24). It does not occur in the LXX. This passage uses three distinct terms to refer to olive trees (1) ἀγριέλαιος verses 17 and 24, "the wild olive tree;" (2) ε λαία in verses 17 and 24, a generic term for any olive tree; and (3) καλλιέλαιος in verse 24, "the cultivated olive tree."

Horticulturally, what is described here is contrary to normal practice. The normal practice would be to graft a cultivated shoot into a wild olive tree. The wild olive would be naturally more resistant to diseases and pests, while the cultivated shoot would bear the better fruit. One should be cautious about reading too much into the imagery here. However, the context does build on the image of the ἀγριέλαιος, describing these branches as grafted in κατὰ φύσιν ("contrary to nature").

The Gentiles by nature had their own "home-grown" civilization, government, law, and administration; however, they had never been in the place of mediatorial responsibility in the administration of God's affairs in the world. Their history had not prepared them for this position. The later negative influence of Greek philosophy on the fourth century church illustrates the inherent dangers associated with grafting these wild olive shoots into the cultivated tree.

THE "CUTTING OFF" OF THE GENTILES

The reason the Gentiles were not to boast about their own position as God's mediatorial agents in the world, is expressed in verse 21, namely, that God would one day remove them from that position and restore national Israel as His mediatorial agent in the world.

The expression "lest perhaps" (μή πως/μήπως[18]) in verse 21 is missing from the most reliable Alexandrian manuscripts (ℵ A B C 81 1739 and many others). However, its inclusion in p[46], as well as in other manuscripts (many Byzantine), has been

---

[18] μή πως (μήπως) in use from the time of Homer (VIII BC) tends to denote a sense of doubt and may be translated into English by "perhaps." When joined with a verb of apprehension (such as φοβεῖσθαι or βλέπετε) it takes on the sense of "lest," BDAG, 901.

influential in convincing modern editors to include this reading in standard Greek texts (USB⁴ and NA²⁷ include the reading in square brackets). Manuscript p⁴⁶, part of the Chester Beatty collection, likely dates from the mid–second to mid–third centuries. All three major versions of the *Textus Receptus* (Stephens 1550, Elzevir 1624, Scrivener 1881) join μήπως with the aorist subjunctive φεισηται ("lest he spare"), resulting in the AV translation, "*take heed* lest he also spare not thee." This requires the editorial addition of a main verb "take heed" which has resulted in a traditional interpretation of this verse that takes it as a warning that the addressees may be in danger of losing God's favor. The Byzantine majority text, however, agrees with the Alexandrian reading of the future indicative φείσεται ("he will [not] spare"). If the future indicative is allowed to stand, then the verse is merely predictive of a future event, rather than a warning of dire consequences. Whether or not μή πως (μήπως) is genuine, the textual evidence is quite conclusive that it is coupled with a future indicative, not an aorist subjunctive. The counterpart to the prediction of the Gentiles' being cut off is the prediction that the Jews will be grafted back in again (ver. 24, ε γκεντρισθήσονται).

The term φείδομαι ("spare") is attested from the time of Homer (VIII BC). Though it may mean "to spare" in the sense of "to rescue from danger" (as in to spare in a time of war), it can also mean merely to retain in the same status quo, with no implication of impending danger (cp. the cognate adverb φειδομένως "sparingly"). This verb does not necessarily connote an idea of impending danger. Such an idea comes from the *Textus Receptus'* reading of the aorist subjunctive, rather than the future indicative, and may be influenced by the presence of μήπως; see discussion above. When a primarily soteriological context is presumed here and the combination of μήπως with an aorist subjunctive is read, this verse takes on a warning about loss of salvation that sounds very Arminian, leading Moo to state, "... if God so judged the Jews, who had a natural connection to the tree and its sustaining root, he will surely judge those who have been grafted in as alien branches."[19] However, the context is not primarily soteriological. At issue here is not one's salvation, but rather one's position as God's mediatorial representative on the earth. When national Israel was "broken off" (vv. 17–18) they did not experience a loss of salvation, for they were already in a non-regenerate condition. Their being broken off consisted in their being removed from a position of representative mediatorial responsibility in the administration of God's affairs on the earth. Likewise, ου δὲ φείσεται here signifies that God will not retain the Gentiles in their place of mediatorial responsibility either. A time will come when national Israel will be grafted back in. At that time, the Gentiles will be removed from that position, possibly via a pretribulational rapture that removes them from the earth.

Similarly, in verse 22, "those who fell" should not be understood in a soteriological sense. Expositors who bring to this passage a preunderstanding of a soteriological theme (as opposed to a dispensational one) become mired in inconsistencies. For example, Morris states with regard to πεσόντας,

> In verse 11 Paul denied that Israel's stumbling was in order that they might fall, and he has the same verb here. But there he was denying that ultimate disaster was the fate of God's Israel; here he is affirming that it is the fate of those branches that were cut off on account of unbelief (v. 20). Those who shut themselves up to unbelief can look forward to nothing but severity.[20]

By presuming that the "fall" here refers to soteriological effects Morris is forced to find two different meanings between verses 11

---

[19] Moo, *The Epistle to the Romans,* 706. Moo does not describe what sort of "judgment" will be visited against "those who have been grafted in," but Paul's clear statement is that "there is now no condemnation to those who are in Christ Jesus" (Rom. 8:1).

[20] Morris, 416.

and 22. But this inconsistency is avoided when one understands the "fall" to refer to a fall from mediatorial administrative responsibility and privilege.

The "kindness" of God (χρηστότης) referred to in verse 22 should also be understood in the dispensational context of the passage. Attested from the time of Euripides (V BC). This term appears to be derived from the cognate χρηστός (from Homer VIII BC) "useful, beneficial." χρηστότης occurs ten times in the New Testament, all in Paul. The LXX uses it 26 times, 17 in the canonical books of Esther and Psalms, the other nine in 1 Esdras (once), Odes of Solomon (once) and Psalms of Solomon (seven times). The original idea of "usefulness, profitableness" has become something more like "goodness, kindness, generosity" by the Hellenistic era. The specific "kindness" ("beneficence"?) in view here should not be understood in a soteriological sense. Though it is true that these believing Gentiles had been justified by faith, the issue here is the privilege that accompanies the responsibility of being God's mediatorial agent. Thus, to be engrafted or to be cut off is not a matter of being saved or lost. It is a matter of God's kindness in the present age that believing Gentiles are serving as His mediatorial agents. But if, at some future point, these Gentiles are to be removed from that position, this does not mean that they will lose their salvation, only that they will be removed from their position of mediatorial agency in the world.

The conjunction ε πεί ("since") introduces the last clause of verse 22 as a causal clause expressing the reason for the uncertainty about the believing Gentiles remaining in the position of God's goodness (χρηστότης). Attested from the time of Homer (VIII BC), ε πεί was used in Classical Greek in either a temporal or causal sense. In the New Testament there are no instances of its use as a temporal conjunction.[21] In the New Testament this conjunction is always causal.

Believing Gentiles will not remain in the position of God's χρηστότης forever because one day God will cut them off from the position of mediatorial responsibility. This will happen at such time as when national Israel is grafted back in to this position. Those who interpret this passage along the lines of a soteriological theme run the danger of coming to Arminian conclusions. For example, Moo states, "... if the believer does not continue in the goodness of God – the believer will, like the Jew, be 'cut off' – severed forever from the people of God and eternally condemned.... Salvation is dependent on continuing faith; therefore, the person who ceases to believe forfeits any hope of salvation."[22]

This conclusion is so surprising that Moo finds it necessary to issue a lengthy and confusing caveat in a footnote.[23] Two kinds of causal clauses may be introduced by ε πεί: (1) directly causal clauses, in which a reason or cause for the preceding clause is given where ε πεί is translated "because, since, for," such as in Matthew 18:32; 21:46; 27:6; Mark 15:42; Luke 1:34; John 13:29; 19:31; 1 Corinthians 14:12; 2 Corinthians 11:18; 13:3; Hebrews 5:2, 11; 6:13; 9:17; 11:11. (2) Clauses introducing a contraindication where ε πεί is translated "otherwise," such as in Romans 3:6; 11:6; 1 Corinthians 5:10; 7:14; 14:16; 15:29; Hebrews 9:26; 10:2. All major English

---

[21] A variant reading at Luke 7:1 has ε πεὶ δέ instead of ε πειδή as a temporal expression. But solid manuscript evidence for this reading is lacking, and no major published edition of the Greek New Testament has adopted it.

[22] Moo, *Epistle to the Romans,* 706–7. Similarly, Stifler states, "The Gentile is responsible for his conduct, and if he fails to honor God he will fall as did the Jew" (193). These statements, from men who would consider themselves to be Calvinistic in doctrine, are quite amazing.

[23] Ibid., n. 57.

translations have understood ε πεί here to introduce a contraindication and translate it as "otherwise."[24] The position taken here is that ε πεί should be understood as directly causal. An analysis of the eight instances of ε πεί as introducing a contraindication reveals that in such instances contraindication is denoted by two characteristics of the grammar:

1.   An expression of uncertainty by means of a question, a subjunctive, a verb of volition (e.g. o φείλω) or a particle like α ´ν. If not uncertainty, then there is the expression of a patently unacceptable result ('grace is no longer grace,' 'your children are unclean').

2.   The implication of some negative to be rejected in the preceding clause.

In Romans 11:22 there is no expression of uncertainty; on the contrary, the verb is a future indicative. It could be argued that ἐκκοπήσῃ ("you will be cut off") expresses a patently unacceptable result, but only on the assumption that the context is soteriological. It has been argued in this chapter that the context is not primarily soteriological, and that the "cutting off" speaks of a dispensational change in the way God administers His affairs in the world. Also, there is no implication of a negative to be rejected in the preceding clause. On the contrary, the preceding clause expresses a positive course of action to which the Gentiles should adhere ("if you remain in His goodness"). For these reasons, the position taken here runs contrary to the major

---

[24] ASV, AV, ESV, HCSB, NASB, NET, NIV, NKJV, NRSV, RSV. So also Cranfield, "The clause is a warning against a false and unevangelical sense of security," 570.

English translations and asserts that ε πεί should be translated "since" or "because."[25]

That the Gentiles will be cut off from the root at some future time is inexplicable in soteriological terms, unless one adopts an Arminian soteriology. But understood in dispensational terms, the future cutting off of the Gentiles simply points to a future change in administration. Gentiles must be removed from the place of administrative responsibility before God can reinstate Israel as His administrative agent in the world for the seventieth week of Daniel. The seventieth week of Daniel will see God's administration carried out by 144,000 sealed Jews (Rev 7:1-8, 14:1-5), two Jewish prophets announcing God's Word in Jerusalem (Rev 11:3-14), and a rebuilt temple in Jerusalem (Dan 9:27; Matt 24:15; 2 Thess 2:4; Rev 11:1-2).

CONCLUSION

The engrafting of the Gentiles referred to in Romans 11:17 is seen by some as support for the view that the Church is somehow involved in Israel's New Covenant. This chapter has put forth an argument that Romans 11:17 is not referring to the Church's participation in the New Covenant at all. Rather, this verse is referring to the Church's dispensational position, serving as God's administrative mediator on the earth during the present age. The "root" into which the church has been grafted is the position of mediatorial responsibility.

The entire context of Romans 9–11 is one which describes Israel's relationship to God in terms of dispensational responsibility and participation. To import a soteriological theme into this dispensational context ultimately leads to Arminian conclusions when discussing the "breaking off," "engrafting," and "cutting off" referred to in this passage. However, when seen from

---

[25] Darby translated it, "since [otherwise]," placing the word "otherwise" in square brackets.

a dispensational perspective of discussing mediatorial respon-sibilities, the "breaking off," "engrafting," and "cutting off" fit neatly, without confusion or contradiction, into a premillennial, pretribulational, dispensational view of the progress of the ages.

7

SECOND CORINTHIANS 3:6 AND THE NEW COVENANT[1]

George Gunn

> *Who also made us adequate as servants of a New Covenant, not of the letter but of the Spirit; for the letter kills, but the Spirit gives life.* (2 Corinthians 3:6 NASB)

Dispensationalists regard the distinction between Israel and the church to be of fundamental importance. Likewise, the question of how the church relates to Israel's covenants must be fundamentally important. If there is "overlap" between Israel and the church in the area of Israel's covenants, then perhaps dispensationalism is built on a faulty foundation. This is a crucial issue, not a peripheral one.

Purpose of This Chapter
This chapter's purpose is to investigate the hermeneutical issues involved in the interpretation of 2 Corinthians 3:6 in light of how the church is related to the New Covenant. Obviously there is a broader theological discussion that must take into consideration numerous other Biblical references, this chapter's purpose will be

---

[1] Initially Addressed to The Council on Dispensational Hermeneutics at Baptist Bible Seminary, September 23, 2009, and later published as "Second Corinthians 3:6 and the Church's Relationship to the New Covenant" in *Journal of Dispensational Theology*, Dec 2009: 25–46.

more limited in scope. The principal goal will be to focus on the matter of authorial intent and how the initial audience (the first century Corinthian congregation) may have been expected to understand 2 Corinthians 3:6.[2]

INTRODUCTION

The relationship of the church to the New Covenant has long been a point of considerable theological discussion among

---

[2] By referring to the way the initial audience may have been expected to understand the text, I do not intend to sanction the various reader–response theories of hermeneutics that seem to have gained much attention with a certain segment of modern scholarship. I merely mean that we need to attempt to understand the shared presupposition pool between original author and original audience. For one such reader–response theory approach, actually based on an interpretation of 2 Cor 3, see Richard B. Hays *Echoes of Scripture in the Letters of Paul* (New Haven: Yale University Press, 1989), 122–125, 129 in which he refers to an "ecclesiocentric hermeneutic" and a "New Covenant hermeneutic"; and a response by Robert B. Sloan, Jr., "2 Corinthians 2:14–4:6 and 'New Covenant Hermeneutics' A Response to Richard Hays" *Bulletin for Biblical Research* 5 (1995), 129–154.

dispensationalists.[3] God's program for Israel's future on the millennial earth is rooted in the four unconditional, eternal covenants: Abrahamic, Land (a.k.a. "Palestinian"[4]), Davidic, and New. These covenants, made between God and national Israel, describe God's administrative/dispensational program for Israel's millennial existence. Traditional dispensationalists believe that God has a separate and distinct administrative/dispensational program for the church. These distinct programs for Israel and the church have led dispensationalists historically to reject covenant theology's view that the church has become the new

---

[3] Some more recent articles: R. Bruce Compton, "Dispensationalism, The Church, And the New Covenant," *Detroit Baptist Seminary Journal* 8 (Fall 2003); Richard Daniels, "How Does the Church Relate to the New Covenant? or, Whose New Covenant is It, Anyway," *Faith and Mission* 16: 2, Spr 1999: 64–98; Rodney J. Decker, "The Church's Relationship to the New Covenant," Part I, *Bibliotheca Sacra Volume 152.* (July 1995): 290–305, Part II, (October 1995), 431–456; Homer A. Kent, Jr., "The New Covenant and the Church," *Grace Theological Journal* 6 (Fall 1985); John Master in chapter 5 ("The New Covenant") of *Issues in Dispensationalism*, edited by Wesley R. Willis and John R. Master (Moody Press, 1994), 93–110; Russell L. Penney "The Relationship of the Church to the New Covenant," *Conservative Theological Journal* 2:7, (December 1998): 457–477; Larry D. Pettegrew, "The New Covenant," *Master's Seminary Journal* 10:2 (Fall 1999): 251–270; Paul R. Thorsell, "The Spirit in the Present Age: Preliminary Fulfillment of the Predicted New Covenant According to Paul" *Journal of the Evangelical Theological Society* 41:3 (September 1998): 397–413.

[4] I have chosen to refrain from using the title "Palestinian Covenant." While this title may have been acceptable in a bygone era, the abuse of the term "Palestinian" by today's Arab claimants to territorial rights in Israel, makes continued use of that term unacceptable, in my opinion. The original application of the term *Palaestina* to *Iudaea* by the Roman emperor Hadrian as an insult to the Jews ought to have been sufficient reason for God-fearing Christians to reject the term in the beginning. However, such, unfortunately, was not the case.

204   *An Introduction to the New Covenant*

replacement party to these covenants. Nevertheless, because the New Testament Scriptures make multiple references to the New Covenant, both covenant theologians and many dispensationalists have argued for some degree of participation by the church in the New Covenant.

THEOLOGICAL ISSUES

Five views of the Church's Relationship to the New Covenant may be defined:[5]

1. Replacement Theology: *Replacement* – The church is entirely fulfilling the New Covenant. National Israel has been superseded by the church, the true, or spiritual, Israel. The church's ministers, by fulfilling the Great Commission, function as ministers of the New Covenant.

2. Dispensational View #1: *Partial Fulfillment* – The church, by fulfilling the Great Commission, is accomplishing a partial fulfillment of the New Covenant, but complete fulfillment awaits the spiritual renewal of national Israel in the millennium.

3. Dispensational View #2: *Participation* – The church, by fulfilling the Great Commission, does not partially fulfill the New Covenant, but does participate in some of the blessings of the New Covenant.

4. Dispensational View #3: *Two New Covenants* – The church has its own "New Covenant" with God that is distinct and separate from Israel's New Covenant of Jeremiah 31.

5. Dispensational View #4: *No Relationship* – The church is not directly related to the New Covenant in any way. The church is related to the Mediator of the New

---

Covenant and to the blood of that covenant, but is not a participant in the covenant itself.

Obviously, these 5 views could be grouped together as suggested above in the following way: The view of Covenant Theology (view #1), the views of Dispensational Theology (views #2–5). However, it is also possible to group these views in another way: the Church has *some* participation in the New Covenant (views #1–4), the Church has *no* participation in the New Covenant (view #5).

In the remainder of this paper, these views will be referred to by the names, "Replacement View," "Partial Fulfillment View," "Participation View," "Two Covenants View," and "No Relationship View."

Darby, often held to be the first systematizer of dispensationalism,[6] held to the No Relationship View; the church is related to the *blood* of the covenant, but not to the covenant itself.[7] Chafer, Ryrie and Walvoord early popularized the Two

---

[6] Charles C. Ryrie *Dispensationalism* (Chicago: Moody Press, 1995), 67.

[7] At least many dispensational theologians claim this to be Darby's position (J. Dwight Pentecost *Things to Come* [Grand Rapids: Zondervan, 1958], 121–122, John F. Walvoord *The Millennial Kingdom* [Grand Rapids: Zondervan, 1959], 210, 218); however, I have read Darby both on Jeremiah, the Gospels, 2 Corinthians and Hebrews, and he is difficult to categorize. It might be possible to argue that he holds to the participation view. Both views are almost merged in this oft quoted excerpt: "The gospel is not a covenant, but the revelation of the salvation of God. It proclaims the great salvation. We enjoy indeed all the essential privileges of the New Covenant, its foundation being laid on God's part in the blood of Christ, but we do so in spirit, not according to the letter.... The New Covenant will be established formally with Israel in the millennium." (Darby, *Synopsis* V, 286, as cited in Pentecost *Things to Come, ibid.*). When all of Darby's statements are examined, however, I suspect that the No Relationship view does, in fact, most closely represent his thinking.

Covenants View,[8] but as of this writing, both Ryrie and Walvoord appear to have moved more in the direction of the Participation View.[9] Most dispensationalists today seem to prefer either the Partial Fulfillment View (notably, progressive dispensationalists[10]) or the Participation View.[11] I will state up front, that my preference is for the No Relationship View. In my opinion, this is the only view that avoids theological confusion and maintains a consistent distinction between Israel and the Church. As I see it theologically, the church has no more place in this age participating in the New Covenant, than it does in the Davidic covenant. However, the question must ultimately be settled on exegetical grounds rather than theological preference.

---

[8] Lewis Sperry Chafer *Systematic Theology* Dallas: Dallas Seminary Press, 1948), VII:98–99; Charles C. Ryrie *The Basis of the Premillennial Faith* (Neptune, NJ: Loizeaux Brothers, 1953), 117; Walvoord *Millennial Kingdom,* 218–219.

[9] Charles C. Ryrie *Dispensationalism,* rev. ed. (Chicago: Moody Press, 1995), 170–174; John F. Walvoord, "Does the Church Fulfill Israel's Program?" Part 3 *Bibliotheca Sacra* 137/547 (July–Sept 1980): 220.

[10] Bruce A. Ware, "The New Covenant and the People(s) of God" in *Dispensationalism, Israel and the Church* edd. C. Blaising and D. Bock (Grand Rapids: Zondervan, 1992), 68–97.

[11] Robert Thomas *Evangelical Hermeneutics* (Grand Rapids: Kregel Publications, 2002), 249; Larry D. Pettegrew *The New Covenant Ministry of the Holy Spirit,* 2nd edition (Grand Rapids: Kregel Publications, 2001), 36–37; J. Dwight Pentecost *Thy Kingdom Come* (Wheaton: Victor Books, 1990), 175; David K. Lowery, "2 Corinthians" in *The Bible Knowledge Commentary"* edd. J. F. Walvoord and R. B. Zuck (Wheaton: Victor Books, 1985), II:560; Compton 47–48.

THE SIGNIFICANCE OF 2 CORINTHIANS 3:6

In 1994, John Master contributed a chapter entitled, "The New Covenant" to the book *Issues in Dispensationalism*.[12] In that chapter, Master argued cogently that the vast majority of NT references to the New Covenant are set in an eschatological[13] context and need not be interpreted in terms of a present realization. The notable exception among these NT references is 2 Corinthians 3:6. Having commented on the references to the New Covenant in the Gospels and the Pauline epistles,[14] Master states:

To this point, the passages that refer to the New Covenant of Jeremiah follow a common thread. All refer to a time when the messianic kingdom is introduced and the people of God are glorifying God through their obedience, brought about by a sovereign work of God. Only if one asserts that 2 Corinthians 3:6 teaches the fulfillment of the New Covenant of Jeremiah 31 by the church (which this author doubts), does the future fulfillment of the New Covenant for national Israel come into question.[15]

I do not intend here to reproduce Master's arguments for the other NT references. Instead, the scope of this paper will be to grant his arguments for the other NT references, but to look in greater depth at how 2 Corinthians 3:6 is to be interpreted. Furthermore, progressive dispensationalism, which prefers the

---

[12] John R. Master, "The New Covenant" in *Issues in Dispensationalism* eds. Wesley R. Willis, John R. Master, Charles C. Ryrie (Chicago: Moody Press, 1994), 93–110.

[13] When I use the term "eschatological" I am not including any reference to a "realized eschatology" or "already–not–yet" scenario that views the present church age as "eschatological."

[14] Mt 26:28; Mk 14:24; Lk 22:20; 1 Co 11:25. The Hebrews references are a slightly different matter, but the specific references are Heb 8:8, 13; 9:15; 10:16–17; 12:24.

[15] Master, 103.

Partial Fulfillment view, places great significance on this verse. Paul Thorsell, for example, speaking of the significance of this passage for proving a present realization of the New Covenant to the church, wrote:

> Traditional dispensationalists have usually argued, however, that Paul's ministry is related to the predicted New Covenant only peripherally or analogically. There is no present fulfillment or inauguration of the New Covenant at all. In contradistinction to this thesis of traditional dispensationalism, *2 Corinthians 3 presents formidable reasons to regard the New Covenant as partially fulfilled or inaugurated* in the gospel–proclaiming ministry of Paul.[16]

Is Thorsell correct in claiming "formidable reasons" supporting a partial fulfillment or inauguration of the New Covenant based on 2 Corinthians 3? To answer this question, a careful exegetical study of how Paul referred to the New Covenant in 2 Corinthians 3 is needed.

HERMENEUTICAL ISSUES

Several questions of a hermeneutical/exegetical nature arise when we seek to understand how Paul envisioned the church's relationship to the New Covenant when he addressed the Corinthians as he did in 2 Corinthians 3:6. These questions include the following:

---

[16]Paul Thorsell, "The Spirit in the Present Age," 406, emphasis mine. Thorsell also states: "2 Corinthians 3 is perhaps the most prominent reference to the New Covenant in the Pauline corpus," 400. Note also Bruce Ware's estimation, "The most extensive treatment Paul gives of the transforming new–covenant work of the Spirit is found in 2 Corinthians 3" (Ware, 88).

1. Is "ministers of a New Covenant" (διακόνους καινῆς διαθήκης *diakonous kainēs diathēkēs*) an objective genitive or a genitive of description?
2. What is the referent to "us" (ἡμᾶς *hēmas*)?
3. What is the context of this statement?
4. Is there significance to the fact that "covenant" (διαθήκης *diathēkēs*)is anarthrous?
5. What was the state of theological development when Paul wrote 2 Corinthians? How well developed was Paul's concept of the church as an entity separate and distinct from Israel?
6. Why would Paul be referring to a passage from the Hebrew Scriptures when addressing a largely Gentile Christian church?

1. Is "ministers of a New Covenant" (διακόνους καινῆς διαθήκης diakonous kainēs diathēkēs) an objective genitive or a genitive of description?
This is probably the most fundamental hermeneutical question in this discussion. In fact, it is a syntactical way of stating the essential problem. If this is an objective genitive,[17] then we may paraphrase, "those who minister (or 'administer') the New Covenant." In other words, Paul would be referring to the New Covenant as the content of his ministry. For example, Hafemann comments, "... he is a minister of the New Covenant (i.e., his function). As a minister, he mediates the Spirit in establishing the

---

[17] Thorsell, "The Spirit in the Present Age," 407; Murray J. Harris, *The Second Epistle to the Corinthians : A commentary on the Greek text.* (Grand Rapids: Eerdmans, 2005), 270. Curiously, Harris sees the roughly parallel διακονία του   πνεύματος in verse 8 as "more probably adjectival ... than objective ... or subjective... (p. 286).

church... The content of Paul's activity as a minister is the 'New Covenant."[18]

On the other hand, if this were a genitive of description, an appropriate paraphrase might be, "'New Covenant-like' ministers." As a genitive of description, the New Covenant does not necessarily point to the content of Paul's ministry, but rather provides a helpful description of the kind of ministry in which he was engaged – in other words, how Paul conducted himself in carrying out the ministry.

I find it interesting that the closest parallel construction using "minister" (διάκονος diakonos) with a genitive in 2 Corinthians occurs in 11:15, διάκονοι δικαιοσύνης (diakonoi dikaiosunēs), "ministers of righteousness" which is almost certainly a genitive of description,[19] not an objective genitive (see in context the parallel ἄγγελον φωτός angelon phōtos, "angel of light"). Although the parallel is suggestive, by itself, this observation is not sufficient proof of the use of the genitive in 3:6, and, on the face of it, both syntactical options are possible in 3:6 and make decent sense. The deciding factors must hinge on other exegetical considerations.

---

[18] Scott J. Hafemann *2 Corinthians* The NIV Application Commentary (Grand Rapids: Zondervan, 2000), 129.

[19] It could be considered a genitive of attribute, which is really only a sub-category of the genitive of description. Thorsell tries to argue for διάκονοι δικαιοσύνης in 11:15 being an objective genitive ("The Spirit in the Present Age," 407, n. 32), but his interpretation here is strained, and does not take into consideration the parallel expression ἄγγελον φωτός. The other examples of διάκονος used with a genitive in 2 Cor. are all possessive genitives: θεου διάκονοι "God's servants" (6:4), διάκονοι αυ του "his servants" (11:15), διάκονοι Χριστου "Christ's servants" (11:23).

2. What is the referent to ἡμᾶς?

When Paul wrote, "... who also has made *us* sufficient as ministers," to whom was he referring? A popular way of looking at this verse might be to see the "us" as referring to all Christians, so that Paul was referring generally to Christian ministry in the carrying out of the Great Commission. Christians, whose responsibility it is to carry out the Great Commission, are made sufficient for such a task by the enablement of God.[20] Such a view would correspond well with taking καινῆς διαθήκης as an objective genitive.

The hermeneutical issue here is: Who is to be included in the reference to the 1st Person Plural? There are several possibilities: First, is Paul alone. "The *editorial 'we'* (also known as the *epistolary plural*) is the use of the first person plural by an author when he is in reality referring only to himself."[21] In this sense, Paul would be seen as addressing the Corinthian congregation regarding criticisms that had been leveled against his own ministry. It is generally recognized among commentators that Paul's defense of his ministry is a major theme of 2 Corinthians.

Second, is Paul and Timothy (and Titus?). Paul and Timothy are mentioned in 1:1 as the co-authors of the epistle.[22] Titus may also be considered as part of the "team" (2:13; 7:6, 13, 14; 8:5, 16, 23; 12:17). In this sense, the meaning would be

---

[20] E.g., *Experiencing the Word New Testament* (Nashville: Holman Bible Publishers, 2001), 408; G. Coleman Luck, *Second Corinthians* (Chicago: Moody Press, 1959), 34; D. E. Garland *The New American Commentary Vol. 29: 2 Corinthians* (Nashville: Broadman & Holman Publishers, 1999), *163*.

[21] Daniel B. Wallace, Greek Grammar Beyond the Basics – Exegetical Syntax of the New Testament (Grand Rapids: Zondervan, 1999), 394.

[22] R.C.H. Lenski, The Interpretation of St. Paul's First and Second Epistles to the Corinthians (Minneapolis: Augsburg Publishing House, 1937), 838–839.

similar to the former possibility, the editorial "we," assuming that Paul's detractors in Corinth would have leveled the same charges against the other members of Paul's ministry team.

A third option is Paul and the Corinthian Christians. In this sense, Paul would be addressing the Corinthian congregation as fellow–laborers with him. As such, he would be describing the gospel ministry in which they were all involved.

A fourth possibility is the apostles. Though less likely, it is possible that Paul was describing the ministry of the apostles in a limited sense, perhaps in inaugurating the New Covenant ministry.

Finally, the reference could be to all believers. In this sense, Paul would be issuing a general statement describing how all believers fulfill the Great Commission as a ministry of the New Covenant.

Paul's use of 1st person deictic indicators in chapters 1–3 is quite interesting. He switches often between the singular ("I/me") and the plural ("we/us"). A personal deixis analysis[23] of these chapters reveals some helpful and interesting observations. Such an analysis can be summarized as follows:

1:1–13a
Plural – In this section, verse 4, "who comforts us in all our affliction so that we will be able to comfort those who are in any affliction with the comfort with which we ourselves are comforted by God," makes it obvious that Paul is distinguishing himself (along with Timothy[24] and Titus?) from the Corinthians ("us" as opposed to "those who").
1:13b,

---

[23] Peter Cotterell and Max Turner, *Linguistics & Biblical Interpretation* (Downers Grove: InterVarsity Press, 1989), 236.

[24] Lenski, 839.

Singular – Verse 13 has an interesting change from the plural to the singular: "For we write nothing else to you than what you read and understand, and I hope you will understand until the end." It is likely that up to this point, Paul has been speaking in the plural in order to include Timothy, and possibly Titus, in his remarks. His switch to the singular makes the comment of 13b a bit more personal and direct, since, after all, Paul was really the focal point of the criticisms emanating from Corinth, and Timothy and Titus were merely "along for the ride."

1:14

Plural – Verse 14 can be considered as a return to the default plural that Paul has been using since verse 1, with the lone exception of 13b.

1:15–17

Singular – In this brief section, Paul's switch to the singular accompanies a switch also to the past tense as Paul makes reference to his past plans to visit Corinth and his subsequent cancellation of those plans. To this point the plural has been the default, and switches to the singular have been the notable exceptions. From 1:15 – 2:13 the singular will become the predominant and default 1st person reference, with plurals constituting the notable exceptions.

1:18–22

Plural – A return, once again to the plural. An interesting note: Paul specifies the plural as a reference to Paul, Silas and Timothy.

1:23

Singular – As with vv. 15–17, Paul's use of the singular here accompanies a past time reference to his previous plans to visit Corinth and his subsequent cancellation of those plans.

1:24
Plural – A return to the plural accompanies a departure from past tense to a gnomic present time frame ("we lord it over" κυριεύομεν, "we are" ε σμεν, "you are standing firm" ε στήκατε) as Paul expresses a timeless generality.

2:1–10
Singular – Once again, Paul's use of the singular here accompanies a past time reference to his previous plans to visit Corinth and his subsequent cancellation of those plans.

2:11
Plural – The plural is used here to make a general statement that is applicable to all.

2:12–13
Singular – This can be considered a return to what has been the default while Paul discusses his past plans.

2:14 – 3:6
Plural – With this verse, Paul brings his discussion of past plans to an end and begins an extended section in which he uses a series of metaphors to describe the nature of his ministry. There is a different reason for his switch to the plural here than there was in 2:11. This can be seen by the observation that in this section (3:3) the 1st person plural is contrasted with the 2nd person plural; whereas, no such contrast is seen in 2:11.[25] Paul's use of the plural in this series of metaphors[26] is intended to depict the ministry as conducted by himself, Timothy and Titus, as distinguished from others (his critics) whose ministry takes on a different character.

---

[25] In fact in 11:3, Paul entertains the possibility that Satan had in fact deceived the minds of some of the Corinthians!

[26] The series of metaphors is discussed below.

This would tend to support the view that "of a New Covenant" (και νης διαθήκης) is a genitive of description.

3. What is the context of this statement?

There are two contextual issues that affect the interpretation of 2 Corinthians 3:6. The first addresses the literary style of the section in which the verse occurs. The second addresses the topic Paul is discussing.

a. Literary Style. A major theme of 2 Corinthians is Paul's defense of his ministry in the face of numerous criticisms.[27] These criticisms seem to have stemmed initially from Paul's failure to visit Corinth as he had planned (1:15–2:2). Interpreted as vacillation on Paul's part (1:17), this seems to have spawned numerous other criticisms about Paul's conduct as well. Beginning in 2:14 and extending at least through 5:5, Paul employs a series of 8 metaphors to explain why he conducted himself the way that he did. Most of the metaphors are based on OT imagery, including the New Covenant. They may, quite possibly, all have been drawn from chapters 30–31 of Jeremiah.

1. The Triumphal Procession, 2:14a
2. The Odor of Life and Death, 2:14b–16a
3. Letters Written on Stone vs. on the Heart, 3:2–3
4. New Covenant Ministers, 3:6
5. The Veil Removed, 3:14–18; 4:3–4

---

[27] In any exposition of the book of 2 Cor I think it is important to point out that in defending his ministry and conduct, Paul's ultimate motive is not to "get back" at those who were harming his reputation. Paul's main concern in defending himself is that the Corinthians were adopting a faulty standard of judgment – a fleshly standard, not a spiritual one. In the end, Paul defends himself, not so much out of a concern for his own reputation, but in order to get the Corinthians to examine themselves (12:19–21; 13:5–6) so that they might be approved at the judgment seat of Christ (5:10).

6. The Light of Creation, 4:6
7. Earthen Vessels, 4:7
8. Earthly House vs. Heavenly House, 5:1–4

Metaphors #3–8 appear to be drawn from Jeremiah 31–32.[28] The 3rd and 4th metaphors are clearly drawn from the Jeremiah 31 New Covenant passage (as well as Ezek 11:19; 36:26). The 5th and 6th metaphors are suggested by the same New Covenant language in that the New Covenant's replacing of the Mosaic law calls to mind the veil that blocked the light of God's glory reflected in Moses' face (Ex 34:29–35). The 7th metaphor may also have been suggested by the same general section of Jeremiah, since the "clay jar" symbolism may well have come from Jeremiah 32:10–14. The 8th metaphor, though more difficult to relate to specific language in Jeremiah, could conceivably be taken from the notion of houses destroyed by the Babylonians and later rebuilt under the New Covenant (32:29, 42–44).

Throughout this passage, the language is metaphorical. For example, when Paul writes, "You are our letter, written in our hearts" (3:2–3), he is formulating a classical metaphor. By using

---

[28] The problem of identifying the source of the first two metaphors has been discussed by various scholars. For example, Richard B. Hayes notes, "... 3:1 ... introduces a new cluster of metaphors .... The difficult metaphors of 2:14–16a belong to an entirely different circle of images" *Echoes of Scripture* 216 n. 5. It is possible that the images of life and death in those metaphors come from Jer 30–31 and their discussion of the Babylonians leading the Israelites away to captivity, some would go away to death while others would live through the captivity in life in hope of a future restoration of Israel. But it is impossible to tell for sure whether this is what Paul had in mind, since there is no overt connection between Paul's language and the language of Jer 30–31. Specifically, Jeremiah speaks neither of triumphal processions (θριαμβεύω) nor of odors (ο σμή, ευ ωδία). Quite possibly Paul is thinking of the Babylonian deportation but is speaking of it in terms of contemporary Roman victory processions (Hafemann, 106–108).

Jeremiah's New Covenant passage as a metaphor for his own ministry, Paul is not using the language of "fulfillment"; that is, he is not saying that his ministry is a realization of what was promised in Jeremiah, but rather that what Jeremiah was describing provides a suitable figure to describe his ministry. Consider how Paul uses the passages from Jeremiah: A letter written on the heart is reminiscent of the New Covenant's provision of God's law written on Israel/Judah's heart (Jer 31:33).

The Corinthian believers are likened to God's law written on Israel's heart, but this is not to say that the Corinthian believers are a fulfillment of this element of the New Covenant. In the fulfillment of the New Covenant, God's law is God's law, not God's people! Similarly, the inability of some to discern the glory of the gospel ministry is likened to the veil that covered Moses' face (3:14–18; 4:3–4; cf. Ex 34:29–35), but clearly this does not mean that the veil is somehow fulfilled by the unbelief of Paul's opponents.

The New Covenant ministry in 3:6 likewise needs to be understood as a metaphor and does not necessarily mean that there is some kind of fulfillment or realization of the New Covenant. Rather, the New Covenant provides a suitable Scriptural figure to describe Paul's ministry in such a way as to respond to the specific criticisms that had been raised against him. In order to understand the point Paul is trying to make with these metaphors, it is necessary to focus on the topic of the passage. This we do in the next section.

b. Topic. Who are Paul's opponents? What is the essence of his defense? Why does he argue the way that he does? The identity of Paul's opponents may affect the way we view the meaning of 3:6. Several writers have attempted to argue on the basis of the context surrounding 3:6 that Paul's point was to contrast the New Covenant with the old covenant, and that therefore he was arguing that the New Covenant was now in force.[29] However in considering the context, the discourse boundaries should not be limited to chapter 3. The passage really needs to be seen in light of the broader discourse boundaries of 2:14 – 5:5 and the series of 8 metaphors Paul employed in this section. This broader context shows that Paul's point had to do with the *character* of his ministry, rather than with the *content* of his ministry. Thorsell recognizes this when he notes about the first four metaphors, "In 2:14–17 the nature of his ministry (as a weak, on–the–way–to–death captive) is compared with a Roman triumphal procession.... Paul continued to develop the theme of adequacy in 3:1–6."[30] Some believe that Paul's opponents were "Judaizers."[31] This "opponents" = "Judaizers" formula makes it easy to say that in 3:6 Paul is answering critics who are seeking to enforce Mosaic legislation.[32] If this were the case, Paul's reply would be to say that we are now administering the New Covenant, as a replacement for the Mosaic covenant. Such a view would favor the

---

[29] Decker, "The Church's Relationship to the New Covenant, Part 2," 450; Penney, "The Relationship of the Church to the New Covenant," 467–468; Thorsell, "The Spirit in the Present Age," 401. Thorsell, however acknowledges that, "The subject under discussion is not primarily the New Covenant but the character of Paul's ministry of proclaiming the gospel," *ibid.*

[30] Thorsell, "The Spirit in the Present Age," 400.

[31] Robert Gromacki *Stand Firm in the Faith* (The Woodlands, TX: Kress Christian Publications, 2002), 162; Alfred Plummer *A Critical and Exegetical Commentary on the Second Epistle of St Paul to the Corinthians* (Edinburgh: T. & T. Clark, 1915), 320; Harris, 76; William MacDonald and Arthur Farstad, *Believer's Bible Commentary : Old and New Testaments* (Nashville: Thomas Nelson, 1995) on 2 Cor 3:6; *et al.*

[32] Rodney J. Decker, "New Covenant, Theology of the" in *Dictionary of Premillennial Theology* ed. Mal Couch (Grand Rapids: Kregel Publications, 1996), 280.

objective genitive. However, identifying Paul's opponents is not quite as simple as claiming that they are "Judaizers."[33] Harris has found at least 19 different identifications of Paul's opponents in the history of the interpretation of 2 Corinthians![34]

There are, in fact, two groups of critics whom Paul answered in this epistle. In chapters 1–9 Paul addressed criticisms that were being directed against him by the Corinthian congregation. In chapters 10–13, he addressed criticisms made by the false apostles/false brothers (ψευδαπόστολοι/ψευδα-δέλφοι).[35] While the false apostles may indeed have been "Judaizers" (though I have my doubts on this) the general makeup of the Corinthian congregation seems to have been of a more Greek or pagan worldview. If the opponents of chapter 3 were of a Greek philosophical worldview, the issue might more likely be one of the teacher's lifestyle and conduct[36] (which favors the genitive of description). This issue is complicated because of the two distinct sources for criticism of Paul. There may have been some intermingling of ideas between these two groups, but they also represent separate sets of criticisms. Chapter 3 falls within the section of the epistle that represents the criticisms of the Corinthian congregation. The outsiders' criticisms are not dealt with until chapters 11–13.

---

[33] An excellent summary of the various views can be found in Harris, 67–87.

[34] Murray J. Harris *The New International Greek Testament Commentary: The Second Epistle to the Corinthians* (W.B. Eerdmans Pub. Co., 2005), 79–80.

[35] Another issue in the interpretation of 2 Corinthians is whether the ὑπερλίαν α πόστολοι represent the same, or a different group than the ψευδαπόστολοι (Harris, 75–76). However that issue does not seem to be relevant to our discussion of 2 Cor 3:6.

[36] See e.g., D. E. Garland, *2 Corinthians,* New American Commentary, Vol 29 (Nashville: Broadman & Holman Publishers, 1999), 166.

Evidence suggesting a Judaizing background for the second group of critics would include 2 Corinthians 11:4 ("another gospel" ευ αγγέλιον ε 'τερον and the parallel in Galatians 1:6) as well as 11:22 ("Are they Hebrews? So am I. Are they Israelites? So am I." Ε βραι οί ει σιν; κα γώ. Ι σραηλι ταί ει σιν; κα γώ.). But these references only suggest a *Jewish* origin, not necessarily a *Judaizing* origin.[37] 2 Corinthians 10:2–3 is interesting in this respect. Paul's use of prepositions is precise here. In v. 2b he refers to some (*tinas* τινάς) who regard Paul as walking "according to the flesh" (κατὰ σάρκα), where "according to" (κατά) gives a standard of measurement. It is not so much that his critics accuse him of walking according to the flesh, but rather that they use the flesh as their own standard of measurement for Paul's walk. Using this standard of measurement, they judge Paul as coming up short (he is poor, he is sick, he is not eloquent, etc.). In verse 3, Paul admits that he walks "in the flesh" (ε ν σαρκί), where "in" (ε ν) indicates the sphere.

Though he does not conduct himself *according to* the flesh, he admits that he walks *in the sphere of* the flesh. Rather, the standard of his conduct (or "warfare") is according to (κατά) a different standard of measurement, i.e., the Spirit. Garland notes with regard to the first group of critics: "They understand him only in part (1:14) because they still evaluate things from the perspective of the flesh."[38] Apparently the same could be said of this second group of critics as well. So it is entirely possible that the second group of critics is not to be characterized as *Judaizers*, but could be of (diaspora?) Jewish origin and simply reflecting a more pagan philosophical perspective. Missing from 2 Corinthians are the specific references to Judaizing teaching found in other

---

[37] Garland, 464 n. 26.

[38] Garland, 32.

epistles of Paul's (e.g., references to circumcision, Jewish dietary restrictions, or observance of special Jewish days).[39]

Regardless of the identity of the second group of Paul's critics, chapter 3 represents Paul's response to the first group of critics. These appear to have very Greek notions of how a successful teacher should be characterized. They criticized Paul for the following reasons:

- He had failed to visit Corinth as he had planned (1:15–2:2).
- He was not a skilled orator (1:12; 10:10; 11:6).
- He was physically weak in presence (10:10).
- He had not been financially successful, and didn't charge an acceptable philosopher's fee (2:17; 6:10; 11:7; cf. 8:9; 12:13).
- He had been in numerous hardships and even jail (1:4–10; 6:4–5, 8–10).

These criticisms have to do with conduct of life, not content of message. As Garland observes:

Today, we may revere Paul for his determined hard work for the gospel that endured the suffering of imprisonments, beatings, shipwrecks, poverty, and fatigue to further its reach into the world. These things did not sap his love for God or his commitment to the cause of Christ. Rather, they only whetted his zeal to do more. Some Corinthians apparently did not share the same appreciation for this selfless suffering. To them Paul cut a shabby figure. Religion, in their mind, is supposed to lift people up, not weigh them down with suffering. They may well have asked how someone so frail, so afflicted, so stumbling in his speech and visibly afflicted with a thorn in the flesh could be a sufficient agent for the power

[39] See also Thorsell, 400 n. 8.

222 An Introduction to the New Covenant

of God's glorious gospel. Paul writes an impressive letter, but his physical presence is disappointingly unimpressive. He is too reticent to boast and to act forcefully. His refusal to accept their financial support and allowing himself to be demeaned as a poor laborer reflected badly on them as well. Such unconventional behavior betrays a lack of dignity appropriate for an apostle.[40]

The five criticisms above reflect a very Greek worldview of what should be expected of a successful philosopher (physical stature, good oratorical skills, evidence of a healthful, wholesome life free of trouble, teaching that is worth a good philosopher's fee). Harris notes on 10:10,

In the ancient rhetorical handbooks ὑπόκρισις denoted an orator's "delivery," which included not only his verbal and elocutionary skills but also his bodily "presence," the impression made by his physical appearance, his dress, and his general demeanor. The dual allegation of Paul's adversaries reflects these two aspects of ὑπόκρισις.[41]

This is basically a "fleshly" view, a focus on the outward man. Paul's reply to such criticisms is to describe the character of his ministry as spiritual not fleshly:

- 2 Corinthians 1:12 For our boast is this: the testimony of our conscience that we have conducted ourselves in the world, and especially toward you, with God-given sincerity and purity, not by fleshly wisdom but by God's grace.

---

[40] Garland, 31–32.

[41] Harris, 700. See also Garland, 446–449 on the physical and rhetorical expectations of a leader in Greek society.

- 2 Corinthians 1:17 So when I planned this, was I irresponsible? Or what I plan, do I plan according to the flesh so that I say "Yes, yes" and "No, no"?
- 2 Corinthians 1:21-22 Now the One who confirms us with you in Christ, and has anointed us, is God; 22 He has also sealed us and given us the Spirit as a down payment in our hearts.
- 2 Corinthians 3:3 since it is plain that you are Christ's letter, produced by us, not written with ink but with the Spirit of the living God; not on stone tablets but on tablets that are hearts of flesh.
- 2 Corinthians 3:6 He has made us competent to be ministers of a New Covenant, not of the letter, but of the Spirit; for the letter kills, but the Spirit produces life.
- 2 Corinthians 3:8 how will the ministry of the Spirit not be more glorious?
- 2 Corinthians 3:17 Now the Lord is the Spirit; and where the Spirit of the Lord is, there is freedom.
- 2 Corinthians 5:12 We are not commending ourselves to you again, but giving you an opportunity to be proud of us, so that you may have a reply for those who take pride in the outward appearance (τοὺς ἐν προσώπῳ) not in the heart.
- 2 Corinthians 5:16 From now on, then, we do not know anyone according to the flesh. Even if we have known Christ according to the flesh, yet now we no longer know Him like that.
- 2 Corinthians 6:6 by purity, by knowledge, by patience, by kindness, by the Holy Spirit, by sincere love,
- 2 Corinthians 10:2-6 I beg you that when I am present I will not need to be bold with the confidence by which I plan to challenge certain people who think we

are walking in a fleshly way. [3] For although we are walking in the flesh, we do not wage war in a fleshly way, [4] since the weapons of our warfare are not fleshly, but are powerful through God for the demolition of strongholds. We demolish arguments [5] and every high-minded thing that is raised up against the knowledge of God, taking every thought captive to the obedience of Christ. [6] And we are ready to punish any disobedience, once your obedience is complete.

- 2 Corinthians 11:18 Since many boast according to the flesh, I will also boast.

This "Greek" worldview of Paul's critics fits in well with what we know of Corinthian society[42] and would suggest that in 3:6 Paul was responding not to criticism about the content of his message, but to his conduct. This fits best with understanding our genitive as a genitive of description. Paul's point is not that he is administering the New Covenant, but rather that his conduct is determined by a Spirit-based standard, not a fleshly standard, or as Master put it, "In 2 Corinthians 3:6, the contrast between 'letter' and 'Spirit' is a contrast between a ministry based on works and self-effort and a ministry dependent upon the Spirit of God."[43] If Paul were to look in the Hebrew Scriptures for support of this idea, Jeremiah's New Covenant provides one of the few suitable metaphors to describe such a phenomenon.

---

[42] Though recently rebuilt and established as a Roman colony, Corinth continued to hold on to its Greek ethos, in contrast with Philippi, another Roman colony. See the review by J. Brian Tucker of *Urban Religion in Roman Corinth: Interdisciplinary Approaches* edd. Daniel Schowalter and Steven J. Friesen (Cambridge, MA: Harvard University Press, 2005) in *JBL* 6/1 (June 2006), 38–54, esp. pp. 41–42.

[43] Master, 101.

c. Putting it all together. When we look at this section (2:14 – 5:5) as: (1) a series of metaphors intended not as fulfillment of OT promises, but as descriptions based on Scriptural language, and (2) Paul's answer to his detractors' criticisms of his conduct based on a Greek worldview, we may understand the metaphors in something like the following way:

1. The Triumphal Procession, 2:14a

Weakness in physical appearance may not meet up with the fleshly standards of cultured Greek society, but it is precisely what characterized the children of Israel who were led in triumphal procession by the Babylonians into captivity. Both the godly and the ungodly alike were led away in weakness; thus weakness in physical appearance is no sign of ungodliness.

2. The Odor of Life and Death, 2:14b–16a

As the presentation of the captive Israelites was accompanied by the offering of incense sacrifices to the pagan gods of their captors, the smell signified death for some, but life for others. Likewise, though Paul appeared no better physically than those ancient captives, yet his message was a powerful one, bringing both life for those who believe, and death for those who rejected it.

3. Letters Written on Stone vs. on the Heart, 3:2–3

Paul's detractors put great confidence in outward fleshly commendation in the form of commendatory letters. But just as the New Covenant points to the superiority of the internal affairs of the heart over an outward written code, Paul's commendation comes from the very transformation that had taken place in the lives of the Corinthians. It was a spiritual commendation, not a fleshly one.

4. New Covenant Ministers, 3:6

The old covenant focused on fleshly matters of outward conformation to a legalistic standard, but Paul's conduct was more like the New Covenant, directed by the Spirit. Thus, his failure to keep his "written itinerary" (planned visit to Corinth, parallel to the written law) was due to the fact that he was sensitive to the Spirit's leading (cf. Ac 16:6–10) and God's sovereign, providential direction.

5.   The Veil Removed, 3:14–18; 4:3–4

After Moses spent time in God's presence, he reflected God's glory. The Israelites were unwilling to look at that glory; they would rather see Moses than God, so they requested that Moses put a veil over his face. Similarly, Paul's detractors were focused on man – what he looked like, how he sounded, how financially successful he was – but Paul desired to conduct himself as one with an unveiled face, so that those who saw him would not focus on his personal appearance, but would see the glory of God.

6.   The Light of Creation, 4:6

"Glory," "light," "appearance": these are the things that pertain to God, not to the creation. The creation exists to glorify God. Paul, as part of God's creation, exists not to be noticed for his physical appearance or oratorical skill, but "to give the light of the knowledge of God in the face of Jesus Christ."

7.   Earthen Vessels, 4:7

On the very eve of the Babylonian captivity Jeremiah purchased the field in Anathoth from his cousin Hanamel and placed the deed of purchase in a clay jar. The clay jar need not be ornamental nor costly; the treasure was what was inside. Paul's outward appearance was like that jar – unimpressive, and not very costly, but inside was a precious treasure – a message of hope.

8.   Earthly House vs. Heavenly House, 5:1–4

The coming of the Babylonians would be accompanied by the destruction of the cities and houses of Judah, but just as surely as God had promised the destruction of those cities, He had also promised the rebuilding of new cities and new houses when He would bring to fulfillment the New Covenant. Similarly, though Paul's body may be wasting away and an embarrassment to the cultured Corinthians, it was symbolic of a future glorified body in the resurrection.[44]

When viewed in this way, the context argues strongly for Paul's referring to the *conduct* of his ministry, not the *content* of his ministry. Thus, the context would suggest the genitive of description in 3:6, rather than the objective genitive.

4. Is there significance to the fact that "covenant" (διαθήκης) is anarthrous?

The anarthrous Greek text is represented in most English translations with the indefinite article ("a New Covenant");[45] although a few translations make it definite by adding the English definite article ("the New Covenant").[46] Master suggested that, "the anarthrous construction [was used] possibly stressing 'quality' more than 'identity.'"[47] If Master's suggestion is correct, then clearly the anarthrous construction is what we would expect to correspond with a genitive of description, as opposed to the objective genitive which might favor a more definite construction (e.g. "ministers of *the* New Covenant" διακόνους τη ς καινη ς διαθήκης *diakonous tēs kainēs diathēkēs*, or "ministers of *His* New Covenant" διακόνους καινη ς διαθήκης αυ του   *diakonous*

---

[44] Both the Stoic and the Epicurean (Acts 17:18–32) Greek philosophical schools had serious problems with the doctrine of the resurrection (see W. J. Conybeare and J. S. Howson *The Life and Epistles of St. Paul* [Grand Rapids: Eerdmans, 1964], 284–285), and this attitude appears to have bled off into the Corinthian congregation (1Cor 15:12–19).

[45] ASV, ESV, HCSB, NASB, NET, NCV, NIV, NRSV, RSV.

[46] TEV, KJV, NKJV, and, surprisingly, Darby.

[47] Master, 101, also Compton, 29.

kainēs diathēkēs autou[48]). Pettegrew, who sees some church participation in the New Covenant, counters this by claiming that the anarthrous construction is the most accurate way to represent Jeremiah's Hebrew original: "Interestingly, by leaving out the article, Paul follows Jeremiah's prophecy precisely: 'I will make a New Covenant with the house of Israel, and with the house of Judah' (Jer 31:31)."[49] Pettegrew may be pressing his point a bit further than is warranted. In fact, twice in the New Testament, Jeremiah's New Covenant *is* referred to using the articular construction (ἡ καινὴ διαθήκη *hē kainē diathēkē* in both Lk 22:20 and 1Cor 11:25). If Pettegrew is correct, and the anarthrous is more accurate, then one might reasonably ask why Paul used the articular construction in his first epistle to the Corinthians. And the logical question to follow is, why did he change to the anarthrous construction in his second epistle? However, we should not dismiss Pettegrew's point altogether, since the anarthrous construction is used in the other three NT references to Jeremiah's New Covenant (Heb 8:8;[50] 9:15; 12:24). More to the point is probably Decker's observation that, "This would seem to be placing too much weight on the lack of an article, particularly when the phrase in question could well be treated as a proper name and consequently definite whether articular or anarthrous."[51]

---

[48] Note the rendering "his New Covenant" in the New Living Translation, "his new agreement" in the Contemporary English Version, or "his new agreement to save them" in The Living Bible.

[49] Pettegrew, 216 n. 45. Also Decker *Premillennial Theology*, 280.

[50] Hebrews 8:13 should probably also be included here, but the noun διαθήκη does not occur here, only the adjective; nevertheless, the adjective is clearly referring back to the expression διαθήκην καινήν in verse 8.

[51] Decker, "The Church's Relationship to the New Covenant, Part 1," 301, n. 35.

It would appear that the most we can say about the anarthrous vs. articular construction is probably that, had the articular construction been used, Paul would *not* have been referring to the quality of the ministry. The anarthrous construction certainly allows for, but does not require our understanding Paul as referring to the quality of the ministry. So the anarthrous construction may be irrelevant to the issue under discussion.

5. What was the state of theological development when Paul wrote 2 Corinthians? How well developed was Paul's concept of the church as an entity separate and distinct from Israel?

Perhaps one of the most challenging hermeneutical tasks we face is that of stepping out of our world and into the world of the ancient writers we study. This requires not only diligent study of the history and sociology surrounding the first century Greco-Roman world, but also an attempt to adjust our own mindset as we read the words of Scripture. It requires not only the mind of the historian, but also the soul of the artist. When Paul wrote to the Corinthians there was a great deal of shared knowledge between author and recipients of which we may be ignorant.[52] For example, as with the discussion above, we may not know precisely who Paul's opponents were, but we can be pretty certain that both Paul and the Corinthian congregation knew exactly who they were.

Likewise, with regard to the subject of the New Covenant and its fulfillment, we may ask just how did a first century believer in Jesus think about it? Our tendency may be to look at this from our 20th/21st century perspective. We see the millennial fulfillment of the New Covenant with Israel as something that has now been postponed for nearly two millennia. As such, if the church is not participating in the covenant, it may seem a bit awkward, maybe even absurd, to use New Covenant language to

---

[52] Cotterell and Turner *Linguistics and Biblical Interpretation*, 90–97.

describe anything relevant to the church of today. The apostolic church, however, likely saw the preaching of the gospel to the Gentiles as a very brief interlude before the second coming, and thus the millennial fulfillment of the New Covenant was anticipated as something quite near. Clearly, the disciples in the upper room did not have anything like the church of our past 2,000 years in mind when Christ uttered His Eucharistic words, "This cup is the New Covenant in my blood" (Lk 22:20). They would have thought, instead, of the millennial fulfillment of the New Covenant and the restoration of the kingdom to Israel. Even for the later apostolic church, the fulfillment of the New Covenant was likely viewed as something to come about very shortly (cf. Acts 1:6; 15:14–17; Gal 6:16; 2 Thess 1:6–10).

So perhaps it should not be too surprising if Paul were to use the New Covenant metaphorically, as somehow loosely descriptive of his gospel ministry. The New Covenant, though not yet operative, would nevertheless have been something very much on the minds of those early believers. As time progressed, however, the metaphor might become less apropos – even, say, for the later epistles of Paul. And perhaps for us this is part of the difficulty we have in accepting "New Covenant language" as something merely metaphorical. We want to make it more highly realized.

If in my mind's eye I transport myself back in time to the upper room, without having any other New Testament revelation, I would find no reason to read into Christ's words at the Last Supper any idea of a realization of the New Covenant in the church. He is simply speaking of the New Covenant's fulfillment in terms of national Israel in the Messianic Kingdom. If I then move forward in time to Paul's use of those same words in 1 Corinthians 11, I only see him quoting the words from the upper room. I am not compelled to understand a church realization of the New Covenant itself. A church realization may be a *possibility* in 1 Corinthians 11, but not a *necessity*. I would need much more evidence to make it a necessity. If I then move on in my mind's journey to 2 Corinthians 3, I am still not convinced of any church realization of the New Covenant. Taken in its context as I have described above, I can easily see Paul's referring to the New Covenant as an apt description of the spiritual standard by which his conduct should be judged, but I am not compelled to come to the conclusion that the church is participating as a party to the New Covenant. It remains to be seen how the relevant Hebrews passages would influence this view of the progress of revelation.

Another issue concerning hermeneutical perspective: Have we been unwittingly influenced by the use of the expression "New Testament" to refer to the Christian Scriptures? For example, Walvoord argued,

> From the very fact that the Bible is divided into the Old Testament and the New Testament, or the Old covenant and the New Covenant, it is clear that Christianity fundamentally is based on a New Covenant brought in by Jesus Christ.[53]

The expression, "New Testament," as a title for the Christian canon, appears first to have been used either by Tertullian or Origen in the third century. Prior to this the Christian canon was not referred to as the "New Testament." By the third century already assumptions of a replacement theology were beginning to influence Gentile Christian thought significantly.[54] But such would not necessarily have been the case either for Paul or for the first century Corinthian congregation (or any other first century Christians, for that matter). Their view of the church was not preconditioned by the title *"Novum Testamentum"* or H KAINH ΔIAΘHKH (*Hē Kainē Diathēkē*) appearing at the beginning of their

---

[53] Walvoord, "Does the Church Fulfill Israel's Program," 218.

[54] Justin Martyr (100–165) in his *Dialogue With Trypho the Jew* represents one of the earliest examples of replacement theology.

Christian Scriptures! I don't know whether we have been unwittingly preconditioned by the use of this title or not, but I wonder about it. When we come to 2 Corinthians 3:6 and read the words "ministers of the New Covenant," do we have a psychological attachment to those words? Do we feel that the "New Covenant" and the "New Testament" are ours, while the "old covenant" and the "Old Testament" are the Jews'? I don't know, but I do wonder.

6. Why would Paul be referring to a passage from the Hebrew Scriptures when addressing a largely Gentile Christian church?
As has already been observed, other NT references to the New Covenant occur in Jewish (Jerusalem upper room) or Hebrew Christian contexts. 2 Corinthians, however, is addressed to a largely Gentile church. Does this observation have any influence on how we might view Paul's use of the Old Testament?

Though it is frequently stated that the church at Corinth was largely "Gentile," this may be overstating the case. According to Acts 18:1–8, the core of early believers in Corinth actually came out of the synagogue. These initial believers would have consisted of both Jews and God–fearing Gentiles, both of whom would have been well acquainted with the Hebrew Scriptures. Thus it is not surprising that Paul would use OT language when referring to church truth, even if doing so metaphorically.

Paul actually makes quite frequent use of the OT in both 1 Corinthians and 2 Corinthians. However, the way Paul used the OT in 1 Corinthians can be contrasted with the way he used it in 2 Corinthians. In 1 Corinthians he tends to cite the OT as authoritative Scripture to prove his point, using such introductory formulae 12 times,[55] as follows:

---

[55] The UBS *Greek New Testament* 4th edition Index of Quotations has 17 OT quotes in 1 Corinthians and 91 OT allusions.

- γέγραπται γὰρ *gegraptai gar* "for it is written" (1:18; 3:19)
- καθὼς γέγραπται *kathōs gegraptai* "just as it is written" (1:31; 2:9)
- γάρ *gar* "for" (2:16; 6:16; 14:27)
- ε ν γὰρ τῷ Μωϋσέως νόμῳ γέγραπται *en gar tō Mōuseōs nomō gegraptai* "for it is written in the law of Moses" (9:9)
- ὥσπερ γέγραπται *hōsper gegraptai* "as it is written" (10:7)
- ε ν τῷ νόμῳ γέγραπται ὅτι *en tō nomō gegraptai hoti* "in the law it is written that" (14:21)
- οὕτως καὶ γέγραπται *houtōs kai gegraptai* "thus also it is written" (15:45)
- τότε γενήσεται ο λόγος ο γεγραμμένος *tote genēsetai ho logos ho gegrammenos* "then the word which was written will come to pass" (15:54)

On the other hand, in 2 Corinthians, Paul tends to quote and allude to OT Scripture much less formally,[56] using introductory formulae only 5 times, as follows:

κατὰ τὸ γεγραμμένον *kata to gegrammenon* "according to what is written" (4:13)

λέγει γάρ *legei gar* "for it says" (6:2)

καθὼς εἶπεν ο θεὸς ὅτι *kathōs eipen ho Theos hoti* "just as God said that" (6:16)

---

[56] The UBS *Greek New Testament* 4th edition Index of Quotations has 11 OT quotes in 2 Corinthians and 44 OT allusions.

καθὼς γέγραπται *kathōs gegraptai* "just as it is written" (8:15; 9:19)
This less formal use of the OT corresponds with what we would expect for a metaphorical use of OT language that refers not to a fulfillment or realization of the OT promise, but rather to a broad, loose description.

CONCLUSION

With reference to the New Covenant, 2 Corinthians 3:6 may be viewed in two possible ways. The expression "New Covenant" expresses either the *content* of Paul's message, or it expresses the *manner in which* Paul conducted his ministry. Having examined various exegetical/hermeneutical issues, it is my studied opinion that Paul was not describing the content of his message, but rather the manner in which he conducted his ministry. Ultimately, the chief exegetical/hermeneutical issue questions whether the expression διακόνους καινη ς διαθήκης represents an objective genitive or a genitive of description.

A consideration of the referent of η μα ς, the context of the statement, the use/non-use of the article, the theological viewpoint of author and recipients and the way in which Paul refers to the OT lead, I believe, to the conclusion that Paul's point was that his ministry is a "new-covenant-like-ministry," not that he was administering the New Covenant. Reference was to the style of his ministry, rather than to the doctrinal content of the New Covenant. Thus, this verse does not support any kind of a realized eschatology, or church participation in the New Covenant. Of the New Testament references to the New Covenant, 2 Corinthians 3:6 is the only one that is set in neither an overtly eschatological nor Hebrew–Christian context. As such, it is something of a *crux interpretum* for those who wish to see some sort of a present realization of the New Covenant.

According to Jeremiah 31:31, the parties to the New Covenant are God and the houses of Israel and Judah. Though

Christ's blood has been shed for the ratification of the New Covenant, the realization of its blessings awaits that time when God brings Israel and Judah into the covenant. Until that time, others (viz. the Church) may be benefitting from the same blood that ratified the New Covenant, but there seems to be no exegetical necessity for seeing the Church as having been brought in as a new party to the covenant. At least, 2 Corinthians 3:6 does not require that we see the church as having been brought into the New Covenant.

8

THE NEW COVENANT IN HEBREWS

Christopher Cone

The New Covenant (hereafter, NC) enjoys more prominence in the book of Hebrews than anywhere else in the NT. Whereas there are six direct and indirect NT references to the NC outside of Hebrews,[1] Hebrews 7–13 contains at least 10 direct references,[2] including an extensive quote in 8:8–12 of Jeremiah 31:27–34.[3] The key question for this present discussion is how the church relates to the NC: as fulfillment, as participant, or as non–related but interested party.

Contextual Considerations

Whether or not Hebrews was written to Jewish believers (as I understand it) or to a mix of Jewish believers and unbelievers, the initial readership is not a dispositive factor in answering the specific question of the relationship of the church to the NC. Of far greater significance to the issue at hand is the writer's *purpose* in citing the NC. Throughout the letter, Hebrews focuses on the

---

[1] Mt 26:28; Mk 14:24; Lk 22:20; Rom 11:27; 1 Cor 11:25; and 2 Cor 3:6.

[2] Heb 7:22; 8:6–8, 10, 13; 9:15; 10:16, 29; and 12:24.

[3] The Hebrews quote is a close, but not exact, following of the LXX (Jer 38:31–34). LXX dependence, rather than Masoretic, is evidenced, for example, by the phrase κἀγὼ ἠμέλησα αὐτῶν, in Heb 8:9 which most closely (though not exactly) resembles the LXX reading of Jer 38:32 (καὶ ἐγὼ ἠμέλησα αὐτῶν).

superiority of Christ and the expected response of His people. The letter identifies Christ as God's final word (1:1-4), and expects readers to respond positively to Him. They are to pay attention (2:1-4), to consider Him (3:1), to beware (3:12), to fear (4:1), to be diligent to enter the rest (4:11), to hold fast their confession (4:14), to draw near with confidence (4:16), to be mature enough to be teachers rather than spiritual children (5:12-13), to mature past the basics and press on to maturity (6:1-2), to show diligence and not be sluggish in imitating the faithful (6:11-12), to draw near with a true heart in full assurance of faith (10:22), to hold fast the confession of our hope without wavering (10:23), to consider how to stimulate one another to good deeds (10:24), to not forsake the assembling but to encourage one another (10:25), to lay aside every encumbrance and the sin that so easily entangles (12:1), to fix our eyes on Him (12:2), to consider Him in order to not grow weary and lose heart (12:3), to strengthen and make straight (12:13), to pursue peace and sanctification (12:14), to avoid lacking in grace (12:15), to avoid bitterness and immorality (12:15-16), to not refuse Him (12:25), to love the brethren (13:1), to show hospitality (13:2), to remember prisoners (13:3), to hold marriage in honor (13:4), to be free from love of money and to be content (13:5), to remember and imitate those who had taught and led them (13:7), to not be carried away by strange teachings (13:9), to bear His reproach (13:13), to offer up continual sacrifice of praise and thanksgiving (13:15), to not neglect good and sharing (13:16), to obey and submit to leaders (13:17), to pray for fellow workers (13:18), to patiently accept the word of exhortation in the letter (13:22), to know that Timothy had been released (13:23) and to greet the leaders and saints (13:24).

In chapters 1-6 there are no less than eleven exhortations, and in chapters 10-13 there are no less than twenty-seven. However, in 7:1-10:18 (where the bulk of the NC discussion is found), there are *no exhortations* – this section being primarily didactic and illustrative. Further, the first application statement following the NC-intensive section is in 10:19-22: "Since therefore, brethren, we have confidence to enter the holy place by the blood of Jesus, by a new and living way which He inaugurated for us through the veil, that is His flesh, and since we have a great high priest over the house of God, let us draw near..." Among other questions, we must consider whether or not the *new and living way* is the NC itself. If it is, then it would seem the writer is indeed recognizing a relationship of church-age believers to the NC.

Does Hebrews Connect the Church and the NC?

Hebrews argues that Christ is superior to the angels (1:4-14; 2:5-9), to His brethren (2:9-18), to Moses, in that He provides a better rest (3:3-4:11), to the Levitical priesthood, being in the order of Melchizedek (4:14-5:10; 6:13-20) and in mediating a better covenant (new being better than old, 7:11-10:18). With His superiority argued in such superlative terms, a positive response to Him would seem common sense. While the desired outcome (positive response) seems obvious, questions persist regarding how Christ's superior NC ministry pertains to the church.

Reformed thinkers view the NC as an iteration of a covenant of grace, which Berkhof so calls because, "it is an unparalleled revelation of the grace of God, and because man receives all its blessings as gifts of divine grace."[4] O.T. Allis's lengthy comment is worthy of representation here, because it is definitive in its Covenant/Reformed explanation of the NC's fulfillment:

> For the gospel age in which we are living is that day foretold by the prophets when the law of God shall be written in the hearts of men (Jer. Xxxi. 33) and when the Spirit of God abiding in their hearts will enable them to keep it (Ezek. Xi. 19, xxxvi. 26f.). The gospel age is the age

---

[4] Louis Berkhof, *Systematic Theology* (Grand Rapids, MI: Eerdmans, 1974), 264.

of the New Covenant; and it is not marked by freedom from the law, by return to a dispensation of promise which knew nothing of obedience as a condition. Rather is it pre-eminently the age when the law of God, the revealed will of God is and will be kept as never before – not as the means of salvation, but as the fruit of a life that is hid with Christ in God![5]

While Allis appeals to OT prophecy, in this instance he does not cite Hebrews as offering any evidence for the NC fulfillment in the "gospel age." Rather he characteristically relies on a non-literal hermeneutic to derive the conclusion.

Gentry and Wellum, in attempting a mediatory position between dispensational and Covenant theology, cite Hebrews to say "it is clear that the New Covenant texts are applied to Christ and the church (Luke 22:20; 2 Corinthians 3; Hebrews 8, 10).[6] Kenneth Barker, in advocating a similar mediatory position (in this case, Progressive Dispensationalism), holds that there are only two eras – old covenant and New Covenant, and cites Hebrews 8–10 as supporting the idea that "the present and future forms of the messianic era (church and Millennium) both fit within the time when the New Covenant is in force."[7] Bock and Blaising add,

> Paul places the New Testament church under this very same New Covenant arrangement when he identifies the

---

[5] O.T. Allis, *Prophecy and the Church* (Phillipsburg, New Jersey: Presbyterian and Reformed, 1947), 42.

[6] Peter Gentry and Stephen Wellum, *Kingdom Through Covenant* (Wheaton, IL: Crossway, 2012), 645.

[7] Kenneth L. Barker, "The Scope and Center of Old and New Testament Theology and Hope" in *Dispensationalism, Israel and the Church* (Grand Rapids, MI: Zondervan, 1992), 295.

church's practice of the Lord's Supper as a sharing of the bread and of the cup which Jesus instituted that night before the crucifixion...The letter to the Hebrews culminates this testimony by quoting Jeremiah 31:31–34 in full (Heb. 8:6–13) and proclaiming Christ to be 'the mediator of a New Covenant'...It goes on to say that Christ's death is the atonement for all sins in accordance with the promise revealed in Jeremiah 31:33–34...It is indisputable that the New Testament views the New Covenant predicted by Jeremiah and Ezekiel as established in the death of Jesus Christ with some of its promised blessings now being granted to Jews and Gentiles who are believers in Jesus.[8]

Note that both Covenant theology and mediatory positions see a clear and indisputable relationship between the NC and the church, due in some part to their understandings of Hebrews. In Covenant theology, the church fulfills the NC. In the mediatory positions the church does not completely fulfill, but receives and participates in blessings of the NC.

Dispensationalists likewise have understood Hebrews as substantiating the idea that the church participates in NC blessings. Arnold Fruchtenbaum is representative of a majority of classical and revised dispensationalists in citing seven passages (7:22; 8:6–13; 9:15; 10:16, 29; 12:24; 13:20) in Hebrews that "connect the New Covenant with the Church."[9] Fruchtenbaum adds that the Mosaic Covenant "kept the Gentiles from enjoying the spiritual blessings of the four unconditional covenants,"[10] and

---

[8] Craig Blaising and Darrell Bock, *Progressive Dispensationalism* (Grand Rapids, MI: Baker Books, 1993), 200–202.

[9] Arnold Fruchtenbaum, *Israelology* (Tustin, CA: Ariel Ministries Press, 1989), 634.

[10] Ibid., 635.

that now "Gentiles can by faith enjoy the spiritual blessings of the four unconditional covenants. That is why Gentiles today are partakers of Jewish spiritual blessings..."[11] Fruchtenbaum does emphasize that "the provisions of the New Covenant cannot be fulfilled in, by, or through the church."[12]

While Elliott Johnson emphasizes, "The writer of Hebrews does not indicate in any way that the covenant is fulfilled with the church,"[13] he understands the NC to be "functioning as a last will and testament,"[14] based on Hebrews 9:15–17. The NC "will be inaugurated with the house of Israel and of Judah at some future day...In the meantime, the New Covenant has been ratified in Christ's death...the inauguration of the covenant was delayed... The covenant was ratified, however, and the benefits are now part of the blessings promised in the gospel."[15] Rodney Decker disagrees with Johnson on some details, but agrees that "The New Testament does not change or reinterpret any of the OT data, it only extends God's revelation to explain how this covenant relates to God's people after the cross."[16] Decker concludes that arguments in Hebrews make it "inescapable that the New

---

[11] Ibid.

[12] Ibid., 636.

[13] Elliott Johnson, "The Church Has an Indirect Relationship to the New Covenant" in *Dispensational Understanding of the New Covenant*, Mike Stallard, ed. (Schaumburg, IL: Regular Baptist Press, 2012), 171.

[14] Ibid., 172.

[15] Ibid., 174–175.

[16] Rodney Decker "Response to Roy E. Beacham" in *Dispensational Understanding of the New Covenant*, 163.

Covenant is related to the church and that believers do indeed...
benefit from it."[17]

Bruce Compton observes, "The fact that the readers are
participating in the forgiveness promised in the New Covenant is
made evident in 10:15–18."[18] He rejects the view that the NC is
exclusively for Israel, in part, based on two arguments he
perceives in Hebrews: first, on the basis of forgiveness of sins, and
second, because of Christ's priesthood. Compton supports his
reasoning as follows:

> Hebrews makes the connection between the new
> covenant and the forgiveness which those in the church
> enjoy even clearer. He establishes in 9:15–18
> (cf. 7:11; 8:6) that the new covenant promised in Jeremiah
> was ratified by the death of Christ. He confirms in 10:14–
> 18 that Christ's death secured the full and final
> forgiveness promised in Jeremiah's new covenant. And, he
> specifically identifies in 10:29 the "blood of the covenant"
> as the basis for his readers' forgiveness (cf. 10:10, 22).[19]

And,

> [Hebrews] inseparably links Christ's role as a priest with
> the new covenant. In other words, just as the Levitical
> priests performed their duties on the basis of the Mosaic
> covenant (7:11), so also Christ functions as a high priest
> on the basis of the new covenant (7:11–12, 20–22; 8:6). At
> the same time, according to the [author of Hebrews],

---

[17] Rodney Decker "Response to Elliott E. Johnson" in *Dispensational
Understanding of the New Covenant*, 163.

[18] R. Bruce Compton, "Dispensationalism, The Church, and the New
Covenant" in *Detroit Baptist Seminary Journal*, 08:1 (Fall 2003): 33.

[19] Ibid., 39.

Christ exercises his role as a high priest on behalf of his readers (4:14–15; 7:26; 8:1).[20]

Each of these thinkers illustrate by their commentary that while there is discord regarding fulfillment and application of the NC, most have no difficulty seeing some type of *already not yet* aspect to the NC in Hebrews. To address the issue of disharmony especially among dispensational thinkers on the NC, John Walvoord identifies three helpful questions pertaining to the NC in the NT:

> The solution of the problem involved in the   new covenant with Israel hinges on several determinative issues: (1) Are all the promises given to Israel under the New Covenant being fulfilled in the present age? If they are, then the postmillennial and amillennial interpretations may be correct. If the promises are not being fulfilled now and cannot be fulfilled under conditions in the present age, then a future fulfillment is called for, and the premillennial interpretation is justified. (2) How does the New Testament use the term new covenant? This approach should confirm findings under the first question and give a ground for certain conclusions. (3) What is the explicit teaching of the New Testament about the new covenant?
>
> The new covenant with Israel is specifically quoted in the New Testament and conclusions drawn from it. How do these passages fit into the doctrine as a whole? The answer to these questions should in a large measure determine the answer to the problem.[21]

---

[20] Ibid., 40.

[21] John Walvoord, "Eschatological Problems X: The New Covenant" in *Bibliotheca Sacra,* 103:409 (Jan 46), 19–20.

To address the question of the relationship of the NC to the church, after exegetically considering each passage, we will apply Walvoord's questions to Hebrews, with slight adjustment: (1) Are any promises given to Israel under the NC operative today in any form? (2) How does Hebrews use the term NC, either directly or indirectly? And (3) what is the explicit teaching of Hebrews about the NC?

Observations From Hebrews 7:11–28
Building on the point established in 6:5–10 and 7:1–10, that Christ is a priest in the superior order of Melchizedek, 7:12 asserts the necessity of a change in law (ἐξ ἀνάγκης καὶ νόμου μετάθεσις γίνεται) to accompany a change in priesthood. Importantly, the writer does not describe a shift from one law to another, but only the departure (μετάθεσις) from an old law. Christ became a priest like Melchizedek, not according to fleshly law (ὃς οὐ κατὰ νόμον ἐντολῆς σαρκίνης), but according to the ability of life that cannot end (ἀλλὰ κατὰ δύναμιν ζωῆς ἀκαταλύτου).

The perfect active indicative γέγονεν, with the conditional εἰ in 7:15 does not reflect merely a hypothetical scenario, as 7:17 shows. It is witnessed (μαρτυρεῖται) that He *is* indeed that very kind of priest. In the 7:17 quotation and in the MT of Psalm 110:4, the phrase, *you are a priest* (σὺ ἱερεὺς and וֹהֵ) זוהי) contains no verb, while the LXX includes the present active indicative *to be* verb in the phrase Σὺ εἶ ἱερεὺς. While they are having become priests (7:20–21, εἰσὶν ἱερεῖς γεγονότες) without an oath, He is having become (γενόμενος, 6:20) with an oath.

A setting aside (ἀθέτησις) of the former commandment (προαγούσης ἐντολῆς) is (γίνεται), because of its inherent limitations (in that the Law made nothing perfect), but on the other hand, there is an introduction of a better hope (ἐπεισαγωγὴ δὲ κρείττονος ἐλπίδος). To this point in 7:19, the better hope has not been identified. Whereas some conclude as Decker does, that "The 'better hope' of verse 19 is surely to be understood in this context as the better covenant (κρείττονος διαθήκης) upon which Jesus' high priesthood is based."[22] There are two assumptions in the statement that need further exegetical examination: (1) the better hope is the better covenant, and (2) Jesus's high priesthood is based upon the covenant.

First, Hebrews references twelve things[23] as *better* using forms of κρείττων: Jesus (1:4), things (6:9), hope (7:19), covenant (7:22; 8:6), promises (8:6), sacrifices (9:23), possession (10:34), country (c.f., 11:14 and 11:16), resurrection (11:35), something provided (11:40), and the sprinkled blood (12:24). While *covenant* in 7:22 and 8:6 is the nearest occurrence to *better hope*, there is some speculation required to equate the two ideas. The association makes an important assumption regarding how believers draw near to God. Decker explains, "It is not our relationship to the High Priest that gains us this access, but it is the covenant itself by which we draw near to God. To conclude otherwise, if I may say so, is to intrude a predetermined system into the text before we allow the text to speak for itself – before we have completed a careful exegesis of the text."[24] He is referencing the last phrase of 7:19: *through which we draw near to God.*

We do, indeed, draw near (ἐγγίζομεν, present active indicative) to God through this better hope. *If the better hope is the*

---

[22] Rodney Decker, *Why Do Dispensationalists Have Such a Hard Time Agreeing on the New Covenant* (Schaumburg, IL: Regular Baptist Press, 2009), 8.

[23] Thirteen total references, with *covenant* cited twice.

[24] Ibid., 9.

New Covenant, then the matter is settled: the recipients of Hebrews (and presumably we too) were benefitting directly from the NC. Of course, this is not an implausible syntactical understanding as Kostenberger illustrates – he views κρείττονος ἐλπίδος and κρείττονος διαθήκης as parallel expressions.[25] However, Kosten-berger also illustrates the deficiency of that conclusion as he later observes that, "The key word   κρείττων and other comparatives are employed to point to the better quality of every constituent element of the new system over the old."[26] Only a few sentences following that summary point Kostenberger concedes, "because Christ is superior to the old system in every way, nothing less will do than complete obedience and faithful allegiance in both belief and practice to *the One who is 'the new and better way'* and who has instituted the New Covenant with His people" [emphasis mine].[27] Kostenberger recognizes that the Hebrews thesis is not the simply the superiority of the new system, but the superiority of Jesus Christ.

Understanding a closer semantic connection between the *drawing near* phrases than between the *better hope* and *better covenant* phrases would allow Kostenberger to maintain both syntactical integrity and the integrity of the thesis. Let's consider that alternative. Decker rightly observes,

> In contrast to the inferiority of the law, the newly introduced "better hope" is the means by which we draw near to God...The languages of perfection (vv. 11,18)

---

[25] For a more detailed exegesis partially agreeing with Decker's equating of better hope and better covenant, see Andreas J. Kostenberger, "Jesus, the Mediator of a 'Better Covenant': Comparatives in the Book of Hebrews" in *Faith and Mission*, 21:2 (Spring 2004): 34–35

[26] Ibid.: 40.

[27] Ibid.

appears to be semantically parallel to drawing near to God
(v. 19): both describe the function of the respective
referents, the law on one hand, the better hope on the
other.[28]

Whereas Decker (like Kostenberger) sees a probable semantic
parallel between the languages of perfection and the drawing
near to God, there is a semantic parallel between the means of our
drawing near to God in 7:19 and in 7:25. While 7:19 utilizes the
verb ἐγγίζομεν (present active indicative) to connote a present
drawing near, 7:25 employs προσερχομένους (present participle) to
indicate the present moving toward God. In this latter context we
discover the exact means of moving toward God – δι' αὐτοῦ. Not
through a covenant, but *through Him*. If we are to understand the
drawing near in 7:19 as the same as the moving toward in 7:25,
then the better hope of 7:19 is *Him* – Jesus Christ Himself is that
better hope.[29]

David MacLeod observes an important aspect of formal
contrast in the employment of adversative particles in Hebrews.[30]
A more exhaustive look at the adversative particles of Hebrews
shows a syllogistic structure in 7:18–24, and considered with
earlier contrasts in the book, evidence a culminating conclusion in
7:25 that supports the idea that Christ is the better hope. If so, the
higher order thesis is sustained: the contrast is not between

[28] Rodney Decker, "The Church Has a Direct Relationship to the New
Covenant" in *Dispensational Understanding of the New Covenant*, 201.

[29] As a lesser point, but still worth noting, in 7:19 the feminine pronoun
ἧς refers to the antecedent, ἐλπίδος, also feminine. Of course, this does
not preclude a reference to Christ, for example. Paul, in 1 Timothy 1:1
refers to Jesus as *our hope* using the identical noun (Χριστοῦ Ἰησοῦ τῆς
ἐλπίδος ἡμῶν).

[30] David J. MacLeod, "The Literary Structure of the Book of Hebrews" in
Bibliotheca Sacra, 146:582 (April 1989): 194.

inferior and superior systems, but between inferior means and the superior Christ:

1:7: μὲν = angels are ministers
1:8: δὲ = Jesus is to rule

3:5: μὲν = Moses a faithful servant
3:6: δὲ = Jesus a son

7:2: μὲν and δὲ (also in 7:3) = both refer to Melchizedek

7:5: μὲν = sons of Levi
7:6: δὲ = Melchizedek
7:7:δὲ = lesser (Abraham) blessed by greater (Melchizedek)

7:8: μὲν = mortal men receive tithes
7:8: δὲ = Melchizedek received a tithe

7:18: μὲν = setting aside of weak commandment
7:19: δὲ = better hope (through which we draw near to God
7:20: μὲν = without oath taking they became priests
7:21: δὲ = Jesus with an oath
7:23: μὲν = priests died
7:24: δὲ = Jesus continues forever
7:25: ὅθεν = Therefore, Jesus is able to save completely those drawing near through Him.

It is notable that in every instance leading up to 7:25, the δὲ clause either refers to Jesus Christ or to Melchizedek – each refers to the superior *person*. Of course it is possible that the δὲ of 7:19 could point to something other than a person, since the μὲν of

7:18 does not appear to reference a person but rather an event. Still, there is no exegetical reason to prefer the δὲ κρείττονος ἐλπίδος δι' ἧς ἐγγίζομεν τῷ θεῷ clause in 7:19 as referring to the NC rather than to Christ – whom Kostenberger calls *the new and better way* (and who is, incidentally, described in a distant context [1 Tim 1:1] using the identical noun [Χριστοῦ Ἰησοῦ τῆς ἐλπίδος ἡμῶν]). The writer of Hebrews to this point has gone a long way in evidencing the supremacy of Christ, and it seems no coincidence that 7:25 culminates the contrastive parallel, and that there Jesus is Himself identified as the means whereby one draws near to God.

One further observation deserving mention in this context is illustrated by Decker's assertion that,

> Just as the Aaronic priesthood is totally replaced by the Melchizedekian priesthood, so that law that authorized the Aaronic priesthood is totally replaced by a new (as of yet unspecified) law. This is a logical and necessary change...Because the previous priesthood is such an intimate part of the law (v. 11b), the priesthood cannot be replaced without replacing the law itself.[31]

Whereas the old, inferior way – the former commandment (προαγούσης ἐντολῆς) is annulled or done away (ἀθέτησις), there is no textual indication *here* (8:6 is significant in this discussion) that it has been *replaced*. While a better hope was introduced, that better hope was not a *replacement* for the former commandment. The Law had one purpose (to serve as a shadow of good things, 10:1), and the better hope has an entirely different one (to bring near to God, 7:19 and 25). If we would argue that there is a new "law" in force under the NC in a present sense, we

---

[31] Rodney Decker, "The Church Has a Direct Relationship to the New Covenant" in *Dispensational Understanding of the New Covenant*, 198.

must also acknowledge that the only NC law described in the original language of the NC would be written on the hearts of all Israel (Jer 31:33). If there is presently a NC law in force, then we have to go much farther than simply saying the church is benefitting from NC blessings. The church would be fulfilling (even if perhaps only alongside Israel) Jeremiah 31:33. The implications of such a maneuver are significant. Jeremiah 31:34 speaks of universal (within Israel and Judah) knowledge of Him and forgiveness of their sin committed under the Mosaic Law (Old Covenant). This hermeneutic drift is one of the inherent dangers of associating *too closely* the Melchizedekian priesthood of Christ with the NC.

Walvoord's questions: (1) Are any promises given to Israel under the NC operative today in any form? No, though the Mediator is identified as the means whereby we draw near to God. (2) How does Hebrews use the term NC, either directly or indirectly? Jesus is the guarantor of a better covenant (7:22). This is a clear reference to the NC, but turns our attention to Jesus rather than the covenant itself. (3) What is the explicit teaching of Hebrews about the NC? Because of the contrastive culmination in 7:25, we can understand the NC as *an evidence* of Jesus's superiority and that He is able to save those who draw near to God through Him.

Observations From Hebrews 8:1–13
Hebrews 8:1–10:18 forms a literary unit as exempla (of how Jesus is a superior high priest), along with the conclusion in 10:19–21 (He is worthy of our confidence), and the exhortation in 10:22–25 (we are to draw near to God with sincerity). The goal of what has been said previously is explicitly identified in 8:1–2. The main point (Κεφάλαιον) of the argument to that point: Jesus is presently a qualified, superior (in every way) high priest. He is a minister of the holy (genitive, τῶν ἁγίων λειτουργὸς) and of the true tabernacle (τῆς σκηνῆς τῆς ἀληθινῆς), which the Lord, not

man, set up (ἣν ἔπηξεν ὁ κύριος, οὐκ ἄνθρωπος). The rest of the section (8:1– 10:18) illustrates the point.

In 8:3 the contrastive structure returns with the summary statement that because (ὅθεν) of the appointment (καθίσταται) of every high priest, it is necessary for them to have something to offer. In 8:4 there is a μὲν clause introducing a contrast between earthly priests who serve a copy and shadow of the heavenly things, according to law (κατὰ νόμον), and Christ (introduced by the δὲ clause). Verse 6 contains three comparative adjectives reiterating reasons Christ is superior. He has obtained a more excellent ministry (νυν[ὶ] διαφορωτέρας τέτυχεν λειτουργίας), insofar as He is a better–covenant mediator (ὅσῳ καὶ κρείττονός ἐστιν διαθήκης μεσίτης). That covenant has been established upon better promises (ἥτις ἐπὶ κρείττοσιν ἐπαγγελίαις νενομοθέτηται). In the second comparative phrase, the genitive adjective κρείττονός modifies διαθήκης, and thus it is the covenant that is better. He is the mediator, so His ministry (λειτουργίας) is more excellent (than that of the high priests (as the summary statement of 8:1 asserts).

It is worth noting, in light of the third comparative adjective in 8:6 that, as is common in other NT epistles, there is a distinction between *promises* and the *promise*. In Hebrews, ἐπαγγελία is used fourteen times, eight in the singular, six in the plural:

Singular
4:1 ἐπαγγελίας a promise of entering rest
6:15 τῆς ἐπαγγελίας Abraham obtained the promise
6:17 τῆς ἐπαγγελίας the heirs of the promise
9:15 τὴν ἐπαγγελίαν the promise of the eternal inheritance
10:36 τὴν ἐπαγγελίαν what was promised
11:9 τῆς ἐπαγγελίας the land of promise

11:9 τῆς ἐπαγγελίας heirs of the same promise
11:39 τὴν ἐπαγγελίαν did not receive what was promised

Plural
6:12 τὰς ἐπαγγελίας imitate those who are inheriting the promises
7:6 τὰς ἐπαγγελίας Abraham had the promises
8:6 ἐπαγγελίαις NC enacted on better promises
11:13 τὰς ἐπαγγελίας without receiving the promises
11:17 τὰς ἐπαγγελίας he who had received the promises
11:33 ἐπαγγελιῶν obtained promises

Of these fourteen references, only 8:6 is explicitly connected to the NC, and no other reference identifies the antecedent of the 8:6 promises. It seems likely that the *better promises* of 8:6 may be simply referring to the promises quoted (in 8:8–12) from Jeremiah's rendering of the NC.

This better covenant has been *established* (νενομο-θέτηται). The use of the perfect passive in this case underscores the importance of how νενομοθέτηται should be translated. The only other NT occurrence of the same form of this verb (perfect passive indicative third person singular) is employed in 7:11 to describe how the people *received law* based upon the Levitical priesthood (ὁ λαὸς γὰρ ἐπ᾽ αὐτῆς νενομοθέτηται).

Roy Beacham understands this to mean the covenant has been "'given' or 'framed'" but not in force.[32] Elliott Johnson

[32] Roy Beacham, "The Church Has No Legal Relationship to or Participation in the New Covenant" in *Dispensational Understanding of the New Covenant*, 134.

distinguishes between "ratified" and "inaugurated,"[33]   and between "existence...functioning...and fulfillment,"[34]   asserting that the NC is in existence and has some present function, but is not being fulfilled. Rodney Decker prefers "enacted...placed in force...ratified."[35]   These diverse understandings highlight the significance of νενομοθέτηται as a pivot point. Whereas I agree with all three that the term does not imply present or past fulfillment, I also would add that the fulfillment of the covenant is imminent in the sense that all that is necessary for the fulfillment (e.g., the establishment of a high priest, the blood to pay for the forgiveness of sins committed under the old covenant, etc.) has already been accomplished (of course there are other prophetic things that will take place first, but not related directly to the covenant itself). In that sense, the covenant has been ratified, established, paid for, or validated.

It would not be improper to say that the covenant has been validated, as long as there is no *already not yet* element read into the covenant. In other words, νενομοθέτηται does connote a past accomplishment in establishing the covenant, but it does not give any indication of blessings being either enjoyed or fulfilled in the present – whether physical or spiritual. It is certainly possible for a covenant to be validated without being fulfilled, though it is difficult to justify that aspects of a covenant can be enjoyed without being fulfilled (unless there is direct exegetical proof to that end– which there is not in this case). Consequently, regardless of the specific translation of νενομοθέτηται, if the term

---

[33] Elliott Johnson, "Response to Roy E. Beacham" in *Dispensational Understanding of the New Covenant*, 148–149.

[34] Elliott Johnson, "The Church Has an Indirect Relationship to the New Covenant" in *Dispensational Understanding of the New Covenant*, 171–172.

[35] Rodney Decker, "The Church Has a Direct Relationship to the New Covenant" in *Dispensational Understanding of the New Covenant*, 204.

is leveraged to argue for present blessing enjoyment or fulfillment then the argument has extended beyond exegetical borders and advanced into theological territory, for better or for worse.

Following the superlative statement regarding Christ in 8:6 is an explanation beginning in 8:7 of how the covenant Christ mediates is better than the first covenant. That first covenant was not faultless (ἄμεμπτος), in that it couldn't make perfect (e.g., 7:19), and consequently it foreshadowed a second. Importantly, there is a difference between a second (δευτέρας) and a replacement – which the second is not. The section following (8:8-12) reproduces closely (though not exactly) the LXX translation (Jer 38:31–34) of Jeremiah 31:33–34. Importantly, the immediate context in Hebrews neither expands the recipients nor distinguishes between physical and spiritual blessings. Rather, it maintains all the original specific recipient language, and gives no alteration to the covenant whatsoever. This fact increases the exegetical burden on those who would argue that the covenant has in some way been expanded – either by present blessings for those not identified as recipients, or by present fulfillment to those who are identified as recipients. That burden is not met in this context. Further, the 8:13 description of the first covenant as obsolete (πεπαλαίωκεν), growing old (γηράσκον), and near disappearing (ἐγγὺς ἀφανισμοῦ), does not constitute a present *replacement* by the NC.

Walvoord's questions: (1) Are any promises given to Israel under the NC operative today in any form? No. In fact, all the original recipient and timing language is intact. (2) How does Hebrews use the term NC, either directly or indirectly? In this section, the term is used both directly and indirectly. In each case the antecedent is obvious. The new is contrasted with the old, the second with the first. (3) What is the explicit teaching of Hebrews about the NC? Here there is no new teaching about the NC; it is cited as a contrast to the old, in order to reinforce earlier assertions that Jesus Christ is superior in every way (in this case, as a mediator of a better covenant). While the covenant has been set in motion, paid for, inaugurated, or enacted (8:6), there is nothing to this point that expands, adds to, or shows present blessings or fulfillment of the NC.

Observations From Hebrews 9:1–28
Beginning with a phrase that includes a hook word repeated from 8:13 (τὴν πρώτην in 8:13, ἡ πρώτη in 9:1), 9:1–10:18 provides more support for Jesus's superiority in that He is the mediator of a better covenant. In 9:1–28 the limitations of the old are emphasized. While 9:1–5 describes the interworking of the tabernacle system, 9:6–7 returns to the adversative particle contrastive structure (μὲν/δὲ) that was prominent earlier in the epistle.

The priests continually enter (εἰσίασιν, present active indicative) on the one hand, into the first tabernacle (εἰς μὲν τὴν πρώτην σκηνὴν). But into the second (εἰς δὲ τὴν δευτέραν), only the high priest enters once a year (ἅπαξ τοῦ ἐνιαυτοῦ μόνος ὁ ἀρχιερεύς), offering sins for himself and the people of ignorant sin (ὑπὲρ ἑαυτοῦ καὶ τῶν τοῦ λαοῦ ἀγνοημάτων). Further, the Holy Spirit is making clear (δηλοῦντος) that the holy way (τὴν τῶν ἁγίων ὁδὸν) has not been revealed (μήπω πεφανερῶσθαι) while the first tabernacle maintains existence (τῆς πρώτης σκηνῆς ἐχούσης στάσιν). The first tabernacle is described as a parable (παραβολὴ) for the present time. This tabernacle and its rituals are related to temporal things but prefigure a time of new order (διορθώσεως). The Levitical priestly ministry was important because it anticipated and illustrated Jesus's future ministry, but the Levitical ministry was inferior, being temporal and unable (by design) to eternally resolve the sin problem for Israel under the covenant.

But Christ appeared (Χριστὸς δὲ παραγενόμενος), a high priest of the good things to come (ἀρχιερεὺς τῶν γενομένων ἀγαθῶν). The phrase τῶν γενομένων ἀγαθῶν is similar to the phrase in 10:1 (τῶν μελλόντων ἀγαθῶν). In 9:11 the good things come into being at some point (γενομένων, aorist middle participle), while in 10:1 the good things are, *at present*, still going to come about (μελλόντων, present active participle, note parallel usage in 11:20). The antecedent of *good things* is not made explicit, but especially by the usage of μελλόντων in 10:1, it would seem that the writer of Hebrews perceived *when he wrote* that those good things had not yet arrived. Still, 9:11 does not focus on the good things, but rather on Christ as the high priest of those good things, and the mechanism whereby He functioned as that high priest. He entered through the greater and complete tabernacle (διὰ τῆς μείζονος καὶ τελειοτέρας σκηνῆς), not made by hands, not of this creation (οὐ χειροποιήτου, τοῦτ᾽ ἔστιν οὐ ταύτης τῆς κτίσεως). This is the true tabernacle of 8:2, the heavenly original (8:5).

Christ entered through His own efficacious blood (9:12), having been found an eternal redemption (λύτρωσιν εὑράμενος). This is reminiscent of Zacharias's prophecy (Lk 1:67–69) that the Lord God of Israel "has visited us and accomplished redemption for His people, and has raised up a horn of salvation for us in the house of David His servant..." Zacharias had in view the promised redemption of Israel, and understood his son to be the forerunner. If David Allen is correct about the linguistic connections between Luke and Hebrews (and I believe he is),[36] then the Hebrews usage of the term redemption (λύτρωσιν) exposes an even more direct

---

[36] David Allen, "The Authorship of Hebrews: The Lukan Proposal" in *Faith and Mission*, FM 18:2 (Spring 2001): 28–37.

connection to NC promises as a national expectation.[37] Verses 13–
14 underscore the contrast between the blood of the old covenant
(cleansing flesh temporarily) and the blood of the NC – Christ's
blood (cleansing the conscience from dead works to serve the
living God). His blood is eternally and comprehensively
efficacious. His blood is, thus, far better. The point here is that *He
is better* because His blood is better.

And because of this He is a New Covenant mediator (Καὶ
διὰ τοῦτο διαθήκης καινῆς μεσίτης ἐστίν). Because of what? The
adverbial purpose conjunction ὅπως introduces a purpose clause:
a death has happened (θανάτου γενομένου) for a redemption
(ἀπολύτρωσιν) of the transgression (τῶν παραβάσεων). Note
that the article τῶν qualifies παραβάσεων (transgression), as
both are genitives. The redemption is of a particular kind of
transgression, and not transgression in general. The redemption
is of the *under the first covenant* (ἐπὶ τῇ πρώτῃ διαθήκῃ)
transgression. In identifying Christ's present role as mediator, the
writer still maintains the original recipient language – the
redemption is for sin committed under the first covenant (just as
is stated in Jer 31:34). This is *not* speaking of redemption for all
sin in every age. The stated consequence (9:15) of this death is
that those having been called (κεκλημένοι) may receive (λάβωσιν,
aorist subjunctive) the promise (τὴν ἐπαγγελίαν, accusative) of
the eternal inheritance (τῆς αἰωνίου κληρονομίας, genitives).

The called are not specifically identified here, though
Hebrews utilizes in six instances forms of the word καλέω. In 2:11
the infinitive is used of Christ calling them (those who are
sanctified) brethren. In 3:13 today is still called today. In 5:4 the
calling is to priesthood. In 9:15 the ones having been called

---

[37] Luke (Lk 21:28), Paul (Rom 3:24; 8:23; 1 Cor 1:30; Eph 1:7, 14; 4:30;
Col 1:14), and the writer of Hebrews all use a derivative of the term
(ἀπολύτρωσις) with broad implications – including personal
redemption. However in each instance of λύτρωσις (Lk 1:68; 2:38; and
Heb 9:12), the reference is to the national expectation.

(κεκλημένοι, perfect passive participle) are those who may receive the promise. In 11:8, by faith when Abraham was being called (καλούμενος, present passive participle) he obeyed. And in 11:18, it is in Isaac that Abraham's descendants would be called (κληθήσεταί, future passive indicative). The connection between the calling and inheritance of the promise reminds us of 6:12–17, which exhorted the readers to be imitators of those who...inherit the promise, and in which readers are reminded of God's faithfulness to the heirs of the promise.

Later, in 11:39 we read, "all these, having gained approval through their faith, did not receive the promise (τὴν ἐπαγγελίαν)." Abraham was given a promise of inheritance regarding the land (11:8). Isaac and Jacob were heirs of that same promise (11:9). But they did not receive what was promised (11:13). Abraham was given promises (11:17), but ultimately has not yet seen their fulfillments (11:39). The reason given for this delayed fulfillment is because something better for us (περὶ ἡμῶν κρεῖττόν τι) was provided of God (τοῦ θεοῦ...προβλεψαμένου). In order that (ἵνα, conjunction in adverbial purpose) apart from us they may not be completed (μὴ χωρὶς ἡμῶν τελειωθῶσιν). The writer distinguishes between us (including himself) and them (those who were approved but did not receive the promise, including those listed in Heb 11).

Despite that distinction, there is no indicator – exegetical or theological – that the NC (or any other covenant) has been adjusted, altered, expanded, or parsed to include the "us." It is at this point – when the distinction between the groups is most explicit – that we might expect the most explicit relating of the NC to the present day believers, but we find no such thing in this context. *Rather, the distinction is maintained.* This is similar to what Paul does in Romans 11:11–12, and 25, indicating that salvation has come to the nations, but that there is a still yet coming fulfillment (πλήρωμα) for Israel, and that fulfillment will not take place until the fulfillment (πλήρωμα) of the nations comes in. God works with both groups – Israel by direct covenant, and the nations by Abraham's covenant. The "us" of Hebrews is church-age believers who are Jewish,[38] and the NC is not theirs in any present sense. However, the Mediator's NC ministry is evidence of His superiority, which is a profound truth with tangible implications for the walk of the readers.

The straightforward statements of 9:1–15 are followed by a puzzling series of statements beginning in 9:16: For where a covenant (Ὅπου γὰρ διαθήκη), a death is necessary (θάνατον ἀνάγκη) to be established (φέρεσθαι) of the one making a covenant (τοῦ διαθεμένου). The question here is whether or not the covenant-maker Himself must die. The next phrase is helpful, but does not resolve the issue: For a covenant upon dead ones is in force or valid (διαθήκη γὰρ ἐπὶ νεκροῖς βεβαία). So far the text has not been definitive about who has to die – somebody or something has to die, but the first two phrases of this pericope give no indication of who, other than to state that death is necessary to render the covenant enacted, valid, or in force (ἐγκεκαίνισται). Verses 18–22 cite the Law as illustrating the principle that the shedding of blood was necessary to validate the covenant. Referring (in 9:19–20) to Exodus 24:8, there is allusion to how Moses signified the obligation of both parties by sprinkling blood on the book and the people.

Whereas the first phrases of 9:16–17 do not indicate who must die, the final phrase of 9:17 is difficult: For it is never in force when lives the covenant-maker (ἐπεὶ μήποτε ἰσχύει ὅτε ζῇ ὁ διαθέμενος). Sir Robert Anderson, dealing with this last phrase,

---

[38] Some argue for a mixed (believing and unbelieving) audience, but in this context, the identity of the audience is only significant in that whoever they may be, they are distinguished from those to whom the covenants were made and with whom they will be fulfilled.

suggests that διαθήκη is employed differently in 9:15–16,[39] a distinction understood by the KJV use of the word *testament* rather than *covenant*, and a distinction supported by Elliott Johnson, who cites that translation as indicating that while the NC is unaltered, there is a will or testament validated (in Christ's death) whereby church age believers are included in spiritual blessings of the NC. Johnson observes, "Thus it was in the purview of one partner [God] to inaugurate the distribution of the benefits based on death, through God's call of His own (3:1; 9:15), after the New Covenant had been ratified. In this way, the New Covenant was inaugurated as a last will and testament for the benefit of believers."[40] Rodney Decker eloquently diagnoses one significant problem with the KJV/Anderson/Johnson view,

> That the writer of Hebrews would use a crucial term such as διαθήκη seventeen times, all in connection with the New Covenant, and yet switch reference in just one sentence (vv. 16, 17) with no explicit indication in the context, seems highly improbable. The preceding statement (v. 15) refers to the New Covenant (διαθήκης καινῆς) in contrast to the first covenant (τῇ πρώτῃ διαθήκῃ), and verse 16 is syntactically linked by γὰρ ("for"). The immediately following statement, introduced with ὅθεν ("therefore"), argues that "therefore not even the first covenant was inaugurated without blood" (v. 18 ESV; ὅθεν οὐδὲ ἡ πρώτη χωρὶς αἵματος ἐγκεκαίνισται).

[39] Robert Anderson, *Types in Hebrews* (Grand Rapids, MI: Kregel, 1978), 56.

[40] Elliott Johnson, "The Church Has an Indirect Relationship to the New Covenant" in *Dispensational Understanding of the New Covenant*, 172.

The context alone would seem adequate to justify the same referent for διαθήκη in the intervening sentence.[41]

If the contextual argument favoring a non-eclectic understanding of διαθήκη (as, for example, the NASB translates it) is correct, then it is most probable that τοῦ διαθεμένου in 9:16 and ὁ διαθέμενος in 9:17 refer not to God as the covenant originator, but to that which would die – the νεκροῖς in 9:17. In keeping with the illustration of 9:18-22, we could simply understand 9:17 as saying that until the covenant is signed in blood, it is not valid. This understanding would be more consistent with the syntactical context, but it carries with it the consequence of removing from the equation the secondary device of a *will* or *testament* as the vehicle for shared blessing under the NC.

After the illustration of the importance of blood, and the description of why Christ's blood is superior in 9:18-22, 9:23-28 advances the explanation of His superiority with a discussion of how, in contrast to first-covenant blood, His blood is shed only once. Note that in 9:24 Christ entered (εἰσῆλθεν) into heaven itself, but now appears (νῦν ἐμφανισθῆναι) for us (ὑπὲρ ἡμῶν). Whereas He entered into heaven in the past, but now He appears in the presence of God on our behalf. Whereas His death validated the NC, and showed Him to be a high priest, He is now in the presence of God, in heaven, on our behalf. Again, there is a distinction in the text between His present ministry and His NC ministry. While the two cannot be fully divorced (because they both involve Him and His blood), we must have exegetical warrant if we are to infer overlap in beneficiaries of these ministries, and in this context we have none.

The uniqueness of His once-shed blood is significant not only in that it puts Him in contrast to the Levitical priests, but also

[41] Rodney Decker "Response to Elliott E. Johnson" in *Dispensational Understanding of the New Covenant*, 192-193.

in that once at the consummation of the ages (νυνὶ δὲ ἅπαξ ἐπὶ συντελείᾳ τῶν αἰώνων), to the removal of the sin He has been manifest (εἰς ἀθέτησιν [τῆς] ἁμαρτίας διὰ τῆς θυσίας αὐτοῦ πεφανέρωται). In several manuscripts *sin* is anarthrous,[42] but in a number of early witnesses, *sin* is articulated. There being a definite article in the phrase is not pivotal, but it would reinforce the idea that there was a particular sin being addressed by His death in 9:26. Still, 9:28 indicates that Christ bore the sins of the many (εἰς τὸ πολλῶν ἀνενεγκεῖν ἁμαρτίας), which appears to be a non-technical reference[43] to his propitiation for all. If there is a distinction between results of His death within the parameters of the NC and outside of those parameters, that distinction is not clear in 9:25-28 as it seems to be in 9:24, for example.

Walvoord's questions: (1) Are any promises given to Israel under the NC operative today in any form? No. There are no specific NC promises mentioned, with the possible exception of 9:15, which maintains the original recipient terminology. Only by changing the meaning of διαθήκη in 9:16-17 can we apply a promise to both the original recipients and the church, yet there is no exegetical or contextual warrant for doing so – even though some argue for theological justification of such an interpretation. It is the view of this writer that the exegetical data renders such a justification implausible if not impossible.

(2) How does Hebrews use the term NC, either directly or indirectly? In this section, the term is used both directly and indirectly. There are six references to the old (9:1, 4 [x2], 15, 18, 20), one to the new (9:15), and two that reference a covenant in general (9:16-17). In each case, as in previous sections, the antecedent is apparent (the debated references in 9:16-17

---

[42] E.g., P46, Majority Text, etc.

[43] As in Is 53:12 and 1 Jn 2:2

notwithstanding). As in the earlier section, the new is contrasted with the old, the second with the first.

(3) What is the explicit teaching of Hebrews about the NC? Like previous sections, there is no new teaching about the content of the NC. It is cited here to advance the argument that Jesus Christ is superior, being the mediator of a better covenant. Whereas there is no new data regarding the content of the NC, there seems to be a pivotal statement in 9:16–17 (complementing 8:6) regarding the present jurisdiction of the NC: it is *validated* by the blood of Christ, just as the Law was validated by the blood in Exodus 24:8. That is not to say that there is a parallel in fulfillment between NC and the first covenant. In the first, Israel accepted and affirmed that the condition of the covenant's blessing was their obedience. Once the Law was validated, it was *being* fulfilled: conditions were being met, or not met, and obedience and disobedience would be rewarded in God's timing. The NC, on the other hand, has, upon its validation, no requirements to be met by the second party. Any conditions in the NC are God's, and its fulfillment awaits His timing. So while the NC can be described as validated (8:6; 9:16–17), there is no indication of it being functional presently in any way, because the stipulated conditions (of Jer 31, for example, which are never redacted or expounded) are not being presently fulfilled or shared.

Observations From Hebrews 10:1–18
Continuing and concluding the argument, especially from 9:22–28, that Christ is superior on the basis of His better sacrifice, 10:1–18 considers the limitations of the Law, particularly with respect to its inferior sacrifices and compares them to Christ's sacrifice. The Law is described as a shadow (Σκιὰν) of the coming good things (τῶν μελλόντων ἀγαθῶν), and had no capability (δύναται) to complete or make perfect the one drawing near (τοὺς προσερχομένους τελειῶσαι). Evidence for this point is offered in

10:2–3: those covered by the sacrifices still had sin-consciences (συνείδησιν ἁμαρτιῶν), and yearly reminders (ἀνάμνησις) of sin. As 10:3 implies and 10:4 explains, continued and repeated sacrifice of bulls and goats was necessary for a reminder, but had no capacity to bear away (ἀφαιρεῖν) sin.

The writer contrasts this limitation with Christ, referencing Psalm 39:7–9 from the LXX (Ps 40:68 in English). Hebrews 10:5 quotes Psalm 39:7 exactly except for substituting the word σῶμα (body) for ὠτία (ear, an accurate rendering of the Masoretic Text). Certainly, the ear is part of the body, so there is no contradiction between the two references, but it is unclear why Hebrews renders the word σῶμα, except in that the whole body of Christ as sacrifice fits the context of Hebrews 7–10 better than focusing on His ear. In 10:6 there are two slight variations (Heb 10:6: ὁλοκαυτώματα [burnt offerings, accusative neuter plural] and Ps 39:7: ὁλοκαύτωμα [a burnt offering, accusative neuter singular]; Heb 10:6: εὐδόκησας [delighted in] and Ps 39:7:ἤτησας [asked]). Hebrews 10:7 includes the phrase ὁ θεὸς τὸ θέλημά σου, adjusting the word order from the LXX (τὸ θέλημά σου, ὁ θεός μου). These variations are not pivotal, and they can be attributed either to quoting from another translation or to the author loosely referencing rather than exactly quoting.

After summarizing in 10:8, the following verse identifies the purpose of the quote: He takes away the first in order to establish the second (ἀναιρεῖ τὸ πρῶτον ἵνα τὸ δεύτερον στήσῃ). While not explicitly identifying the antecedent of the *first* and *second*, the passage implies from the context that the covenants are in view. In 10:9, Jesus is portrayed as having come to do the will of the Father, which is considered in the second phrase of 10:9 to be the taking away of the first and establishing of the second. By this will (θελήματι) we have been sanctified. Note the distinction between the second (covenant) and the will. The sanctification is by *this* will of God, not through (διὰ) the covenant, but through the one time offering of the body of Jesus Christ (τῆς προσφορᾶς τοῦ σώματος Ἰησοῦ Χριστοῦ ἐφάπαξ). Here the multiple purposes of Christ's death come into view. He came to do the will of the Father. That *will* includes taking away the first and establishing the second. By His will we are sanctified through Christ's body. In 10:29 the sanctification (ἡγιάσθη) is described as being through (by which, ἐν ᾧ) the blood (τὸ αἷμα, accusative) of the covenant (τῆς διαθήκης, genitives). The genitives in 10:29 denote that *of the covenant* modifies *the blood*, but it is the blood itself that sanctifies us – not the covenant. Notably, in 10:10 present age believers are said to be sanctified by His body, and in 10:29, by His blood. Here are two more opportunities for the writer of Hebrews to connect the church to the NC, and he doesn't do it in either case. Again, he connects the church to the One who validates the NC, but is very careful not to create any connection between the NC itself and the church.

Whereas the Levitical priestly ministry of presenting offerings and sacrifices was necessarily continuous due to its inefficacy (10:11), Christ, after His once–offering sat down at the right hand of God where He awaits the time His enemies are made a footstool for His feet (10:12, referencing Ps 110:1). This allusion to His future kingdom rule is a reminder that *it is not already, it is only not yet.* He sits (not on David's throne) at the right hand of the Father, waiting (10:13). In the meantime, while He awaits the inauguration of His Davidic and earthly kingdom at His coronation, He has completed (τετελείωκεν, perfect active indicative) for always (εἰς τὸ διηνεκὲς) those being sanctified (τοὺς ἁγιαζομένους) (10:14).

Building on the assertion of 10:11–14, that His work is accomplished, 10:15–18 provides one last piece of evidence for Christ's superiority, citing the work of forgiveness that has already been validated by His offering. Note in 10:15 the Holy Spirit testifies *to us* (Μαρτυρεῖ δὲ ἡμῖν καὶ τὸ πνεῦμα τὸ ἅγιον). The passage distinguishes in 10:15–17 once again – as Hebrews has consistently – between *us* and *them* (this is the covenant I will make with *them*). The NC of Jeremiah 31:33 is loosely summarized in 10:16–17 with the original recipient language maintained. The distinction is further emphasized in 10:18 citing forgiveness of these things (τούτων). What things? *Their* sins. *Their* lawless deeds. And because He already offered Himself for sin, there is no more offering needed – no sacrifice remains yet unoffered (11:26). He has accomplished all. And therein is the significance of the NC to the church age believer: Jesus's death validated the NC, thus providing for the forgiveness of Israel's sins committed under the first covenant, and His death also provided the means whereby *we* (who haven't committed sins under the first covenant) draw near to God and are sanctified. For the writer of Hebrews, the NC is Exhibit A in the inventory of evidence for the superiority of Christ. It proves His ministry is efficacious. It proves that He is superior.

Consequently, 10:19–25 begins with an exhortation to the readers: Since therefore brethren we have confidence to enter the holy place by the blood of Jesus (not the covenant, but the *blood* shed to also validate the covenant) by a new and living way (ὁδὸν πρόσφατον καὶ ζῶσαν) which He brought into existence for us (ἣν ἐνεκαίνισεν ἡμῖν) – a way through the curtain (διὰ τοῦ καταπετάσματος) that is, the flesh of Him (τοῦτ' ἔστιν τῆς σαρκὸς αὐτοῦ), and we have a great priest over the house of God (καὶ ἱερέα μέγαν ἐπὶ τὸν οἶκον τοῦ θεοῦ), let us draw near (προσερχώμεθα).

Because of His superiority, present–age believers are to have confidence and draw near. The thesis of the Hebrews argument is that He is superior, therefore He can be trusted, therefore, believers have a responsibility to fix our eyes upon Him (e.g., 12:2). In light of these truths, Hebrews contains repeated warnings about neglecting Him (e.g., 2:3–4; 4:1,11; 6:1–8; 10:26–31; 12:25). He is faithful. He is true. He is the Author and Perfecter of faith, and if we attempt to walk without Him – either by trying to place ourselves under the Law or by any other focus, we are being entangled and failing to run the race as He has designed. In other words, we are failing. Instead, we should show gratitude by which we may offer to God an acceptable service with reverence and awe; for our God is a consuming fire (12:28–29).

Walvoord's questions: (1) Are any promises given to Israel under the NC operative today in any form? No. In 10:1–18 there is no mention of promises, though there is reference in 10:23 to He who has promised as faithful – and that is the point. He who has promised is faithful. The NC is a powerful demonstration of that truth. There are promises not yet received (e.g., 11:39–40), but they will be received in His timing and for His glory.

(2) How does Hebrews use the term NC, either directly or indirectly? In this section, the term is used both directly and indirectly. The NC is only directly referenced in 10:16 (quoting Jeremiah), and is possibly indirectly alluded to in 10:9 (He takes away the first to establish the second). In neither instance is there any implication that the NC has been expanded to involve the church, either in fulfillment or in blessings presently enjoyed.

(3) What is the explicit teaching of Hebrews about the NC? In this section the NC is cited as evidence of Christ's superiority and as a reason we may have confidence in Him. Because of the consistency of this message in Hebrews, the NC has great significance to the church – but not because the church is related either directly or indirectly to the NC (Hebrews does not suggest a relationship, either direct or indirect). Whereas the NC provides for Israel her future national and individual hope – ultimately to fulfill God's promises to Abraham, Isaac, Jacob, and David – the NC demonstrates His ability to keep His word and helps the church to have confidence (10:19), to have full assurance of faith (10:22), and to provide us yet another reason to fix our eyes on Him.

But you have come to Mount Zion and to the city of the living God, the heavenly Jerusalem, and to myriads of angels, to the general assembly and church of the firstborn who are enrolled in heaven, and to God the Judge of all, and to the spirits of the righteous made perfect, *and to Jesus the mediator of a New Covenant*, and to the sprinkled blood, which speaks better than the blood of Abel (12:22–24). We *have not* come to the covenant. We have come to *Him*.

9

SOCIAL–POLITICAL IMPLICATIONS OF THE NEW COVENANT

Charlie Clough

As Christopher Cone has pointed out, dispensationalists have offered several views of how the New Covenant relates to the Church.[1]   The three major views are: (1) the Multiple New Covenant View (MC) advocated by Lewis Sperry Chafer and John Walvoord; (2) the Single Covenant Multiple Participants View (SCMP) held by C. I. Scofield, J. Carl Laney and Stanley Toussaint; and (3) the Single Covenant Israel Only View (SCIO) promoted by J. N. Darby.   The MC view distinguishes the New Covenant promised to Israel from another New Covenant that appears in the New Testament connected to the Church.   The SCMP view holds to the one New Covenant promised to Israel but separates its physical blessings to Israel from its spiritual blessings and has the Church sharing the latter with future Israel.   Cone criticizes the MC and SCMP views as compromising the literal grammatical-historical hermeneutic methodology central to dispensationalism. These approaches either construct covenants inferred theologically without direct exegetical support or utilize an "already/not yet"

---

[1] Christopher Cone, "Hermeneutical Ramifications of Applying the New Covenant to the Church: An Appeal to Consistency," *Journal of Dispensational Theology* 13 (December 2009): 5–22.

hermeneutic--both of which open the door to covenant theology and progressive dispensationalism.[2]

In defense of the SCIO view Cone points out that the New Covenant was ratified at the crucifixion among Jews and prior to the creation of the Church (Matt 26:28; Mark 14:24; Luke 22:20) so "it would not have been at all inappropriate for Him to discuss an entirely Jewish covenant."[3]   Paul's mention of the New Covenant in 1 Corinthians 11:25-26 emphasizes the Lord's death not the covenant itself. Cone's discussion of every New Testament passage that mentions the covenant also notes the striking absence of all mention of the covenant in John's writings that so thoroughly deal with spiritual blessings of the Church. Paul as a minister of the New Covenant, Cone suggests, could refer to the gospel message provoking the Jews to jealousy so they would call upon their Messiah and thus trigger His return and historical implementation of that covenant (2 Cor 3:6 cf. Matt 23:39). Another extensive discussion of 2 Corinthians 3:6 on which progressive dispensationalists place much emphasis is by George Gunn.[4] He concludes that the expression "New Covenant" here metaphorically expresses the manner of Paul's ministry (a "new-covenant-like-ministry"), the spiritual standard by which his conduct should be judged, not its message.

---

[2] Cone asks, "how can one apply 'already not yet' to the New Covenant and yet argue that it should not be applied to the Davidic covenant?" Ibid., 15.

[3] Ibid., 18.

[4] George A. Gunn, "Second Corinthians 3:6 and the Church's Relationship to the New Covenant," *Journal of Dispensational Theology* 13 (December 2009): 25-45.

THE PURPOSE OF THIS CHAPTER

As we see contemporary culture deteriorating back to the likeness of pre–Christian Roman paganism, a trend we facetiously could call "going forward into the past," Christians, particularly in the West, face increasingly the challenge of how to interact with the social and political consequences. Do Christian parents capitulate to civil authorities who demand that all education, including home–school and Christian–school, conform to the anti–Biblical enlightenment philosophy?[5] How do Christian graduate students cope with department requirements to deny the truth claims of Biblical history and ethics or face expulsion?   What about a Christian employee who is forced to pay union dues to further

---

[5] For example, consider these articles in prominent law journals that influence judges' thinking about adjudicating future cases:: "If a parent subscribes to an absolutist belief system premised on the notion that it was handed down by a creator, that it (like the Ten Commandments) is etched in stone and that all other systems are wrong, the essential lessons of a civic education (i.e., tolerance and mutual respect) often seem deeply challenging and suspect. . . .Such 'private truths' have no place in the public arena, including the public schools." Catherine Ross, "Fundamentalist Challenges to Core Democratic Values: Exit and Homeschooling", *William and Mary Bill of Rights Journal* 18 (May 2010): 1006; and from a professor at the Northwestern University School of Law a claim that there are legal and constitutional limits on the ability of homeschooling parents "to teach their children idiosyncratic and illiberal beliefs and values". . .[Government control must be exercised against] "parents [who] want to teach against the enlightenment. . . .Parental control over children's basic education flows from the state (rather than vise versa). States delegate power over children's basic education to parents. . . ." Kimberly A. Yurako, "Education Off the Grid...", *California Law Review 96* (February 2008): 183, 132. The reference to "enlightenment" clearly declares total war by civil bureaucrats against the Christian faith by demanding universal replacement of the authority of the self–revealing Triune God of the Bible with man's imagined ultimate intellectual authority espoused for the past 300 years by the Enlightenment tradition.

anti-Biblical political agendas? How should a Christian medical practitioner respond to government requirements to participate in abortion and denial of parental notification? Since Christian citizens of modern states are legally part of civil governance, what Biblical guidance for exercising this responsibility exists?

The famous five categories of the Church-culture relationship articulated by H. Richard Niebuhr in his book *Christ and Culture* (1951) aren't just academic notions for scholars to debate. They are vital means for believers today to think through their social and political roles. After excluding the Roman Catholic position of "Christ above culture" that led to the supremacy of the institutional church over the civil government and the Liberal Protestant position of "Christ of culture" that led to accommodation of Biblical faith to whatever cultural view prevailed, Bible-believing Christians are left with three possibilities. First, there is the "Christ against culture" position often followed by those of the Anabaptist tradition of shunning cultural life altogether because it is hopelessly contaminated by sin. Second, there is the "Christ and culture in paradox" position of the Lutheran tradition of intruding redemptively into the culture only to evangelize and disciple converts while passively letting God use civil government to providentially retard the spread of evil. And finally there is the Reformed "Christ the transformer of culture" position of restructuring culture by Biblical standards.

The first position tries to establish a safe religious ghetto which increasingly appears impossible to do in modern culture.[6] The second position lulled German evangelicals during the 1930s

---

[6] A recent example of typically unavoidable economic interaction with surrounding culture: totalitarian health regulations of the US Food and Drug Administration have now resulted in arrests and fines against Amish farmers who sell unpasteurized milk to supply customers who reject the enzyme-destructive consequences of pasteurization. Social isolation is not a realistic option.

into allowing Hitler's Nazi minions to take over their country.[7] The third option has been extensively developed within Reformed circles in recent decades largely by the Christian reconstruction (theonomic) community. When dispensationalists had accommodated their interpretation of early Genesis to the radical nineteenth century innovations of natural history in spite of their claim of a grammatical–historical–literal hermeneutic, it was the Reformed reconstructionist community that dared to publish *The Genesis Flood* book by two dispensationalists in 1961 which began the restoration of Scriptural authority to construction of natural history models.[8] Moreover, it was the reconstructionists who, following the implications of the presuppositionalist apologetic of Cornelius Van Til, developed incisive critiques of economics,

---

[7] Reformed resistance to a position very similar to the classical Lutheran model is expressed in the recent work by John Frame, *The Escondido Theology: A Reformed Response to Two Kingdom Theology* (Lakeland, FL: Whitefield Media Productions, 2011).

[8] The philosophy of uniformitarianism which Charles Lyell (1797–1875) substituted for the absence of direct observational data of past geophysical processes had permeated by the 1830s geological science and had necessarily led to rejection of the traditional "young earth" view of the Bible. Terry Mortenson has published his PhD dissertation on this subject as *The Great Turning Point: The Church's Catastrophic Mistake on Geology--Before Darwin* (Green Forest, AL: Master Books, 2004). His work refutes the claim by Mark A. Noll in *The Scandal of the Evangelical Mind* (Grand Rapids: Eerdmans, 1994) that young earth creationism was imported into dispensationalism by John Whitcomb and Henry Morris from Seventh Day Adventism, i.e., it arose from a cult rather than from a consistent hermeneutic that supported eighteen centuries of interpretation. The truth is that the dispensational publishing house of Moody Press refused to publish the Whitcomb-Morris book. It was reconstructionist Rousas Rushdoony who immediately recognized its historic validity and implications and helped get it published by Presbyterian and Reformed Publishing Company. I was told this account years ago by Henry Morris who with John Whitcomb were both unabashed dispensationalists. See Henry M. Morris, *History of Modern Creationism* (San Diego, California: Master Book Publishers, 1984) 154.

education (including mathematics), philosophy, politics, and sociology.[9] As any home–schooling parent who has researched curricula materials will admit, some of the finest Christian educational materials have come from Reformed circles heavily influenced by reconstructionism and theonomy. Clearly this group of Christians have acted on the Reformed view that Christ transforms culture.[10]

So, then, what is a consistent dispensational response to today's deteriorating culture? While the next chapter will attempt an overall answer, this chapter explores the narrower facet of how one's conception of the New Covenant–Church connection may affect his interaction with the culture.[11]

COVENANT STRUCTURE

That the God of the universe would come down to our human level on this planet and enter into a covenant with us ought to provoke great wonderment. Unfortunately because the word "covenant" has become a much–used title for doctrinal controversy by theological specialists, the wonderment in

---

[9] An early example of such comprehensive critique is Gary North, ed., *Foundations of Christian Scholarship: Essays in the Van Til Perspective* (Vallecito, CA: Ross House Books, 1976). Even the so–called neutral nature of mathematics was challenged in this volume by Vern S. Poythress in his fascinating essay, "A Biblical View of Mathematics, " 159–188.

[10] This is not to dismiss the contributions of dispensationist scholars and educators. My participation in creationist circles since 1964 has made me appreciated the insights that dispensational theology uniquely provides in interpreting nature. See Charles A Clough, "Dispensational Implications for Universal Historiography and Apologetics," *Chafer Theological Seminary Journal* 7 (September 2001): 34–61.

[11] "Church" in this chapter and the next refers to the universal church of all regenerated people.

ordinary Bible readers is too–often missed.[12] It might be better translated as "contract" since it refers to a formal agreement between two parties (e.g., Abraham made a business contract with Abimelech in Gen 21:22–34). What is stunning about this term in the Bible is that it refers to contracts between God and man. In his discussion of the term, Albright wrote: "Contracts and treaties were common everywhere, but only the Hebrews, so far as we know, made covenants with their gods or God."[13]

Several important implications follow from this unique form of revelation. First, it reinforces the point that the transcendent Triune God condescends to come down to man's level to bargain (Gen 18), to argue (Job 38–41), and, yes, to commit Himself to defined behavior for the duration of such

---

[12] "Covenant" occurs over 300 times in the English Bible generally translating the Hebrew berith and the Greek diatheke.

[13] He noted the provisional nature of his claim, but his discussion of the cultural milieu clearly shows the ordinary commercial meaning of the term berith: "Being prevailingly caravaneers and so ethno–political intruders in the West, the early Hebrews were in constant need of contractual and treaty protection." William F. Albright, Yahweh and the Gods of Canaan: A Historical Analysis of Two Contrasting Faiths (Garden City, NY: Doubleday & Co., 1968), 106–108. Of course, we biblicists would insist that it was God that made the contracts with man, not the other way around.

contracts.[14] After all, specification of future behavior by parties to a contract is the very reason for contracts. Second, it presupposes positional sanctification since there must exist righteousness on the part of man adequate to enter into a personal relationship with the God of absolute righteousness.[15] Third, it establishes the legitimacy of a literal hermeneutic since all contracts necessarily are interpreted in terms of ordinary language for validation of the parties' behaviors. Finally, it assumes that the meaning of the contract terminology must be conserved throughout the duration

---

[14] In his thorough discussion of such condescension Oliphint points out that this Old Testament "coming down" is preparation for the ultimate "coming down" in the Incarnation. See K. Scott Oliphint, *Reasons for Faith: Philosophy in the Service of Theology* (Phillipsburg, NJ: Presbyterian & Reformed Publishing Co., 2006), 232–255. God's condescension also answers the challenge of "open theology" concerning passages like Genesis 18 that depict God involved in "fact-finding" conversations with man. It also sharply contrasts with Islam's Allah. Condescension by such a transcendent deity in binding himself to any contract with man is seen by Muslim theologians as an impossible contradiction. The price paid for denying such condescension is a deity that can never be known personally. Thus Biblical contracts by revealing God's interest in personal relationships can play a key role in Muslim evangelism.

[15] Note the occurrence of sacrifices with Biblical contracts: the ecological Noahic contract (Gen 8:20–9:17), the land–seed–global blessing Abrahamic contract (Gen 15), the theocratic Mosaic contract (Exod 24:1–8); and the New contract (Matt 26:26–29). It is precisely with the first redemptive contract that revelation of justification based upon imputed righteousness occurs which the Apostle Paul so carefully later expounds (Gen 15:6; Rom 4:1–8). Modern contract law faintly reflects this truth in the doctrine of "legal capacity" which requires that all parties to a contract must be legally competent to enter into such a relationship.

of the contract.   Terms cannot be reinterpreted later in the relationship.[16]

The contractual form of revelation, therefore, sharply distinguishes the Creator–creature relationship from the casual concept of relationship in pagan unbelieving society.[17]   God doesn't enter relationships casually. And the specific nature of His contractual stipulations demands that each contract stand on its own. Dispensational theology has therefore resisted the theological synthesizing of Covenant theology in this regard. Instead of locating continuity at the level of a generic redemptive covenant synthesized from later New Testament revelation and read back into the Old Testament, dispensational theology prefers instead to locate continuity in God's immutable character behind each Biblical contract and maintain the integrity of each contract's terminology.[18]

---

[16] Imagine, for example, that after a tornado destroyed your house (but allowed you and your family to survive), your insurance company read back a "deeper meaning" into your homeowners policy that the term "house" really meant "family."

[17] In his analysis of pagan society Paul characterized it as *asunthetous*, translated in modern Bibles as "untrustworthy" but more insightfully translated in the King James Bible as "covenant-breaking" (Rom 1:31). Today it can be readily observed in government policy departure from the Constitution, corporate contract-breaking, and cohabitating couples lacking the social maturity and trust in each other to enter a marriage contract.

[18] For a detailed development of this argument see my article, "A Meta-Hermeneutical Comparison of Covenant and Dispensational Theologies," *Chafer Theological Seminary Journal* 7 (April–June 2001): 59–80. Rousas J Rushdoony, like many Reformed critics of dispensationalism, errs in failing to see where it locates continuity and thus accuses it of polytheism in *The Institutes of Biblical Law* (Nutley, NJ: Craig Press, 1973), 18.

THE FOUNDATIONAL "CONTRACTS"

The New Covenant rests upon prior Biblical covenants or contracts which form its historical, social and legal context. The first clearly explicit Biblical divine–human contract is the Noahic covenant. It provided the basis for civil authority to use lethal force to execute some of God's judgments to protect human life (Gen 9:5-6); it defined the variability limits of the post–flood geophysical environment (Gen 8:21-22, 9:11-15; Isa 54:9-10); and it laid out the biological relationship between man and animal life (Gen 9:1-4, 8-17). Its contract parties included not only all humanity but also those animals whose DNA was preserved in the ark of Noah (Gen 9:9-10). These social and environmental features by formal divine agreement continue through history into the millennial era when the New Covenant becomes functional. The Noahic covenant is a *preservative,* but not a *redemptive* contract.

In sharp contrast the Abrahamic contract defined God's plan of post–Babel *redemption* through His promise of progeny to Abraham, His land allotment to that progeny, and His exclusive selection of that progeny as the means of blessing all humanity (Gen 12:1-3). Its land provisions were later unfolded in the so-called Palestinian contract (Deut 29:1-30:10); and its progeny provisions were later revealed to include an everlasting Davidic dynasty (2 Sam 7:4-16; Ps 89:3-4, 28-29, 34-37). When God established this formal agreement with Abraham and his progeny in the early second millennium, BC, it made *a fundamental change in His relation with mankind that continues through today until the end of time.* Before this agreement, post–flood civilization had access to previous special revelation given from Adam to Noah (the "Noahic Bible") with possible isolated additional prophetic revelation (Job?). The various people groups apparently were then ruled by king–priests who combined civil and religious authority (Gen 14:18-24). Afterward, special revelation comes only through Abraham's progeny. God's relation with mankind that had shown itself universally corruptible at Babel thus began anew with *revelational exclusivism* (cf. Deut 4:19–20; John 14:6; Acts 4:12).[19] With this change comes the necessity for communicating the Word of God outward into the world beginning with Israel and continuing today with the Church.[20] All subsequent blessing to the Gentile world, therefore, exists in accordance with this covenant.

By the second millennium, BC, then, a known contractual framework between God and His terrestrial creation had been established. Although fear of post–flood geophysical catastrophes no doubt lingered after Babel, those who feared the Lord had revelational assurance of a reasonable natural environment. Human life was to be protected with lethal force if necessary by civil government. Moreover, God had provided specific contractual terminology that outlined the shape of all future redemption including any additional contracts He would make. The physical, social, and spiritual foundation of subsequent history was, therefore, *legally established* in utter contrast to the idolatrous and chaotic imaginations of unbelieving minds.

THE MOSAIC COVENANT SETS THE STAGE

If the Noahic covenant revealed details of the physical and social environment in which the future New Covenant would function,

---

[19] Religious exclusivism angers religious egalitarianism like that referenced in footnote 5 that presumes all religious dogma originates in man's imagination so no religion can claim absolute truth (of course, that presumption begs the question of whether God has verbally spoken in history). Forgotten is the *cause* of this change: the apostasy of Babel when mankind collectively rejected Noahic revelation that had been universally available to every postdiluvian people group (Gen 11:1–9).

[20] George Peters years ago pointed out that here arose the concept of a "missionary book" and a "missionary people" in *A Biblical Theology of Missions* (Chicago: Moody Press, 1972), 130.

and if the Abrahamic covenant established the global strategy of redemption, the Mosaic covenant set the stage to demonstrate the necessity of the New Covenant. To view the Mosaic covenant in the socio–political perspective of this chapter a look at the exodus event is in order.

The Abrahamic family was led into Egypt for molding it into a tribal community with its own associated civil government. Egypt of the pharaohs was a classic example of the tyrannical state where civil government incarnated the pagan metaphysic of one–level of existence (a continuity of nature–man–gods). Egyptologist Frankfort describes the political–religious situation:

> [Pharaoh] was the fountainhead of all authority, all power, and all wealth. The famous saying of Louis XIV, *l'etat c'est moi* [I am the state], was levity and presumption when it was uttered, but could have been offered by Pharaoh as a statement of fact in which his subjects concurred. It would have summed up adequately [Egyptian] political philosophy.[21]

The claim of total civil authority led to absolute civil power. Why? Because this idea directly follows from the pagan metaphysical presupposition. When the Creator-creature distinction – the two-level existence – is denied, there can be no authority transcending the state. As Rushdoony writes:

> Wherever a society has a naturalistic religion, grounded on the concept of continuity, man faces the total power of the state. . . .Where there is no transcendental law and power in a separate and omnipotent being, then *power has a wholly immanent and immediate source in a state, group, or person, and it is beyond appeal.* The state

---

[21]Henri Frankfort, *Ancient Egyptian Religion* (Torchback ed.; New York: Harper & Row, 1961 [1948]), 31.

becomes the saving power and the source of law; . . . [It] becomes god walking on earth. . . .In this faith, for man to be free means to be in the state.[22] [Emphasis supplied]

The exodus event by which Israel *physically* came out of Egypt thus marked a major disruption of pagan civilization which, it will be seen later, speaks to the contemporary expansion of the modern secular state. So profound was this cultural break that the first generation of Israel still could not *spiritually* come out of Egypt in their worldview. In spite of the public geophysical miracles, they continued to imagine God, man, and nature in Egyptian categories (Ex 32:1–6). They feared a freedom in which they would have to trust God for food, clothing, and survival and so reverted to seeking the security of slavery: "Who will give us meat to eat? We remember the fish which we ate freely in Egypt, the cucumbers, the melons, the leeks, the onions, and the garlic" (Num 11:4–5). Rushdoony describes the political implications of this kind of thinking:

[Man] will perpetually demand of the state a redemptive role. What he cannot do personally, i.e., to save himself, he demands that the state do for him, so that the state, as man enlarged, becomes the human savior of man. . . .[This

---

[22] Rousas J. Rushdoony, *The One and the Many* (Nutley, NJ: Craig Press, 1971), 60–61. This dilemma of civil authority rooted in man inevitably becoming absolute power was classically described by Hobbes: "It makes no difference, Hobbes argues, whether the sovereignty is held by one man or by an assembly. In either case 'the sovereign of a commonwealth. . .is not subject to the civil laws. For having the power to make and repeal laws, he may when he pleases, free himself from that subjection by repealing those laws that trouble him. . . . he that is bound to himself only is not bound.'" Mortimer J. Adler and William Gorman, "Government," Vol. 1: *The Great Ideas: A Syntopicon of Great Books of the Western World*, ed. Robert Maynard Hutchins (Chicago: The University of Chicago, 1952), 640.

political arrangement] cultivates the slave mind in order to enslave men, and to have people themselves demand an end to liberty. . . .The slave mind clings to statist. . .slavery, cradle-to-grave welfare care, as a fearful child clings to his mother. The advantage of slavery is precisely this, security in the. . . state.[23]

That was the background of the Mosaic covenant. The Israelites quickly discovered that Yahweh God was going to call the shots, not their Egypt-conditioned hearts. The exodus event had physically separated them from Egypt; now Sinai would begin a painful, all-encompassing conflict with surrounding Gentile culture and the ideas emanating from it. They learned that they had joined a really unique community. The Creator-creature distinction was no longer going to be suppressed. Yahweh God gave to the people the constitution and original legislation of the nation by direct revelation in the ten commandments and indirectly through Moses in the statutes and judgments. *No other legal document in history can claim to be the publicly-heard words of God* (Deut 5:22-27). This event is one of the most astounding occurrences in all of political history, and yet pagan suppression continues today to omit it as a supernatural public revelatory event from the modern educational system.

Unlike the Noahic and Abrahamic contracts the Mosaic contract was neither preservative nor redemptive; it was a test for a kingdom relationship with God and therefore *provisional*. Merrill puts it well:

The Mosaic [covenant] is subservient to the Abrahamic, a special arrangement with Abraham's seed to put it in a position to become the means of blessing which the Lord had promised to his descendants...For Israel to be a holy

---

[23] Rousas J. Rushdoony, *The Politics of Guilt and Pity* (Nutley, NJ: Craig Press, 1970), 28-29.

nation called for a deportment that would cause the peoples of the earth to see in Israel's behavior a reflection of the God they professed to serve...Theirs would be an inestimable privilege, but at the same time the commitment they made would entail enormous responsibility. Should they refuse God's gracious overtures, he surely would work out his redemptive program by some other means, the nature of which defies human imagination.[24]

It challenged Abraham's progeny to bring into existence the Kingdom of God on earth.[25] As such it spelled out the details of what loving God and neighbor actually should have looked like in the second millennium BC.

Because Yahweh's call for submission to His Kingdom rule covered all facets of daily life, it inescapably pierced to the fallen hearts of unbelievers. It brought out into the open more clearly than all previous revelation the need for repentance and a heart change because *it brought out more clearly what true social justice actually looks like.* From the beginning Yahweh expressed the problem: "Oh, that they had such a heart in them that they would fear Me and always keep all My commandments" (Deut 5:29 NKJ). No sooner had the contract been ratified on Mt. Sinai than the nation reverted to pagan idolatry (Ex 32–34; Deut 9–10). Having watched the exodus generation fail to properly respond to Yahweh, Moses, in his address to the second generation just prior

---

[24] Eugene H. Merrill, *Everlasting Dominion: A Theology of the Old Testament* (Nashville, TN: Broadman & Holman Publishers, 2006), 327, 271–272.

[25] I use the term "Kingdom of God" in the way Alva J. McClain used the term "Mediatorial Kingdom" to distinguish it from the universal, ever present Kingdom reign of God over all His creation. See his book, *The Greatness of the Kingdom* (Chicago: Moody Press, 1959), 41–51.

to the conquest, reiterated the need for them to *internalize* the ritual of circumcision: "Circumcise the foreskin of your heart, and be stiff-necked no longer" (Deut 10:16 NKJ).

To understand what Moses meant we have to reflect upon the ritual of circumcision. Circumcision was the sign of the redemptive Abrahamic contract which promised numerous natural descendants as well as a special spiritual progeny. Circumcision demonstrated that natural human propagation—specifically the male seed—was somehow flawed and needed a corrective action to be capable of producing the promised progeny.[26] Circumcision said in effect: "God has promised to produce a special line of children within the Abrahamic family, but those children won't come by natural reproduction using your male seed." In calling for spiritual circumcision of the heart Moses implied that the natural state of the heart was incapable of fulfilling the Kingdom imperatives of Yahweh; surgery was needed to correct the problem. To circumcise their hearts and participate as a national society and culture in the stipulated blessings of the Mosaic contract, Israelites had to believe like their father Abraham; they had to join the special line within his natural progeny.[27]

Unfortunately, the subsequent historical record of theocratic Israel – the contract performance data – demonstrated the failure of both the people and their leaders to circumcise their hearts. Jeremiah and Ezekiel gave last-minute exhortations: "Circumcise yourselves to the LORD, And take away the foreskins

---

[26] The Ishmael-Isaac narrative illustrated that supernatural action was needed to produce the true covenant-carrying progeny—the seed of promise—as Paul discusses in Rom 9:6-13.

[27] Subsequent history of the theocracy gave rise to the concept of the faithful Jewish "remnant." See discussion of 1 Kings 19:18 and ensuing development by the classic writing prophets in Arnold G. Fruchtenbaum, *Israelology: The Missing Link in Systematic Theology* (rev. ed., San Antonio, TX: Ariel Ministries, 2001), 601-604.

of your hearts" (Jer. 4:4 NKJ); "Cast away from you all the transgressions which you have committed, and get yourselves a new heart and a new spirit" (Ezek. 18:31 NKJ). In spite of all the warnings to respond positively, the cursings provision of the Mosaic contract had to be applied to the nation and into exile it went (Lev. 26:14–39; Deut. 28:15–68). The Mosaic contract did not redeem because it could not by itself bring about the inner transformation in the people that was needed for its blessings provisions to be applied.[28] The theocracy, therefore, ended with the exile. Nevertheless, some individuals did show a circumcised heart of loyalty to Yahweh's commands (e.g., Ps 19:7–11; 37:31; 40:8; 119:11,36,111–112; Is 51:7) and did so *before the New Covenant was promised.*

The exile event posed a dilemma. How would the prophetic promises of the Abrahamic contract and their unfolding details via the so-called Palestinian and the Davidic contracts come to pass if the nation could not meet the prerequisite for blessing? Moses had foreseen the dilemma and prophesied that "God will circumcise your heart and the heart of your descendants" (Deut. 30:6). As the time of the exile drew close God revealed through His prophets that He would initiate a new contract with Israel to replace the Mosaic and to provide the proper heart condition for national blessing (Jer 30–31; Ezek. 36:24–32). McClain explains:

> The moral problem posed by the failure of the Mosaic Covenant will under the New Covenant be met by God's own sovereign grace and power...the benefits of the

---

[28] Here is the historic proof that all attempts to convert civil authority into a redemptive agency—Marxist-Communism, Fascism, Euro-spawned "Christian Socialism," and Islamic Sharia—fail. They violate God's design of man and, as mere external legalisms, lack spiritually transforming power and thus inevitably lead to totalitarian civil government.

Mosaic Covenant will be attained, and at the same time its moral requirements will be secured... The New Covenant, therefore, is in the gracious spirit of the earlier Abrahamic Covenant... [It] is not on the basis of any surviving rights in the broken Covenant of Sinai but simply because Jehovah remembers His earlier 'covenant with Jacob...with Isaac, and...with Abraham' (Lev. 26:42).[29]

The Mosaic covenant thus set the stage for the New Covenant by exposing the need for genuine and comprehensive conformity to God's righteous standards in order for Israel to enjoy its promised blessings. Five elements of this new contract are important for the present discussion: (1) the covenant assured Israel that one day circumcised hearts would characterize the *entire nation*, not just a remnant, and do so *to the end of history* (Isa 59:21; Jer 31:33–37; 32:40; Ezek 37:26) ; (2) it was to be made with the *nation Israel* in the future, not with as yet non-existent transnational Church (Isa 59:20; Jer 31:31; Ezek 16:60–63); (3) it flowed out of the Abrahamic covenant, not out of the Mosaic, and therefore would comport with the earlier covenant's *global strategy objective of blessing the world* (Gen 12:3); (4) it was to enable observance of the *same righteousness* required by the law, statutes and ordnances of the Mosaic system (Jer 31:33–34; Ezek 37:22–24); and (5) the resultant blessings would be those offered under the Mosaic listing in Leviticus 26 and Deuteronomy 28 – actual publicly–observable climate, botanical, zoological, economic and social blessings (Jer 32:41–44; Ezek 34:25–29) . All its blessings, spiritual and material, were *bound inextricably together.*

---

[29] McClain, 158.

THE NEW COVENANT, CHRIST, AND ISRAEL

Much can be learned from the eight-centuries of theocracy under the old covenant of Moses. Here we had an actual community, a state, established by God as a local model of His Kingdom, one ruled by Him in an arrangement unique in world history. In the closing centuries of its declining existence we observe more and more prophetic focusing upon a future solution to be brought about by divine intervention that included more than just a New Covenant. Out of the historical experience of corruptible rulers there emerges the additional concept of a coming *Ideal Ruler* through some sort of convergence of Yahweh God's intent to dwell with man and the very human Davidic dynasty (Is 9:6-7; 11:1-2; Jer 33:15; Ps 110). A Messianic figure emerges as a longed-for Ideal King. Whereas the New Covenant would solve the corrupt people problem, the Messiah would solve the corrupt leadership problem. Together they would bring into historic existence the Kingdom of God which would reach outward from Israel to the entire globe.

Because Israel was chosen as the unique holy nation of all the nations (Ex 19:6), as the conduit of special revelation to mankind, and as the sole human party to all divine contracts after Noah (Rom 3:2; 9:4), it comes as no surprise that its Ideal King was to have global hegemony (Ps 2; Zech 14:9). To enlarge Israel's awareness of their God's global reach, His discipline for the nation's disobedience consisted of dispersion among the pagan cultures of the Gentile nations. The Jewish Diaspora would endure five centuries of suffering in pagan culture under Gentile rule before the coming of Jesus. But they had a source of enduring hope in the revelation God gave through His prophets that even the greatest Gentile nations beyond the promised land were under His control. Daniel, while holding a high office in two pagan empires, was given a panorama of history from that day (603 BC) until the final re-establishment of the Kingdom of God in all its completeness. Although the transfer of political supremacy from

Israel to four successive Gentile kingdoms would occur, Jewish hope was to center on the Son of Man—the Ideal Leader not just of Israel but of all mankind—whose domain would certainly encompass the world (Dan 7:13).[30]

So in the fullness of time Christ came to Israel (Gal 4:4) and offered it the Kingdom (Mark 1:15), but Israel rejected which led to His death. Ironically that death established the very New Covenant that would be so necessary for the Kingdom. Without submitting to the King, however, Israel could not experience it. Israel was left under Gentile hegemony referred by Jesus as "the times of the Gentiles" (Luke 21:24). Until the nation formally welcomes Him back, Christ will not return (Matt 23:39). Implementation of the New Covenant for the nation is thus *contingent upon its response to Christ*.[31] Until then Israel cannot be in the proper condition to assume its chief position among the nations, Christ cannot rule from the Davidic throne, the material environmental blessings will not come, and world peace cannot be achieved. The New Covenant is shaped by its historic, social and legal context, resting as it does upon the prior divine contractual agreements. These set the parameters within which the New Covenant is expressed: a natural environment safe for human survival, a redemptive worldwide agenda operating

---

[30] "During that long [pre-exilic] period the power and authority of the Theocracy was never in question. No nation, regardless of its size or strength, could stand successfully against Israel as long as that people followed the will of its divine King. . . .Israel went down in defeat only when she turned aside from the divinely written charter of her kingdom." McClain, 125.

[31] Some, particularly in the Reformed community, are troubled by the idea of contingency because of their focus on ends to the neglect of means. However, the condescension of God in His willingness to enter into contractual relationships with man inevitably generate historic trails of real interactions between them. Viewed from the creature level outcomes are "contingent" upon behaviors that are the *means* to the prophesied *end*.

exclusively through Abraham's progeny, and a historic entree of the Kingdom of God by means of an elect nation and the Ideal King.

THE NEW COVENANT, CHRIST, AND THE CHURCH

The divine response to Israel's rejection of the its King–Messiah followed an oft repeated pattern: failure of "Plan A" followed by what appears as "Plan B" except with God Plan B reveals more of His glory in expanded revelation – revelation which nearly always is unanticipated. In Eden the *offer* to man to dominate (manage) and subdue the earth was *rejected*, and resulted in fallen, death-filled history which led to the revelation of the gospel of God's grace that would reach to the heavens (cf. Rom 8:18–39). What would have happened if Adam had not sinned? In the centuries after the flood, the *offer* to build a new civilization was *rejected* (most clearly at Babel) which led to God beginning an everlasting counter-culture through Abraham that would both safeguard and expand special revelation for all mankind (note the contrasting sources of "naming" in Gen 11:4 and 12:2). What would have happened if the sons of Noah had established a God-fearing re-colonization of the earth? In the days of Samuel the *offer* of a politically simple and liberated theocracy was *rejected* which led to a monarchy that defined the role of a Messiah (1 Sam 8; Jer 23:5-6). What would have happened if Israel's tribal confederacy had honored Yahweh as their king? And what would have happened had Israel received Him when He became incarnate?

Let's think about the "unanticipated expanded revelation" resulting from the Israel's official rejection of Jesus. We know that his death established the legal basis for the New Covenant.[32] But is that all? What about its effect on believers who died before this ratification? What about its relationship to the myriad of Gentiles who have believed and are not comprehensively addressed in any

---

[32] See summary of Cone's discussion at the beginning of this chapter.

of Israel's covenants with God? Instead of trying to reinterpret the human parties of the New Covenant to get "coverage" (thereby breaking the contractual structure and its associated hermeneutic), why not admit that the crucifixion's redemptive work extended beyond the nation Israel as part of the Abrahamic covenant's global strategy clause (Gen. 12:2) and thus *beyond the New Covenant's national scope*?

There's an easy-to-understand physical example of this notion of unexpected expansion of God's work beyond the scope of a contract. At the inauguration of the Noahic covenant, God made promises to uphold limits on terrestrial geophysical processes (Gen 8:21-22; 9:10-16). However, creation is a designed unit; causing a local effect at given point in time ultimately causes effects throughout creation at all subsequent points in time. To uphold His promises to postdiluvian civilization on planet earth, God had to control every extra-terrestrial physical process affecting the earth's geophysics, viz., processes of solar system, constellation, nebula, etc. Were these entities specified parties to the Noahic covenant? Was upholding a distant constellation in a far off nebula part of the covenant's stipulations? Is there some sort of "discontinuity" problem between the covenant with those on planet earth and the surprising involvement of all extraterrestrial creation? Here's the point: ratifying the Noahic covenant *did more, to more, of creation than what appears in the contract language.*[33]

There's more to this theme of unanticipated expansion of God's work in response to Israel's rejection of Jesus Christ than just His crucifixion. There's His resurrection that created the first immortal physical component of the eternal state. There's His ascension and session that placed a human being permanently at the helm of the universe. And there's the Pentecost event that confirmed Jesus' authority within the Trinity and initiated a new kind of believing community, viz., His "body," the Church. In the next chapter we will delve into some of the implications of these momentous events, but now, using the background discussion so far, we consider the New Covenant as we've traced it in the Old Testament, as a contract between God and Israel, and its relation to the newly-created entity, the Church.

As Cone has shown, dispensationalists have held to at least three views in this matter. He has argued that the MC and SCMP views require inconsistencies in applying the literal grammatical-historical hermeneutic. In trying to account for some apparent similarities in New Covenant promises with post-Pentecost revelation of the Church, proponents of these two views connect them. The forgiveness of sin, circumcision of the heart or regeneration, and the indwelling of the Holy Spirit occur in the

---

[33] For this reason the hermeneutical principle used often by covenant theologians against dispensationalists that the simple Biblical text should interpret the more complex text isn't necessarily true in the case of prophecy. Old Testament passages promising the Messiah did not clarify His two advents brought about by His rejection by Israel as Peter noted in 1 Pet 1:10-11. The two advents of Christ certainly complicated the preparatory role of Elijah not seen in the "simple" text of Malachi 4:5 that predicted the role of Elijah to include restoring the hearts of the nation to avoid the curse. As the angel said in Luke 1:17 and as Christ repeated in Matt 11:14 John the Baptist was "in spirit" Elijah for the first advent. Yet Elijah is to come again prior to the second advent (Matt 17:11). There is always "room" in prophecy for the interplay of true moral choice in response to God's initiatives.

Church, they think, only because of promises in the New Covenant that had been ratified by the death of Jesus.

The problem with these two approaches is that the three supposed similarities turn out either to antedate the New Covenant or to be not so similar upon closer examination. Forgiveness of sins began with Adam, not with the New Covenant. Circumcision of the heart occurred before the New Covenant was revealed. And the indwelling of the Holy Spirit mentioned in the New Covenant probably refers to His indwelling the nation rather than indwelling individuals.[34] It is unnecessary, therefore, to consider these two sets of phenomena as identical. Moreover, to do so alters the contract structure by changing the addressees, ignoring certain stipulations and severing the cause–effect relationship between spiritual enablement and physical blessings

---

[34] In his thorough study of the indwelling of the Holy Spirit James M. Hamilton, Jr. notes concerning Ezekiel's rendition of the new contract ("I will put My spirit within you and cause you to walk in My statutes, and you will keep My judgments and do them") (Ezek. 36:27) that he uses the Hebrew phrase "in your [plural] midst" (*beqirbekem*—translated in the NKJV as "within you"). That terminology, Hamilton argues, would probably "have been understood against the vision of God's glory leaving the temple in Ezekiel 8–11. Not only does this interpretation fit contextually, it also has grammatical probability on its side. Each time this term, which is the equivalent of 'in the midst of you all,' occurs in the Old Testament, it signifies something that is in the midst of the community collectively rather than something that is in the midst of each individual in the community. It would be remarkable if the uses of the form in Ezek. 36:26 and 27 were the lone exceptions to this pattern of usage in the Old Testament," *God's Indwelling Presence: the Holy Spirit in the Old & New Testaments* (Nashville: Broadman and Holman Publishers, 2006), 49.

in the Israel's promised land.[35] Of course, MC and SCMP advocates (and progressive dispensationalists for that matter) don't go so far as to claim the New Covenant is fully operational today. But in so doing they necessarily create a theologically–derived, *interim version of the New Covenant* using a methodology similar if not identical to that of traditional Covenant theology. One wonders if there's an unwitting influence operating here from the common expression, "New Testament," for the Christian canonical Scriptures so New Testament truths are just subliminally considered part of the New Covenant.[36]

With the SCIO view the contract structure of the New Covenant remains intact. The creation of the Church with its numerous positional blessings forms a progressive flow of God's words and works––unanticipated in most of the details–– resulting from Israel's rejection of Christ. This rejection and death of Christ with His subsequent resurrection, ascension and session, while indeed establishing the legal basis for the New Covenant, "did more, to more, of creation than what appears in the contract language" (to quote from the preceding discussion). They lie outside of the Old Testament's New Covenant content while occurring because of its ratification. The New Covenant, Christ and the Church in this view retain their separate identities within the ever advancing plan of God.

---

[35] The addressees shift from Israel to the Church. The stipulations that circumcised hearts would characterize the entire nation Israel and would last to the end of history are thus glossed over. And the linkage between obedience to God and the blessings in the geophysical, biological, and health environment in the land of Israel are disconnected.

[36] George Gunn has pointed how unrecognized preconditioning in loading the term "New Covenant" with Church truths simply from using the New Testament entitled part of the Bible can be highly influential, See Gunn, 43–44.

SOCIO–POLITICAL IMPLICATIONS OF A PRESENTLY FUNCTIONAL NEW COVENANT

Do the MC and SCMP views on one hand and the SCIO view on the other logically affect the Church's interaction with the culture in different ways? If the Church operates under some sort of interim version of the New Covenant, does its cultural role take on similarities with how it operates in the view of traditional Reformed covenant theology? To answer that question a brief but detailed treatment is in order of the lively discussion that occurred within Reformed circles in the 1980s and 1990s concerning the Church and culture. All parties of that discussion viewed the Church as functioning under a theologically-synthesized New Covenant with King Jesus reigning over the earth from "David's throne." Understanding the socio–political ideas discussed and debated within that perspective, therefore, may help us discern the implications of linking the Church to a currently functioning New Covenant.

By the late 1980s at least four distinct socio–political viewpoints had appeared within the American Reformed community: theonomy, principled pluralism, Christian America, and national confessionalism. As editor of a volume dedicated to discussion of these four views, Gary Scott Smith first enumerated the major areas of agreement:

> Christians have a cultural. . .mandate in the world. The task of God's people is not simply to help individuals commit a dimension of their lives to Christ – the spiritual (as opposed to, say, the physical, aesthetic, and psychological dimensions). Christians are called to subdue the earth in God's name and to have dominion over all aspects of life...Christians are God's ambas-sadors...the force He uses to renew the world...With regard to government, Reformed Christians have agreed on several basic principles. Because Jesus is the ascended

King over all creation, all governments are under His authority...Reformed Christians agree that the primary task of government is to insure justice among its citizens...All Christians...have political responsibilities... Christians should seek to challenge other views [of moral sources of law] at the presuppositional level."[37]

He then noted the significant disagreements that emerged among the four views such as:

"What is the nature of the continuity and discontinuity between the Old Testament and the New Testament, especially regarding the Mosaic law?

How does Christ exercise His kingship over the nations?

How may the creedal distinction between the moral, ceremonial, and civil laws of Old Testament Israel be applied to contemporary political life?

To what extent should the state tolerate the practice and promulgation of non–Christian world views and religious confessions?[38]

Of the four views the Christian reconstructionist/ theonomic view was the most published and influential. So around the same time of the Smith volume, the faculties of Westminster Theological Seminaries in Philadelphia and in California responded to the theonomic claim that it was the real guardian of the Westminster Creed. The editors of their published response summarized the leading characteristics of the theonomic concept of Christian reconstructionism:

---

[37]Gary Scott Smith, ed., *God and Politics: Four Views on the Reformation of Civil Government* (Phillipsburg, NJ: Presbyterian and Reformed Pub. Co., 1989), 11–13.

[38] Ibid., 286.

[There is] an emphasis on the Old Testament law; stress on the continued normativity not only of the moral law but also of the judicial law of Old Testament Israel, including its penal sanctions; and belief that the Old Testament judicial law applies not only to Israel, but also to Gentile nations, including modern America, so that it is the duty of the civil government to enforce that law and execute its penalties.   Christian reconstruction hence has the appeal of claiming to apply Biblical principles to contemporary society in a way that will express the dominion of Christ.   Usually, Christian reconstruction is characterized by a postmillennial eschatology.[39]

The concern of the Reformed faculties was two-fold. First, the theonomic approach in its treatment of civil law departed from the historic Westminster Confession which stated in Chapter XIX, 4 that to Israel "as a body politic, He gave sundry judicial laws, which expired together with the State of that people; not obliging any other now, further than the general equity thereof may require." Theonomy advocates had seemed to

---

[39] William S. Barker and W. Robert Godfrey, ed., "Preface," *Theonomy: A Reformed Critique*, ed. (Grand Rapids, MI: Zondervan, 1990), 9–10.

disregard this "expiration" clause.[40] Second, by 1990 the growing popularity of theonomy among Reformed laity, who saw in theonomy a blueprint to cope with cultural deterioration, was becoming disruptive in claiming to be the only Scriptural view of cultural interaction. The Westminster volume argued that Christians ought to press for social regulations that implement the general equity observed in the Mosaic code but must recognize that we live outside of ancient and theocratic Israel and so cannot apply the details of civil case law to our modern pluralistic society.   Specifically, civil rulers are not to enforce Biblical penology.

The Westminster critique in turn inspired a detailed and sharp theonomic rejoinder. At least three key questions emerged during the interchange: (1) what is the *proper methodology of extracting God's justice for society at large from the Bible*--is it merely relying upon generic equity principles observed in the Mosaic code and elsewhere, or is it to be seen by exegesis of case-law details which have not expired but continue in force for all nations? (2) what is the *proper goal of socio-political transformation of a state of believers and unbelievers*--a pluralistic tolerance of all religious viewpoints or an official subordination of the state to King Jesus? and (3) what is the *proper motivation for Christian socio-political action* - is loyalty to God's ethical

---

[40] Historical theology professor Sinclair Ferguson pointed out that the term theonomy had always been understood in a comprehensive either-or sense as in "theonomy vs. autonomy" referring to the only two possible ultimate authorities, God or man. However, the new use of the term had become far more narrowly focused upon Mosaic case law and penology. He notes, "The Westminster Divines chose their emphasis and wording for Chapter XIX with great care, for by the time of the Westminster Assembly, the issue of the continuing validity of the Mosaic civil laws had been widely discussed for more than a century....Theoretical theonomy as such is not the teaching of the Westminster Confession of Faith.," Sinclair Ferguson, "An Assembly of Theonomists? The Teaching of the Westminster Divines on the Law of God," Ibid., 327, 348.

standards sufficient, or does it also require the hope of continual progress toward the goal of maximum transformation (i.e., postmillennialism)?

The first question centers on general equity and specific case-law. At issue is the authority of Mosaic case law today. Bahnsen, who had written the major apologetic for theonomy, *Theonomy in Christian Ethics* in 1977, argued on the basis of Matthew 5:17–18 ("...one jot or one tittle will by no means pass from the law till all is fulfilled"–NKJ) that all details of Mosaic case law remain authoritative for everyone unless they are explicitly modified by New Testament revelation. The logic appears straightforward: God is righteous and immutable; He revealed His righteousness in the Mosaic law; therefore the law must apply to all men for all time. The problem here, pointed out by Waltke, is that Bahnsen allowed abrogation of ceremonial laws and "fails to realize...that his concessions undermine his thesis. Jesus cannot be establishing every jot and tittle of the law...and at the same time abrogate some of its laws."[41] Bahnsen also conceded that when it came to applying case law details to modern society, theonomists disagreed among themselves.[42] This concession prompted John Frame to comment that neither the theonomist view of case law nor the non–theonomist view "taken in itself,

---

[41] Bruce K. Waltke, "Theonomy in Relation to Dispensational and Covenant Theologies," Ibid., 81.

[42] Bahnsen distinguished his work as presenting the "underlying theonomic orientation" from attempts by R. J. Rushdoony, Gary North, and James Jordan to "interpret and apply the details"––an area that "leaves much room for controversy and disagreement" and adds that "at a number of places I myself cannot agree with the exegesis or reasoning attempted in them," Greg L. Bahnsen, "The Theonomic Position," *God and Politics*, 23 footnote 5.

requires or forbids the continuing normativity of any Biblical law. That question must be answered by exegesis of individual texts."[43]

Bahnsen responded by repeating his major point that in light of Matthew 5:17-19, one cannot argue from New Testament silence on moral imperatives of the Mosaic law that they have been rescinded (Lev 20:15). His example: the New Testament nowhere deals with bestiality, but this silence doesn't mean Old Testament prohibition and punishment is done away. The burden of proof, therefore, lies with the non-theonomist who claims that a particular case law has no abiding authority. "The appeal to silence as a tool of abrogation is *selective* and *arbitrary*" [Emphasis original].[44] As this exchange shows, central to the matter of applying Mosaic case law was the matter of *penology*. Without sanctions, imperatives have no force, and without accepting details of the Biblical text there can be no sanctions. In particular which crimes warrant capital punishment? Some theonomists like Gary North insist that Mosaic capital punishment sanctions ought to be in force today:

> The most widely shared Christian myth of our era [is] that Jesus Christ abolished the civil sanctions that the Trinitarian God established in Israel...The capital sanctions established by God in Old Covenant Israel were to serve as public warnings - pledges - of what would take place when the criminal's soul was transferred by an act of the civil government - execution - into God's court of primary jurisdiction.[45]

---

[43] John M. Frame, "The One, The Many, and Theonomy," *Theonomy: A Reformed Critique*, 97.

[44] Greg L. Bahnsen, "Westminster Seminary on Penology," Gary North, ed., *Theonomy: An Informed Response* (Tyler, TX: Institute for Christian Economics, 1991), 122.

[45] "Editor's Conclusion," Ibid., 319.

Though he cited New England Puritans as examples of invoking Mosaic penology, North did not interact with then Westminster Professor of Church history Samuel Logan, Jr., who had addressed the Puritan use of Mosaic law in the prior Westminster volume. Logan showed that it took Massachusetts Bay Colony eighteen years to establish their law code. "If Winthrop and the other magistrates had been absolutely sure what the laws should be, the process would certainly have been much quicker. . . .The Mosaic judicial law was directly relevant to Massachusetts Bay, but the circumstances within which the colony found itself demanded a flexible appropriation of that Mosaic law."[46]

The first key question – what is the proper *methodology* of extracting God's justice for society at large from the Bible – was thoroughly discussed during those years and given a spectrum of answers from adaption of general principles of equity within the whole Bible to a detailed casuistic study of specific Mosaic case-law texts. All the answers assumed that Jesus now reigns via the theologically–constructed New Covenant over all nations. The gospel thus calls rulers everywhere to recognize Jesus' present reign by implementing Biblical policies as soon as possible. In nations like the United States where citizens share in political rule each citizen is included in this call.

Whereas the debate over the first key question resulted in consideration of political details like the troublesome matter of penology, the second question – what is the proper *goal* of socio-political transformation of a state of believers and unbelievers – necessarily raised a second troublesome matter: *religious pluralism.* The issue had earlier been discussed in *God and Politics* where, of the four views, only Spykman had argued for an enduring confessional pluralism that "refers to the right of the various religious groups that make up a society to...promote their views" as compatible with a program of reclaiming "every sphere

---

[46] Samuel T. Logan, Jr., "New England Puritans and the State," *Theonomy: A Reformed Critique*, 378–379.

of life for the King."[47] Carson in response admitted that the other three non-pluralist views were not politically viable in the US presently: "whatever our goals and hopes for the future, we cannot now simply elect to have a national confession, a Christian America, or a theonomic society...[Confessional pluralism] is attractive for historical reasons.   The results of the exercise of political power by Christians have often been frightening."[48] Nevertheless he questioned "how can one reclaim all of life for Christ and still recognize the rights of all faiths?...Can a pluralist model handle the wide differences in a heterogeneous society like our own?[49] He also had to admit that pluralism isn't Biblical; it is not the proper goal of society. Although pluralism is unavoidable now, Carson called for Christians "to persuade Americans to submit to the sovereignty of Jesus Christ over our nation."[50]

In response to this earlier advocacy of pluralism Bahnsen had noted that the discussion showed that three of the four views – theonomy, national confessionalism, and Christian America – shared the same general political theory. Pluralism was the outlier, he said, that violated "the Biblical demand that all the kings and judges of the earth 'serve Jehovah' specifically (Ps. 2:10-11)...[and] is logically impossible. When one religious philosophy requires the death penalty for murder and another forbids the death penalty for murder, the state cannot conceivably give 'equal protection' to both viewpoints...As faithful disciples of the Lord, we must urge the state to base its sanctions and policies

---

[47] Gordon J. Spykman, "The Principled Pluralist Position," *God and Politics*, 79.

[48] David M. Carson, "The National Confessional Response to Principled Pluralism," Ibid., 115, 117.

[49] Ibid., 118.

[50] Ibid., 120.

upon the one and only sound moral perspective, the one revealed by Christ--not some blend of 'plural' religious views...[51]

In the Westminster-Theonomy exchange the pluralism discussion surfaced again. Westminster faculty member Barker insisted that pluralism of religious belief was God's will for this time in history. He noted that as the gospel began to reach outward into Gentile nations, "all that missionaries could rightly ask of civil authority was the freedom to preach the Gospel so that people might be freely persuaded by the word and by the Spirit. To have the state in any way coerce belief or worship could only compromise the free nature of the Gospel..."[52] To the theonomic appeal to Old Testament Gentile kings who publicly acknowledged the God of Israel, Barker pointed out that neither Nebuchadnezzar nor Darius "destroyed the other religions as the civil ruler was required to do in God's covenant nation" (cf. Dan 4:2,37 and Dan 4:8). He further argued that Jesus' exchange with the Pharisees over paying the poll tax in Matthew 22:15-22 shows that "*in the New Testament situation, under a Gentile regime, [Jesus] did not expect the civil authority to support the true religion*" [emphasis original].[53]   Asking civil authority merely for the freedom to pursue the missionary mandate is the intention of King Jesus today. The standard to which we must appeal for political policy in a mixed society is conscience and natural [general] revelation, done so, however, with our knowledge of special revelation.[54]

---

[51] Greg L. Bahnsen, "The Thenomic Major Response," *God and Politics*, 246.

[52] William S. Barker, "Theonomy, Pluralism, and the Bible," *Theonomy: A Reformed Critique*, 238.

[53] Ibid., 236.

[54] Ibid., 240.

To this Westminster-supported pluralism Bahnsen responded that Westminster seminary (Philadelphia) had departed from the vision of its founder, J. Gresham Machen who had insisted that every country on earth should be subject to God's law. Machen's position was shown in his political opposition to the state monopoly on education, even testifying to such before Congress.[55] Specifically addressing Barker, Bahnsen countered that Jesus' distinction between God and Caesar during the coin incident merely referred to the age-old distinction in function between king and priest, not between two standards of ultimate authority. Since no pluralist can advocate "a completely open religious toleration...The real question is where and how we morally ought to draw the line. Theonomists believe that this – like all other moral questions – must be answered according to Biblical instruction."[56]

Bahnsen thus claimed that pluralism cannot consistently be advocated by a Christian conception of the state. Either anything goes, which all agree is intolerable, or some ethical restraint is eventually imposed which is either some sort of natural law or Biblical law. If natural law, it is subject to unbelieving suppression of general revelation within and around man (Rom 1:18–32). But such suppression needs to be corrected by special revelation which, when done, simply uncovers the moral guidelines of general revelation that all along mirror those

---

[55] Bahnsen cites sources of Machen's quotes during the 1920s and 1930s like the following: "A monopolistic system of education controlled by the State is far more efficient in crushing our liberty than the cruder weapons of fire and sword. . . .If liberty is not maintained with regard to education, there is no use trying to maintain it in any other sphere. If you give bureaucrats the children, you might as well give them everything else," "Westminster Seminary on Pluralism," *Theonomy: An Informed Response*, 94.

[56] Greg L. Bahnsen, Ibid., 98n18.

of special revelation. How then, he asks, can Bible-believing Christians argue for religious pluralism as a civil policy?

Thus the debate involving the second key question – what is the proper *goal* of socio-political transformation of a state of believers and unbelievers – exposed significant differences over what degree of transformation is to be expected, ranging from an enduring pluralism to a formal state allegiance to King Jesus. To sustain this effort at transforming culture proper *motivation* is needed. A third key question arose, therefore, during the years of the 1980s and 1990s. Is loyalty to the ethical demands of the presently-reigning King Jesus sufficient, or is an eschatology of continual progress toward the goal of maximum transformation also necessary (i.e., postmillenialism)?

The Westminster response to theonomy noted that postmillennialism has usually characterized the theonomic/ reconstructionist community. Gaffin wrote that essential to theonomy was a revival of postmillennialism that had occurred "almost entirely within the English-speaking, especially American, Reformed community" and nowhere else in the world whether in Reformed or non-Reformed circles.[57] As an advocate of "realized millennialism" Gaffin opposed both postmillennialism and premillennialism as forms of chiliasm that shift "the eschatological center of gravity into the future" and away from the church era under the present reign of King Jesus.[58] The end result, he pointed out, is that postmillennial triumphalism undermines

---

[57] Richard B. Gaffin, Jr., "Theonomy and Eschatology: Reflections on Postmillennialism," *Theonomy: A Reformed Critique*, 197.

[58] Ibid., 206.

the New Testament teachings of the present suffering service of the Church and of the imminent expectation of Christ's return.[59]

Concern over postmillennialism was also expressed in *God and Politics* by Harrington who held to a political philosophy akin to theonomy but was clearly annoyed by the idea that postmillennialism was a motivational necessity:

> Basing theonomy on postmillennialism...is a constant irritant...Those who are not postmillennialists, but who fervently believe in the ethical demands of Christ upon men and nations, are not happy when they are sneeringly referred to as 'pessimillennialists' by a number of theonomists...Theonomists, having rid themselves of natural theology and natural ethics, ought also to rid themselves of natural psychology. Christians are motivated by something other than an expectation of temporal success.[60]

He thus accused theonomists of choosing postmillennialism for purely psychological reasons.

In his rejoinders in both *God and Politics* and *Theonomy: An Informed Response* Bahnsen clarified this issue of motivation.

---

[59] Discussing Romans 8:18ff, Gaffin writes, "The notion that this frustration factor will be demonstrably reduced, and the church's suffering service noticeably alleviated. . .in a future era before Christ's return is not merely foreign to this passage; it trivializes as well as blurs both the present suffering and future hope/glory in view. . . .Whatever has happened to this theology of the cross in much of contemporary postmillennialism?. . . .Postmillennialism deprives the church of the imminent expectation of Christ's return and so undermines the quality of watchfulness that is incumbent on the church." Ibid., 214–215, 216, 218.

[60] H. B. Harrington, "The National Confessional Response to Theonomy," *God and Politics*, 71.

He argued that ethics apart from eschatology would be sufficient motivation:

> One's *eschatological* (especially millennial) interpretation has no logical bearing upon the *ethical* aspect of the present, unconsummated kingdom. We should agree that men, including their political leaders, *ought* to submit obediently to the will of Jesus Christ, regardless of our differing views about *whether* (or when) many will do so or not.[Emphasis original][61]

At another place he wrote:

> Theonomists of all eschatological convictions would confess that the ultimate social state 'wherein righteousness dwells' lies beyond the present age of history...Christ's present kingdom is the world, in which there shall always be a mixture of wheat and tares (Matt 13:36–43). The 'sons of the evil One' and all 'things causing inequity' will not be removed until 'the end of the world,' Until that time, our aim is to let the light of Jesus Christ and His Word dispel *as much as possible* the darkness of our rebellious world.[Emphasis original][62]

This was his reply to Gaffin's warning about nascent triumphalism within theonomy.

Over the ensuing years since these debates the bulk of theonomic publishing has shifted from Gary North's Institute for Christian Economics to Gary DeMar's American Vision. Both North and DeMar are much less tolerant eschatologically than

---

[61] Greg L. Bahnsen, "The Theonomic Position," Ibid., 28fn10.

[62] Greg L. Bahnsen, "Westminster Seminary on Pluralism," *Theonomy: An Informed Response* 104–105.

Bahnsen.[63] American Vision regularly publishes books and videos that vilify dispensationalism – most of the time with very little understanding of it. Obviously DeMar and his staff think postmillennialism is needed for psychological reasons to motivate Biblical transformation of the culture.

This decades-old, but very thorough, Reformed discussion illuminated three key questions that every believer who is concerned with the Church's interaction with culture needs to ask: (1) what *methodology* should we use in obtaining our view of God's justice for human society? (2) what ought to be the *goal* of any socio-political efforts at transformation of culture? and (3) what ought to be our *motivation* in cultural interaction? The various answers given to these questions, of course, all came out of the view that we are now under the New Covenant and are establishing Christ's kingdom on earth. As dispensationalists living in the rapidly-deteriorating Western culture, we can be thankful for the great effort that our Covenant theology brethren have devoted to thinking through the task of how to respond. We, too, must do the same.

Most dispensationalist discussion of the New Covenant has been exegetical and theological but not involved with the socio-political implications.[64] We need to ask what the MC and SCMP (and progressive 'already/not yet') dispensational views of the New Covenant imply concerning the socio-political role of the

---

[63] Gary North wrote of Bahnsen, "We in Tyler are nervous about [his position's] self-conscious separation of theonomy (ethics) from postmillennialism." "Stones and Cornerstones in Christian Reconstruction," *Christian Reconstruction*, March–April 1988, 2.

[64] Thus ex-dispensationalist Bruce K. Waltke complained that dispensationalism is indifferent to the lordship of Christ over society and pointed to "its failure to address the questions of church-state relationships and of the ethical principles that ought to guide the state," in "Theonomy in Relationship to Dispensational and Covenant Theologies," *Theonomy: A Reformed Critique,* 66.

Church. Under the various proposed interim New Covenant arrangements what is Christ now doing? If He is on David's throne and implementing His kingdom now, do we concentrate on mining Scripture for installing Biblically–just policies in society at large to reflect that reign? How far should this effort go in challenging pluralist policies? Should our motivation as premillennialists simply be loyalty to the King?

If Christ is not ruling from David's throne, yet some sort of interim New Covenant is functioning, how are the righteous standards of the Mosaic covenant – which are supposed to be fulfilled *society–wide* under the New Covenant – to be applied and to which culture?   Where? As a local concentration of believers grows when, if ever, should pluralism be challenged? If this sort of interim New Covenant cannot answer these questions, it would seem to be a useless concept without practical effect.

SOCIO–POLITICAL IMPLICATIONS OF THE SINGLE–COVENANT ISRAEL ONLY (SCIO) VIEW

The Single–Covenant Israel Only (SCIO) View preserves the New Covenant contractual format as given in the Old Testament. The nation Israel remains as the sole human party to the contract. Contract terminology retains its original meaning. No attempt is made to invent a new version. Therefore, it cannot now be functioning, and the Church is not under it. This state of affairs at once simplifies discussion of the Church's place in world culture and at the same time allows us to benefit from previous discussions like those that have occurred within the Reformed Covenant community.

If the Church's positional blessings are not received through the New Covenant, they must come directly from union with Christ and thus follow from the global aspect of the Abrahamic Covenant as Cone has shown. Christ's position at the Father's right hand resulting from the crucifixion, resurrection, ascension and session involves work unanticipated by New

Covenant terminology and on a far larger scale. The sending of the Holy Spirit to indwell the Church as a result of Christ's subsequent request to the Father validated His standing within the Trinity (John 14:16–17; 16:7; Acts 2). His present reign is that of a divine–human being at the helm of the universe over not only mankind but also over the invisible world (Matt 28:18; 1 Cor 15:24–28). It is a *cosmic* reign involving far more than what was envisioned in the Old Testament prophecies concerning the Davidic dynasty as I will suggest in the following chapter.

The post–Pentecostal imagery of the Church is not that of a king and a domain governed by contracts and treaties. It is overwhelmingly that of a Body (e.g., Rom 12:4–5; 1 Cor 10:17; 12:12–27; Eph 1:22–23; 2:16; 3:6; 4:4–16; Col 1:18–24). And this body metaphor, like all Biblical metaphors, isn't an arbitrary literary choice by the writer. It deliberately points to the phenomenal structure of the human body thoughtfully designed and created in advance as an analog to this spiritual union of believers with Christ. As the union of vine and branches in Jesus' vine metaphor in John 15, there is a systemic communion within the body that operates more deeply than just the self-conscious interaction between a king and his subjects. Perhaps Paul was led to think in these terms by Jesus' remark on the road to Damascus that by persecuting Christians Paul was actually persecuting Him even though He was physically absent (Acts 9:4).

Another important image of the Church is that of a temple (1 Cor 3:16–17; Eph 2:21). As that part of the Body of Christ on earth the Church is Christ's presence amidst all people groups. That presence is *spatially limited* just as Yahweh's presence was spatially located in the Old Testament tabernacle, Temple and elsewhere (e.g., Eden, Bethel, Sinai). These locations were "sacred spaces" designated by God for face-to-face meetings with man.[65]

---

[65] See the discussion on sacred spaces in Eugene H. Merrill, *Everlasting Dominion: A Theology of the Old Testament* (Nashville, TN: Broadman & Holman Publishers, 2006), 281–292, 351–59, 452–454.

As finite spaces they obviously must be distinguished from His omnipresence. In this dispensation the Church as Christ's presence – as His meeting place (with unbelievers 'outside' in need of the gospel and believers 'inside' in need of sanctification) – demarks the boundaries of His redemptive work. Instead, therefore, of a vaguely defined kingly reign over all nations through some sort of theologically–constructed New Covenant, we have sharply defined spatial areas within socio–political entities where He "lives." The issue of transformation of culture now focuses upon the effects of Christ's immanent presence in the Church upon the cultural environment of its locations and not merely upon the transcendent providential administration of history from His seat within the Trinity.

How does this perspective of the Church's union with Christ view cultural transformation? Let's start with Jesus' model as the apostle John urges us to do: "He who says he abides in Him ought himself also to walk just as He walked" (1 John 2:6 NKJ). How did Jesus walk? He walked in occupied Israel under Gentile domination, and He offered the kingdom if they would accept Him. What were His priorities? His calling was "to save His people from their sins" as "the Lamb of God" (Matt 1:21; John 1:29). Thus He affirmed that He came "to seek and to save that which was lost" (Luke 19:10). While he did heal and feed people, these efforts were quite limited and subordinated to His first priority.[66] This consistent subordination to His Father's calling modeled true humility as the cardinal virtue in stunning contrast

---

[66] Jesus clearly was careful not to compromise His agenda of gaining peoples' trust in Himself as Messiah by His efforts at social welfare. Note His response to those whom He had fed: "You seek Me, not because you saw signs, but because you ate of the loaves, and were filled" (John 6:26 NKJ). As Ryrie concluded: "The Lord gave top priority to spiritual needs. Though sensitive to physical needs, He met relatively few of them. Though always obedient to government, He led no attempt to reform the system or correct injustices." Charles C. Ryrie, *The Christian and Social Responsibility* (Ft Worth, TX: Tyndale Seminary Press, 2008), 61.

to the chief pagan virtue of hubris (Phil 2:5–8). Ironically, however, His seemingly passive behavior has left a centuries–long record of significant cultural transformation unmatched by anyone else.[67]

This historic cultural transformation came about through His presence in the Church. And how was that implemented? He sent the Holy Spirit who had been "in" Him while He was physically present "among" the disciples so that the Holy Spirit would now be "in" His disciples and thus "among" mankind wherever Christians might be (John 14:17). The Old Testament divine presence in the tabernacle and temple thus came again in Christ (John 1:14) and after that in His Body, the Church (John 14:23). Yet we must remember that this past socio–political impact did not come easily. Just as Israel overwhelmingly resisted Christ's kingdom offer, so the world at large resists Him as Savior and Judge. Luke's history in the book of Acts provides many examples of debate, angry mobs, imprisonments and physical assaults as the apostle Paul confronted the culture with the absolute claim that God "has appointed a day on which He will judge the world in righteousness by the Man whom He has ordained. He has given assurance of this to all by raising Him from the dead" (Acts 17:31 NKJ). Having learned at the feet of Jesus, John warns us that the whole world "lies under the sway of the wicked one," that it "does not know us, because it did not know Him," and that it "hates us" (1 John 5:19b; 3:1,13 NKJ). The presence of God's sacred space in the fallen world always provokes conflict – especially so since the day when religious exclusivism began with the Abrahamic covenant, an exclusivism which continues right up to the present moment (John 14:6; Acts 4:12).

---

[67] Numerous books tell of his unprecedented effect on world culture. See, for example, Bruce Bickel and Stan Jantz, *Why Jesus Matters: The Impact of One Extraordinary Life* (Uhrichsville, OH: Barbour Pub. Co., 2003).

So, if instead of functioning under Jesus reigning in *absentia* as King from David's throne according to New Covenant stipulations, the Church functions as the Body of Christ in union with Him and as God's temple or sacred space on earth, how does transformation of culture take place? Well, no man is an island; everyone necessarily interacts with other people. By virtue of creation structures such as ordinary verbal communication, labor with its economic exchanges involving value choices, marriage and family with its life-producing and educational activities, Christians in all ages have always had some impact on their social environment. It is precisely these ordinary life activities that create credibility and inquisitiveness for the gospel (e.g., 1 Pet 3:1-2, 14-16). Robbins has called our attention to how politically powerless Christians changed foundational concepts of pagan Roman culture. Addressing *political theory*, he writes,

> Christ founded a church whose government is representative and republican, whose officers are elected by the people, and whose constitution – the Bible – is written...The early Christians, condemned by pagans such as Celsus and Porphyry as stupid, foolish, and super-stitious, were not killed for their stupidity, but because they rejected the highest value of pagan society: worship of the state in the person of the Emperor...[68]

Addressing the *value and responsibility of man*, he writes,

> Christ taught that man is a creature of God and the lord of creation...what [men] believe and do on Earth will have eternal consequences...The classes and nations of ancient society – the nobles, the proletariat, the slaves, the

---

[68] John W. Robbins, *Christ and Civilization* (Unicoi, TN: The Trinity Foundation, 2003), 25.

citizens, the men, the women, the Jews, the barbarians –
mean nothing to God....[69]

Addressing *social welfare* and *education*, he writes, "The early
Christians rescued thousands of children discarded by the
pagans...Christianity...made theological and moral knowledge and
teaching...available to all."[70]   This all was accomplished with
neither political power nor postmillennial motivation.

That was then, but during the last three or four centuries
ordinary Christians have gained political capacities beyond
anything experienced by the early Christians in the Roman
Empire. We now have citizenship responsibilities for influencing
the ethical standards that determine our social and political lives.
We must point out here that, contrary to the repeated charge of
political indifference against dispensational premillennialists by
church historians like Mark Noll and most covenant theologians,
dispensationalist leaders have publicly argued for Christian

---

[69] Ibid., 26.

[70] Ibid., 19.

involvement in civil affairs for many years.[71]   To fulfill those responsibilities now, however, it would be wise to think about our answers to those three key questions of the relatively recent discussion within Reformed circles.

The first question is how to extract clear notions of God's just order for society from the Bible.   Theonomists can be thanked for raising the issue of going to the specific content in the Mosaic case–law for information.   After all, that is precisely the Scripture that shows God's will for an actual national society that He ruled as His Kingdom.   It clearly states that outside observers can recognize in its statutes and judgments the qualities of righteousness and wisdom (Deut 4:6–8).   In a somewhat similar manner theonomists have done for socio–political involvement

---

[71] See the repeated claim in Mark Noll, *The Scandal of the Evangelical Mind* (Grand Rapids: William B. Eerdmans Publishing Co., 1994). What he and others of like–mind ignore is the clear socio–political involvement of dispensational premillennialists such as that documented in Jim Owen, *The Hidden History of Historic Fundamentalists, 1933–1948* (Lanham, MD: University Press of America, 2004). Owen uses original source documents to show how dispensationalists correctly identified the threats of communist/ socialist ideas and of Nazi anti–Semitism long before they were acknowledged by mainstream culture and how they had organized relief efforts for those afflicted well in advance of government–sponsored efforts. They also within a few years of the implementation of New Deal policies correctly identified its threats to individual liberty and had undertaken efforts to relieve the economic suffering of the Depression on a deeply personal level. Owen cites Dr. James Congdon's talk on "Christian Patriotism" in 1936 to the student body of Moody Bible Institute in which he criticized evangelical neglect of citizenship duties as much as he did participation in left–wing Social Gospel action groups. He also reports on similar published statements by Paul Rood, president of Biola in 1936 and editor of *The King's Business* (see pages 82–83). The argument that lack of political involvement by some dispensationalists proves a flaw in their theology is no more valid than the argument that because some Reformed Christians don't share Christ with their neighbors, their theology of salvation is defective. In both examples the problem isn't their theology; it's lack of personal growth.

what creationists have done for cosmogony, and both have been ridiculed by the same evangelical accommodationists. The basic conclusion of their interaction with non-theonomists was that detailed exegesis of specific texts is needed to which all who seek His will agree.[72] The exegetical struggle involves extracting the unchanging moral elements from the ceremonial elements and then transferring from ancient Israel's circumstance to the present situation – no easy job as Bahnsen has admitted.

Use of the Mosaic covenant for defining social justice quickly raised the controversial issue of penology, specifically the many uses of capital punishment. Reformed and non Reformed critics of theonomy have usually resisted invoking these sanctions today presumably due to concerns that it represents "cruel and unusual punishment." However, it is likely that actual capital punishment was not very common in theocratic Israel since the rules of evidence, requiring two or more eyewitnesses (e.g., Deut 17:6-7), were far more strict than those that allow circumstantial evidence for indictment in capital cases today.[73] Yet, if the Mosaic covenant really was the local expression of God's social justice, then its sanctions can't be arbitrarily abrogated. If one takes the strict interpretation of the New Covenant followed here, that covenant was designed to empower the elect nation to live as the Kingdom of God under the future, direct, physical presence of God

---

[72] See footnote 42. One can observe why exegesis of Mosaic law is so important in the exchange concerning economic justice between theonomist Gary North who cited specific texts in context and non-theonomists who argued on the basis of abstract equity mixed with New Testament personal ethics in *Wealth and Poverty*, ed. Robert G. Clouse (Downers Grove, IL: InterVarsity Press, 1984).

[73] See the account of the famous Bloodsworth case in which a former Marine was sentenced to death on the basis of circumstantial evidence for the rape-murder of a nine-year old girl but years later DNA evidence exonerated him at Northwestern University School of Law's legal database online at: http://www.law.northwestern.edu/ wrongfulconvictions/exonerations/mdBloodsworthSummary.html.

beginning with King Jesus' return. All statutes with their corresponding sanctions (the legislative component) and administration (executive and judicial components) should then immediately come into effect as an integrated governing system at His future inauguration just as they did at Sinai and Moab (Deut 5:2; 29:1). Covenant theology gets into an internal debate over penology not only because of the exegetical difficulties in extracting universal moral principles and translating them for today. It also has to deal with the practical problem of how to implement the relevant sanctions with their related statutes piecemeal by persuasion in different societies with different governmental organizations at different times without the King present to assume authoritative, comprehensive and capable leadership. And, as the next chapter will show, there is the matter of the invisible powers and principalities as well as man's synergistic relationship with his geophysical environment.

With the New Covenant installed, but not yet functioning, the dispensationalist SCIO perspective clearly sees Jesus in *absentia* today growing His Body in preparation for His kingdom. Those relevant sanctions and their related statutes as part of an integrated civil rule in the physical presence of the King, while temporarily held in abeyance to be re-implemented in the Millennial Kingdom, provide *an enduring and sobering view of what true social justice under God looks like.* Instead of trying to modify them or apologize for them, we ought to decisively affirm them as God's evaluation of the specific behaviors listed as capital crimes. Those behaviors and the mental attitudes prompting them warrant death in His sight. If we had lived in the theocracy and participated in those behaviors, we could have been stoned to death. We should challenge our contemporaries who casually throw around the term "social justice" too often as political manipulation. We should seriously ask them, "do you want *real* social justice? Take a look at what it is." That is the proper use of the law which Paul employed in his analysis of pagan society (Rom 1:32; 1 Tim 1:8-10). That directly confronts the pagan notion that justice is whatever man's fallen mind happens to imagine with the Biblical truth that justice derives from God's immutable nature as revealed in His Word. The contrast in authority and content between Mosaic case–law that emanated from the transcendent Creator and the laws of ancient Egypt that emanated from the ruling elite still exists.

Rigorous exegesis of Scripture will yield a wealth of truths about the creation design of society. From the creation account one obtains foundational truths of man's conscience, his responsibility for the environment, the necessity of labor and economic value choices in use of private property, the distinct male and female aspects of God's image in man, marriage and family as well as the effect of the fall on each. From the Noahic covenant one obtains the reason for lethal civil power to judge evil (pro–life, not social vengeance). From the Abrahamic covenant one obtains the justification of the exclusive authority of revelation mediated through Israel (i.e., Biblical authority). These are truths universal applicable to all mankind, whether acknowledged or not, and form the context for additional truths available from the Mosaic covenant. From the New Testament one obtains Jesus' model behavior toward society–at–large and the apostles' directives to the Church concerning it. Sufficient revelation, therefore, exists for socio–political policy making in areas as diverse as court proceedings, labor and contract law, economic and education policies, public health regulations, and environmental protection.[74]

The next question we have to answer is with what priority and how far should Christian "citizen–kings" attempt to influence our pluralistic cultural environment? Unquestionably there will always be some influence as the early centuries of Christianity demonstrated. And the centuries since bear testimony to the

---

[74] One can observe even today fragments of Biblical influence on civic policy such as the distinction between murder and homicide and the debt relief in bankruptcy regulations.

influence of the Ten Commandments on Western law from late Rome through Alfred the Great to Blackstone and others.[75] Dispensationalists have pointed out that by building His Body as a step toward eventually bringing about the Kingdom of God, Jesus closely follows the pre–coronation pattern of David (cf. 1 Sam 16– 2 Sam 2). Like David He was chosen by a prophet and proved His qualifications through public actions, but could not yet sit on His throne. Just as David was a fugitive pursued by delegitimized Saul, so Jesus was despised by Israel and now (through His body) is despised by the world that still lies in some sense under the Evil One. Yet just as David gathered the distressed of Israel in the interim, so now Jesus gathers members of His Body one by one though He doesn't rule as David didn't prior to his coronation.[76]

Jesus priority for His Body is the same as He followed while on earth, viz., "to seek and save that which was lost" (Luke 19:10). Although Jesus did heal and feed some of those not His disciples, that work was always subordinated to His first priority since the Kingdom could not come until the nation recognized Him and believed. Likewise, in this era of gracious postponement of the coming Day of the Lord among Gentiles, the priority of His Body is to complete itself so that the Lamb can finally begin the judgments that will bring about the Kingdom (Rev 5). The means of gathering members of the Body, of course, is the gospel, and the gospel as Paul describes it in 1 Corinthians 15:3–8 and as John does in John 20:31 has no reference to socio–political action. That action belongs to post–justification sanctification, not evangelism. Interestingly, however, in order to carry out successful evangelism and missions, there must be a challenge to pluralistic unbelief.

---

[75] John Eidsmoe presents a detailed history of how the Mosaic code has left its mark on the foundations of Western jurisprudence in John Eidsmoe, *Historical and Theological Foundations of Law* (Powder Springs, GA: Telle Lege Press, 2012) 3 vols.

[76] Alva J McClain, *The Greatness of the Kingdom*, 440; Charles C. Ryrie, *Dispensationalism* (Chicago: Moody Press, 1995), 169.

Metaphysically, pagan notions of reality must be replaced with the Creator-creature distinction. Epistemologically and ethically, the subjective authority of the fallen finite mind must be replaced with the divine authority of the Word of God. So it turns out that pluralism is confronted with the age-old exclusivism from Abraham's day. Christian convert after convert experiences his own micro-exodus from a society always facing Hobbesian totalitarianism to a community that knows liberty. Thus *excluding cultural transformation from the gospel does not negate it.*[77]

How far pluralism is challenged and to what degree the culture is transformed depends upon the spiritual state of a society as we will see in the next chapter. In the discussion described above, it will be remembered that few disputants were happy with pluralism as the final end state or even as a Biblically justifiable view of civil government because pluralism is inherently relativistic. However, most, if not all, agreed that in present history it must be tolerated while attempts are made to persuade unbelieving society to accept Jesus' present kingly authority. From a dispensational non-kingdom, Body-centered standpoint there are at least two angles of attack upon relativistic pluralism.

The primary one is evangelism and then sanctification of the individuals who are saved. Any believer who is involved in

---

[77] Jim Owen reports how dispensationalists historically affected US culture primarily through Christian individuals acting as citizens rather than through local churches acting collectively. Collective action during the 1920s and 1930s was done by liberals who as heirs of nineteenth-century postmillennialism added social action to the gospel and made it first priority through the Federal Council of Churches. *The Hidden History of Historic Fundamentalists, 1933-1948* 52, 55-57. A classic answer about dispensational anti-communist political influence during the cold war was given by my former pastor, R. B. Thieme, Jr., to an *Atlantic Monthly* reporter who asked, "Do you tell your people how to vote?" Pastor Thieme replied, "No, I don't tell them how to vote. I teach them Bible doctrine, and they know how to vote!" (I do not possess the issue but remember the cover title: "The Temple of the Super-Patriots").

evangelism or missions or who seeks to conform his living to Biblical imperatives knows very well that he is challenging pluralism.[78] The secondary attack on pluralism is a "pragmatic sell" of social policies to those who have not yet responded to the gospel. Daniel 1 is the model. Daniel put forward a pragmatic appeal to "see what works." Daniel did it to keep pagan folly at bay. We do it for the same reason. Since the real world works best when it is treated according to its design, policies that fit that design should work better than foolish policies, all other things being equal. For example, divorce and fornication violate the in-His-image design of men and women. There are psychological, health, and economic consequences for acting contrary to creation design. Policies, therefore, that reward traditional marriage and impede divorce and fornication should result in lower social costs.[79] Godliness is demonstrably cheaper. Both of these attacks on the relativism of a pluralist culture are free of coercion, give room to the Holy Spirit to convince unbelievers from within, and maintain the commitment to absolute truth.

We've outlined some answers to the first and second key questions from the perspective of the Church as functioning directly in union with Christ in preparation for the complete, fully-installed Kingdom rather than functioning under a New Covenant construct that is somehow gradually bringing in the Kingdom. To the third and last question we now respond. Does

---

[78] As president of the MIT Christian Fellowship during 1961, I was regularly interrogated by the Dean of Students and the Protestant liberal chaplains for our group's challenging of scientific, liberal art, and political ideologies in the classroom and in the dormitories. Relativistic pluralism pushed back!

[79] An excellent documentation of the $112B annual cost to the US taxpayers is the detailed study: Benjamin Scafidi, *The Taxpayer Costs of Divorce and Unwed Childbearing: First-Ever Estimates for the Nation and All Fifty States* (New York, NY: Institute for American Values, 2008) available at www.americanvalues.org.

the motivation for affecting the social and political elements of culture come primarily from one's eschatology or from simple loyalty to God's imperatives?   Bahnsen, it will be remembered, argued that ethics (what ought to be) is not logically related to eschatology (what will be).   Another disputant in *God and Politics* pointed out that requiring postmillennialism for motivation smacks of naturalistic psychology.[80]   However, North, DeMar, and other theonomists insisted, and still do, upon the necessity of the postmillennial hope of continuous progress toward maximum cultural transformation in this age.   Perhaps it is wise to say that as long as an eschatology promises an ultimate ethical resolution to history, it offers sufficient motivation. Premillennial eschatology, while offering hope of ultimate ethical resolution, does not support *irreversible* cultural transformation as will be seen in the next chapter.

The dispensational SCIO view, then, adequately answers the major questions about socio–political involvement without altering the originally prophesied New Covenant. Moreover, by seeing the Church as made possible by Christ's work in ratifying the New Covenant but functioning apart from it, the SCIO view offers straightforward guidance for Christian citizenship responsibilities without altering gospel priorities.

CONCLUSION

This chapter explored the varying socio–political consequences of placing or not placing the Church under some form of the New Covenant so that dispensationalists can respond to the contemporary cultural decline. Reformed Covenant theology traditionally sees the Church operating under a theologically-constructed New Covenant differing in significant details from that prophesied in the Old Testament to Israel. Dispensationalists, however, traditionally try to honor its connection with national

---

[80] See footnote 60.

Israel but do so with varying hermeneutical approaches as analyzed previously by Christopher Cone.[81] Since most discussion of the Church's relation to the New Covenant within dispensational circles has focused only upon exegetical and theological matters, this chapter focused upon the implications for our response as dispensationalists to the re–paganization of America.

Because extensive debate occurred within Reformed circles concerning the Church and culture during the 1980s and 1990s, we surveyed that discussion in order to identify the key questions to answer from the dispensational single–covenant-Israel-only (SCIO) perspective. Subsequent analysis showed that the SCIO view with its consistent hermeneutic maintains a clear picture of the Body of Christ functioning in pagan Gentile nations analogously to how Jesus functioned in Gentile–controlled Israel. This approach avoided modification to the New Covenant promises, avoided tampering with the content and priority of the gospel, yet encouraged usage of revelatory source material for Christian citizenship responsibilities.

What was not discussed is how this dispensational view connects the Church age with the coming full implementation of the New Covenant. What insights can be derived from this perspective for a consistent dispensationalist interaction with culture? That is the subject of the next chapter.

[81] See footnote 1.

10

HISTORICAL PROGRESS WHILE THE NEW COVENANT AWAITS IMPLEMENTATION

Charlie Clough

The usual impression people get from dispensational prophecy charts is that the Church age is a "parenthesis," an interruption in God's progressive movement in history.[1] But is the Church age with its world-wide proclamation of the gospel really only a temporary interruption unrelated to God's prophesied tribulation and millennial kingdom that follow? Yet, if the Church involves a distinct "heavenly people" in contrast to "earthly peoples," where is the unity amid this obvious discontinuity in God's redemptive program? The previous chapter pointed out that the dispensational SCIO view does not recognize the Church as a formal party to the New Covenant but does recognize that the Church resulted from the New Covenant's ratification as part of the largely unanticipated expansion of God's work that followed. Given this position what progress is the Church making to move history along to activate that covenant and thus the Kingdom of God on earth?

---

[1] Diagramming the Church age as a parenthesis, of course, is done from the perspective of God's contractual relationship with His elect nation Israel. In this chapter we will "zoom out" to a larger perspective of His doxological program with all of creation including its visible, invisible, mortal and immortal components.

326   *An Introduction to the New Covenant*

THE PURPOSE OF THIS CHAPTER

The subject of historical progress in God's revelation and redemption covers a vast amount of material. For the purposes of the previous chapter and the present one we will confine attention to answering two questions – one having to do with the present Church age and another having to do with the full implementation of the New Covenant. These questions arise because when one asks for the intended accomplishment of an age or dispensation, one necessarily must relate that dispensation to the next one that follows and then relate both to God's overall strategy. As in the previous chapter we will be looking for the practical implications regarding dispensationalists' interaction with a rapidly declining culture.

The first question looks at just what is being accomplished in the present age. We know that the Church as the Body of Christ is growing into a holy temple in the Lord (Eph 2:21). We know it is in union with Christ (Rom 12:5) and has a heavenly citizenship (Phil 3:20). We've seen in the previous discussion that successful evangelism with proper follow-up will have socio-political consequences. The question, though, goes deeper. Just what is it about the growth of the Body of Christ and its effects in this age that moves history onward to the tribulation and millennial kingdom with its full-orbed New Covenant?

The second question concerns why there should be an age that intervenes between the Church age and the eternal state. If the dispensational SCIO view pushes the functioning New Covenant into a future age other than the eternal state, doesn't that millennial age appear as an anticlimactic follow-on to the Church age? As lofty as Church positional truth is in union with the crucified, resurrected and ascended Christ, wouldn't the only appropriate progress be directly into the new heavens and earth of the eternal state? While this question isn't often raised by dispensationalists, it certainly is raised by its critics. They have endlessly accused dispensational premillennialism of unscientific fantasy and crippling effect on all Christian socio-political impact. Answering it provides an opportunity to show another advantage of the dispensational SCIO view.

JESUS' ASCENT AND SESSION

Each dispensation builds on the preceding one. If the real reason why Jesus hasn't set up His kingdom and inaugurated the New Covenant is Israel's rejection of Him (Matt 23:39), how can it then be said that the Church accomplishes something that is also required before that kingdom can come? Could that "something" be provoking Israel to believe in the Messiah through evangelism? Perhaps that effect of evangelism can be seen with regard to individual Jews today, but prophecy seems clear that it's the suffering of the tribulation or some other historic judgment associated with the second advent that causes Israel's national repentance (Zech 13:8-9; Ezek 20:33-44).[2] And what, after all, ends the Church age and begins the tribulation itself prior to this provocation upon the nation Israel?

I suggest there is another significantly different "something," an accomplishment by the Church, that is also required to usher in the kingdom with its implemented New Covenant. It stems from the work of God that accompanied the New Covenant's ratification but which reached beyond its promised scope. Nowhere in the contractual terminology of the New Covenant is there mention of the Messiah or of His crucifixion, resurrection, ascension, and session. The previous chapter mentioned that similar unanticipated phenomena accompanied ratification of the Noahic covenant – phenomena of vastly bigger scale than mentioned in Genesis 9:9-17 terminology.

---

[2] See the extensive discussion in Arnold G. Fruchtenbaum, *Israelology: The Missing Link in Systematic Theology* (Tustin, CA: Ariel Ministries, 1994), 539-552.

When Christ shed His blood for the New Covenant, He also provided propitiation for the sins of the whole world (1 John 2:2). When He rose from the dead, there came into existence for the first time a human body with the material physics of the new universe.[3] *No other religion or political vision can claim the present existence of the final future.* As John Pilkey observes:

> Wherever it is clearly conceived as a metaphysical reality, resurrection annihilates every premise and every conclusion of the Marxist, Freudian, and Darwinian schools of thought. It erases the premise of Marxism by positing a version of humanity independent of the natural food chain; it cancels the premise of Freudianism by furnishing a degree of vitality so absolute that temporary sexual euphoria loses all meaning; and it destroys the whole point of evolution by bringing mankind to absolute physical perfection in an instant of transformation.[4]

When Jesus disappeared in a cloud during His ascension just east of the Temple before the apostolic witnesses, He showed that His return won't be an imaginary mystical event of speculative theology but will be quite physical and publicly observable (Acts 1:10–11). The unseen remainder of His ascent to the throne of God is revealed in the New Testament as a *journey through multiple heavens to the supreme position over the entire creation* (Eph 1:20–21; Heb 4:14; 1 Pet 3:22).

---

[3] George Eldon Ladd described the resurrection act in these terms: "a piece of the eschatological resurrection has been split off and planted in the midst of history. The first act of the drama of the Last Day has taken place before the Day of the Lord" in his book, *A Theology of the New Testament* (Grand Rapids, MI: William B. Eerdmans Publishing Co., 1974), 326.

[4] John Pilkey, *The Origin of the Nations* (San Diego, CA: Master Book Publishers, 1984), 260.

The complex of events from crucifixion through session, unanticipated in the covenant stipulations though partially foreseen in the prophetic texts, extends the dimensions of God's work far beyond not only Israel but also the empirically-observable universe. The New Testament always speaks of Christ's new position as that of a genuine human at the helm of the universe outranking all angels, elect and fallen. Since man had lived under the invisible world of angelic dominion (Ps 8:4–6 as interpreted by Heb 2:5–9), Jesus's session at the right hand of the Father *radically altered the place of man in the universe.* With the ascension and session, therefore, we come face-to-face with the relation of man to the invisible world. Whereas in the Old Testament one observes occasional glimpses of it (e.g., Job 1–2, 1 Kings 22:17–23; 2 Kings 6:17), no man is ever seen to be over it.

When New Testament writers interpret Jesus' unobserved ascension and session, they draw upon three key Old Testament passages for their imagery: Psalm 2, 110; Daniel 7. In Psalm 2 the Ideal King, the royal Son of God, reigns in victory from geographical Mt. Zion. He is to pray to Yahweh for dominion over all nations so he can "break them with a rod of iron" (Ps 2:8–9). The New Testament uses this imagery to speak of the formal session of Jesus thus identifying Him as the King ("today I have begotten thee" – as in Heb 1:1–5; Phil 2:6–9; Eph 1:20–22). The persecuted Church uses the same imagery to interpret and pray against the opposition of Jewish–Roman civil government (Acts 4:24–30). Some elements of the psalm are analogous to the early Church situation, but there are other elements not analogous. For example, Jesus now rules from heaven, not from literal Mt. Zion. Nor is he globally governing with a "rod of iron." In Psalm 110 the Ideal King fulfills the pre-Israelite Gentile office of king–priest thus nullifying any Israelite provincialism and revealing the global outreach that Israel was called to have in the Abrahamic covenant (Ps 110:4). The New Testament uses this imagery to show Jesus' full acceptance before the Father as a non–Levite priest and His need to wait for eventual global conquest (1 Cor 15:23–28; Heb

10:13; 12:2). Again not all elements are analogous to the Church age: Jesus isn't ruling from Mt. Zion nor is this the Day of God's wrath. In Daniel 7 the Son of Man, obviously representing man in his original position of dominion, is given an everlasting kingdom after the destruction of each of the Gentile empires in the previous visions. The New Testament uses this imagery to show the total authority given to Jesus over both visible and invisible realms (Matt 28:18). The violent destruction of the beast and the sub-human, animal-like empires, however, has not yet occurred.

Jesus' ascent above the clouds and subsequent session in heaven took place beyond empirical observation. The Holy Spirit therefore led New Testament authors to employ elements of Biblical imagery to understand what happened. We learn from their efforts that Jesus now outranks all creatures including the myriads of angelic beings. We also learn that there is an intriguing "waiting period" for the kingdom during which God's enemies are somehow being subdued. Since some of these enemies appear to reside in the invisible realm, we must now consider the nature of what the Bible calls the "cosmos."

THE NATURE OF THE COSMOS

With whatever activities the Church is involved, they take place within the post-session created order. How does the Bible characterize this order, especially as man interacts with it? We first note that according to Jesus' resurrection, ascension, and session, reality is not necessarily what it appears. There is evidently a sort of parallel universe inhabited by angelic beings, dead humans, and the resurrected Jesus. Not only does such a realm exist, but there is cause-effect between it and our physical realm. Under God angelic beings can control biological processes (e.g., 1 Chron 21:14-15), geophysical phenomena (e.g., Rev 7:1), and human intellects (e.g., 1 Kings 22:22). In opposite fashion the unseen world reacts to what happens in our world (e.g., Luke 15:7,10).

Add to this *metaphysical* complexity of contemporary creation, the *ethical* complexity of good and evil introduced by the fall in both the angelic and human realms. New Testament authors use the word "cosmos" to describe what we might consider the post-fall configuration of visible, physical creation that is now aligned with the evil segment of the invisible angelic world. Satan is the now "god of this world" (John 12:31; 14:30; 16:11; 2 Cor 4:4; Eph 2:2). Chafer described the cosmos as: "a vast order or system that Satan has promoted, which conforms to his ideals, aims, and methods. It is a civilization now functioning apart from God."[5] Though the configuration may be evil, the physical creation has many components good in themselves. Food, whether sacrificed to idols or not, is still good to eat (1 Cor 8:4–8). Possessions are not evil in themselves as modern socialists imply. As Ryrie has pointed out,

> [Jesus']circle of friends included well-to-do people like Joseph of Arimathaea (Matthew 27:57), Nicodemus (John 3:1), the centurion of Capernaum (Luke 7:2), the family of Lazarus, Mary and Martha of Bethany (Luke 10:38), and the several women who contributed to His and the disciples' support from their private funds (Luke 8:3). None was condemned for possessing wealth nor expected to redistribute it evenly among fellow Jews.[6]

Paul wrote to the Corinthians to "use (*chraomai*) the cosmos" but not "make full use (*katachraomai*) of it" (1 Cor 7:31), that is, use things with careful discrimination. The apostle John cautions us to use this world's goods in acute situations to help fellow

---

[5] Lewis S. Chafer, *Systematic Theology* (Dallas Theological Seminary Press, 1947) II, 77.

[6] Charles C. Ryrie, *The Christian and Social Responsibility* (Fort Worth, TX: Tyndale Seminary Press, 2008), 42–43.

believers (1 John 3:17). Today we are well aware that technological advances can be wonderful or destructive depending upon the purpose we put them toward. We have to discern how to use objects in our physical environment without conforming to its evil configuration (1 John 2:15-17).

Finally, we should note a few other features of true Biblical cosmology important to our argument. In spite of accommodationist attempts to conform Biblical narrative to the latest speculations of historical science, there is no way to avoid the many discrepancies. Piecemeal harmonizations fail to account for the fourth-day problem in Genesis 1, the narrative of woman's creation, the transformation of the biosphere by the post-fall curse, the high longevity of antediluvians and exponential decay of human longevity after the flood, the exodus event, the long day of Joshua, etc. In a word Biblical cosmology features unavoidable, catastrophic, high-power processes both in past history *and in the prophesied future.*[7]

---

[7] High-power processes accomplish work over short time intervals (power = work/time). They thus integrate with a young universe and a short history to which all Biblical genealogies testify. Postmillennial conceptions of tens of thousands of years of possible Church growth promote a time scale at odds with a young earth and Biblical cosmology. Postmillennial full preterists sense this dilemma and have now produced a book with a consistent long time scale for the past as well as for the future. Only low-power processes are supposed to have occurred in the past (old universe view) and are to occur in the future (long history). Timothy P. Martin and Jeffrey L. Vaughn, *Beyond Creation Science: New Covenant Creation From Genesis to Revelation* (Whitehall, MT: Apocalyptic Vision Press, 2007). To observe how the dispensational hermeneutic should work regarding cosmology when it isn't compromised by accommodationism see Charles A. Clough, "Dispensational Implications for Universal Historiography and Apologetics," *Chafer Theological Seminary Journal* 7 (July-September, 2001): 34-61.

THE CHURCH AND THE COSMOS

If the Church currently functions within a creation having the metaphysical and ethical features the Bible describes rather than within the impersonal material universe conceived by modern culture, what implications does that have for the question at hand? What does the current age accomplish in this cosmos? One way to look at the situation is to view it from "below", i.e., here in readily observable human history, and then try to see matters from "above", i.e., through Scriptural accounts of what is going on in the invisible realm.

Throughout both testaments there is an unceasing struggle between man and Satan that is always ethical in nature and sometimes involves the physical. It begins in Genesis 3 and continues all the way to the present age. One result is that God cursed the natural environment with observable changes in both botanical and zoological realms (Gen 3:14–19; Rom 5:12–14; 8:18–23). Further divine cursing during the flood judgment lowered human longevity by over 90% and probably affected the rest of nature similarly. Additional cursing upon Israel's natural environment, if warranted, would (and did) follow according to the Mosaic covenant's sanctions enumerated in Leviticus 26 and Deuteronomy 28. In a day of heightened ecological awareness how can we not take seriously the relationship between man as lord of creation and the natural environment by neglecting how such texts establish the literal interpretation of tribulation and millennium environment texts? From Genesis to Revelation there is a consistent theme "as goes man, so goes the environment."[8]

---

[8] Terrence E. Fretheim, previous editor of the *Journal of Biblical Literature*, described this often unrecognized feature of Biblical cosmology as a "symbiosis between the human and the non-human orders commonly observed in the OT from Genesis 3 on (e.g., Hos 4:1–3; Jer 9:10–16,20–22)," *Interpretation Bible Commentary: Exodus* (Louisville, KY: John Knox Press, 1991), 112.

The greatest ecological disaster was a consequence of man's fall. The greatest ecological deliverance so far in history was Noah's role in salvaging the DNA that made possible the survival of all current air-breathing creatures. Although these physical judgments came from the hand of God, they came not because of man's abuses of the environment but because man aligned himself with the evil of the invisible world.[9] Besides God's judgments on man's environment, there are the direct physical attacks of Satan (Job 1:13-19; 2:7; 2 Cor 12:7).

Besides observable natural evil in all of the past ages, there is the strictly ethical resistance to straightforward obedience to God--often involving sophisticated deception. With Job it was on a personal scale. With Israel it was usually on a national scale involving the kings (e.g., 1 Kings 22; 1 Chron 21). With Gentile nations it was evil powers behind the rulers (e.g., Isa 14; Ezek 28; Dan 9). With Jesus it was trying to get Him to violate the terms of His kenosis (Matt 4:3-11; Phil 2:5-8). And with the

---

[9] Some evangelicals who have adopted the modern environmental hostility toward Genesis 1:26-28, try to justify their position by quoting Scripture out of context. For example, Wesley Granberg-Michaelson interprets Jeremiah 2:7 ("I brought you to a bountiful country, To eat its fruit and its goodness. But when you entered, you defiled My land. And made My heritage an abomination"-NKJ) as referring to environmental abuse when, if he had noticed the next verse, Jeremiah was clearly speaking of the defilement of religious apostasy. Wesley Granberg-Michaelson, "Ecology and Life: Accepting Our Environmental Responsibility," *Issues of Christian Conscience*, ed. Vernon Grounds (Waco, TX: Word Books, 1988) 57. Of course, we are to take care of the creation, but in the Biblical cosmos the over-riding cause-effect is NOT that insisted upon by the green movement. The Bible is radically different: first the cause--man ethically and religiously sins against the Creator with sin primarily not at all involving the environment; then the effect--God directly curses it. Thus on one hand man is far more responsible for environmental conditions than the most avid green lobbyist would admit, yet on the other hand the Biblically revealed responsibility is of a vastly different and socio-politically unacceptable kind.

Church it seems to be all of the above. It can be personal (e.g., Acts 5:3; 1 John 3:8; 1 Pet 5:8–10). It can involve people in the surrounding culture (e.g., Rev 2:7,10; 3:9) or rulers (Rev 2:13) or all of unregenerate humanity (e.g., Acts 26:18; Eph 2:2).[10] The Church as the present location of God's sacred space on earth is now Satan's central target.[11]

It's easy to see that "down here" the Church exists in a terrestrial environment that has been seriously degraded and in a condition subject to nearly constant assault from the unseen realm of Satan. It is not so easy to see what simultaneously is going on "up there" in the invisible realm. However, on at least three occasions the Scripture provides us with parts of actual conversation between Satan and the Lord. In all three cases Satan requests and receives permission to afflict believers. The dialogues are *forensic*; they center on debating the ethical character of God. In Job 1–2 Satan tries to argue that Job really doesn't trust in God's good and just character; he trusts God only because God "pays him off" with favors. In Zech 3:1–5 Satan seems ready to challenge the legitimacy of God's acceptance of the high priest Joshua, clothed as he is with dirty garments which evidently portray iniquity. God's counter argument is a visual image of imputed righteousness. In Luke 22:31–32 Satan demands permission to test Peter apparently by insinuating that God won't protect him. Jesus' intercession somehow limits the intensity of the test so that Peter can emerge faithful.

The forensic center of the ethical clash in the unseen world "up there" points to what dispensational theology has always made central: the doxological purpose of history. In

---

[10] Thomas suggests that the "throne of Satan" in Rev 2:13 refers to Pergamum's temple to "the divine Augustus and goddess Roma" and hence to the prominent Asian location of Caesar-worship. Robert L. Thomas, *Revelation 1–7: An Exegetical Commentary* (Chicago: Moody Press, 1992), 184.

[11] See discussion of sacred space in the previous chapter.

discussing the grand climax of history given in the book of Revelation, Pilkey uses a very simple argument to show the all-encompassing nature of the doxological compared with the redemptive:

> As mortals, we remain in various kinds of trouble; and salvation strikes us as an all-consuming, universal concern. Yet the angels of heaven have never been saved; the demons cannot be saved; and the redeemed in heaven have nothing from which to be saved. If life in the resurrected state has a purpose, goals must exist beyond salvation...In [Revelation] the doors of the third heaven have swung open exposing mankind to a new note of confrontation, defiance, and universal intrigue. To possess such a book now, under the limitations of the present age, is to distinguish between the Christian religion, as it must exist today, and the Christian faith, as it exists in all ages and in eternity.[12]

Redemption applies to only part of creation. The ethical struggle extends throughout all creation, encompassing angelic beings as well as mankind. In their abode the struggle centers on vindication of the character of God and lasts from the fall to ultimate judgment when good and evil will be forever separated never to mix together again (Rev 22). Once the eternal state begins, redemption and grace end and are eclipsed by the doxological purpose.   Here is the unifying theme larger than redemption as dispensationalism has always claimed.

The Church as the Body of Christ also extends across the boundary between the empirically observable world "down here" and the invisible world "up there." While similar to Old Testament conditions, there is a radically different new thing here. Since Jesus' ascent and session, *two divergent metaphysical orderings*

---

[12] Pilkey, 279–280.

now exist: the old rank-order of angel-man-nature and the new rank-order of man-angel-nature. A representative of the human race, the Son of Man and God-man, Jesus, for the first time in the age-old conflict now occupies the high ground. This new state-of-affairs leaves the Body of Christ at the crossroads like as never has happened to believers previously in history. Living saints now exist in the visible world of the old rank-order but are united spiritually with Christ Who is of the new rank-order. Since they know that the Church in union with Christ is supplanting them in the metaphysical order as well as successfully defeating their ethical challenges, one can only imagine the hatred that Satan and his minions have toward the Church on earth. They can reach only that portion of the Body of Christ to vent their rage (1 Pet 5:8). With this understanding of the cosmos, we again ask the question: what is being accomplished during the Church age? We now anticipate the forensic-doxological element as well as the redemptive element.

In the vision of Rev 5 the pre-kingdom judgments upon mankind begin with the qualification of Jesus Christ: *"Worthy art Thou to take the book, and to break its seals; for Thou wast slain, and didst purchase for God with Thy blood men from every tribe and tongue and people and nation. And Thou hast made them to be a kingdom and priests to our God; and they will reign upon the earth .*" (Rev 5:9-10 NASB).[13] According to the vision Jesus alone is qualified by virtue of His substitutionary atonement that has by then enabled the redemption of people from every subset of mankind. A representative body of Adam has thus come into

---

[13] I cite the NASB that follows the textual tradition of the third person plural pronouns in 5:10 rather than the second person plural pronoun readings in the NKJ. Dr. John Niemela using an extensive study of manuscript evidence persuasively argued for the third plural reading at the 2006 Chafer Seminary Pastors Conference but unfortunately did not submit a paper of his talk.

existence.[14] It satisfies all the forensic requirements of heaven and thus makes possible the tribulation judgments which in turn will bring about Israel's repentance. When Israel then nationally welcomes Jesus, He will return to earth as He ascended and establish His kingdom with a fully–functioning New Covenant (Matt 23:39; Acts 1:11). There seems to be a similarity in strategy here between Jesus in the Church age and that of David prior to his accession to his throne. Just as David gathered refugees from Israel while he waited for God to subdue his enemies (1 Sam 16–2 Sam 2), so the Greater David has gathered refugees from the cosmos while He has waited to begin the violent judgments that re–establish the earthly throne of David and the Kingdom on earth (cf. Ps 2:8; 110:1; Heb 1:13).[15] It seems fairly clear that the Body of Christ must be complete before the scroll can be opened that begins global judgments of the next era. But what is involved in the notion of "complete"? And how does the Church become complete redemptively such that all the background forensic issues are also settled?

A feature of church history that scholars have thought about since the nineteenth century is the observed sequence of doctrinal development. Various schemes have been used to organize and explain the data. Some historians such as Roman Catholic John Henry Newman and German liberal Adolf von Harnack used evolutionary schemes, explaining doctrinal expansion beyond that of the early church variously as sign of health or decay or sociological maturity. Conservative evangelical historians like John Hannah recognize that doctrinal development has taken place but claim that is it explanatory, not expansive. It

---

[14] All five of Daniel's images in Dan 2 and 7 seem to refer to the individual founding kings as well as the people in each kingdom. The first four are beastly (sub–human) in nature. Only the fifth, the Son of Man, is truly human and fitting for the race of Adam.

[15] See footnote 76 of the previous chapter for older references to this idea.

is the response to threats to the church.[16] Indeed, it seems that the development cycle often begins with some sort of cultural trend that starts to shape adversely how Christians think. Then, to more and more believers, its lack of conformity to the Word of God becomes troubling. As special revelation is at last brought to bear upon the situation, there is spirited debate within the Church over what is the truth. Finally, carefully-worded doctrinal statements are published.

Using Hannah's outline, for example, during the first 400 years the Church encountered the philosophical legacy of the Greeks in trying to preach the authority of Scripture, the divine-human nature of Jesus, and the nature of the Biblical God. The doctrines of Christology and Trinitarianism were developed from Old and New Testament texts that, in principle at least, denied metaphysical concepts the Church was inheriting from Plato and the Neoplatonists as well as indiscriminate use of Aristotelian logic.[17]   The cluster of soteriological doctrines was developed during the next twelve centuries up through the Reformation. These doctrines denied the seductive epistemological self-sufficiency and merit of fallen man. During the last 400 years doctrines of sanctification, ecclesiology and eschatology have been developed and still are being debated. These doctrines challenge the threats from naturalist psychology, state domination

---

[16] John Hannah, *Our Legacy: The History of Christian Doctrine* (Colorado Springs, CO: Navpress, 2001), 24–28.

[17] The far-reaching metaphysical challenges that Christology and Trinitarianism give to unbelieving thought still cause thoughtful Christians to marvel. For examples, see the socio-political implications of Trinitarianism in Rousas J. Rushdoony, *The One and the Many* (Nutley, NJ: Craig Press, 1971); the logical implications in Vern S. Poythress, "Reforming Ontology and Logic in the Light of the Trinity: An Application of Van Til's Idea of Analogy," *Westminster Theological Journal* 57 (1995): 187–219; and the theological implications in John W. Cooper, *Panentheism: The Other God of the Philosophers* (Grand Rapids, MI: Baker Publishing Group, 2006).

of church organizations, naturalist cosmology and utopian "new orders" like Marxism, Fascism, Islamic Sharia and more recently global governance.[18]

History thus shows a Church encountering major cultural deceptions that literally force it to become more self-consciousness of the implications of Biblical doctrine. One day there will be corporate victory in rejection of every deception thrown at the Body by the Evil One including those emanating from antichrists within the organized church (e.g., 1 John 2:19). There will be an accumulated corporate skill in trusting the Lord in every kind of trial including martyrdom (e.g., Rev 2:10). Redemptively there will be growth that Paul prayed for (e.g., Eph 1:15-23; 3:14-19). From world-wide missionary effort there will be saints from every people group. Forensically there will be a record of choices to trust in God's saving grace that alone satisfies His justice, a cleansing of all sin by the substitutionary atonement, a recognition of every lie and deception and a final purging of all falsely accomplished works at the Bema Seat (1 Cor 3:12-15).

Some might object that the picture of Church completeness here discussed is one of unattainable perfection. Every generation of Christians had faced different circumstances and have never perfectly overcome all of them. True, but somewhere in church history there have been *some* believers who were individually successful at *particular* trials. There have been *some* believers who did correctly perceive the error of *particular* deceptions. None of them were ever without sin, but in a specific situation they were overcomers (1 John 1:8). Only Jesus did it all.

Others might object that this view has nothing observable "down here" in visible history that could be construed as progress. Victories here and there don't constitute progress whether smooth or erratic. Perhaps an analogy from business

---

[18]For important source documents on the increasingly influential global governance movement, see the ministry of Canadian evangelical Carl Teichrib at http://www.forcingchange.org/.

accounting will help. Businesses have two views of their condition: a balance sheet and an income statement. A growing (progressing) business will show growing total assets in its balance sheet. However, for any particular accounting period (historical situation) it may show widely varying income.[19] Growing assets is an analogy to the accumulating historical victories of the total Church in heaven and on earth--both the numerical additions from various people groups as well as the increasing variety of experience in managing different historical circumstances with Biblical doctrine. Varying income is an analogy to victories and defeats of believers in particular locations at particular times. Looking just at the observed sequence of events in church history neglects the accumulated carryover in the invisible world of the accomplishments of the dead in Christ. Unilinear progress "down here" isn't necessary for unilinear progress "up there." The Church's historical progress has to be viewed from the metaphysical complexity of creation and not purely as a sociological phenomenon. This is one reason why the Church can be considered as a "heavenly" people in contrast to an "earthly" people like historic Israel the accomplishments of which belong "down here."

Another analogy may also illustrate. After surveying every major military conflict over the past 2500 years, the famous British strategist and military editor of the *Encyclopedia Britannica*, B. H. Liddell Hart, concluded that "effective results in war have rarely been attained unless the approach has had such indirectness as to ensure the opponent's unreadiness to meet it.

---

[19] No apologies here for using an economic illustration. Paul employed economic modeling to the spiritual dynamic of imputation so much so that I've heard liberal scholars actually ridicule the doctrine purely because of their anti-capitalist mentality. What they fail to realize is that Biblical metaphors presuppose God's design of specifically created objects just for illustrative purposes. Biblical metaphors are not arbitrary literary accidents and economic metaphors come from God's design of labor, ownership, and value.

The indirectness has usually been physical, and always psychological. In strategy, the longest way round is often the shortest way home."[20] The indirect strategy contrasts with brute force frontal assaults so common in the Civil War and First World War. Liddell Hart gives examples of flanking maneuvers more common in the Second World War and in the Arab–Israeli wars. He writes, "The aim is to weaken resistance before attempting to overcome it; and the effect is best attained by drawing the other party out of his defenses."[21] This appears to be the strategy the Father is using in the Church's cosmic conflict. By placing us in circumstances where we are compelled to learn humility, it gives the impression of weakness and cultural impotency to casual observers. This was the pattern Jesus followed with what theologians call His kenosis, i.e., His submission to the Father in the use of His divine attributes (Phil 2:5–8). Such perfect submission was profoundly misinterpreted by Satan, luring him to initiate an attack to exploit what he thought was a weakness. He inspired Judas to have Jesus executed and out of the way only to discover that his direct offensive thrust ended in the unraveling of his claim upon mankind (e.g., Matt 26:23; John 16:11). Is this not the same with the Church? Is it not the apparent weakness that Paul refers to in 1 Corinthians 2 and the daily life–style of submission that Peter refers to in 1 Peter 3:15–16 that lures unbelievers and evil principalities and powers into action? The defensive nature of our spiritual armor in Ephesians 6 implies that the *apparent* initiative lies with our opposition. However, because of a clever indirect strategy each such encounter by bringing cosmic vanity into contact with the Word of God advances both the invisible battle over the nature of God and the visible growth of the Body of Christ.

---

[20] B. H. Liddell Hart, *Strategy*, 2nd ed., (New York: Frederick A. Praeger Publishers, 1967), 25.

[21] Ibid., 18.

The Church age, therefore, does show historical progress when considered as a body of believers in union with the ascended Christ at the Father's right hand. Over the centuries the Body of Christ has grown quantitatively and qualitatively. It has spread throughout mankind in spite of cultural resistance. It has also demonstrated in varied locations at various times victory against the deceptions and persecutions thrown at it from the evil principalities and powers of the invisible world. Moreover, at every step of the way it has been under angelic surveillance which would have exposed it to any forensic accusations before God (1 Cor 11:10; Eph 3:10 and the meaning of 'satan').[22] Historical progress continues until worldwide redemption goals are reached that can withstand all forensic accusations by Satan. When the Body of Christ is at last completed, Jesus can break the seals on the scroll. The judgments upon both mankind and the evil angelic powers will have begun. Thus the completion of the Church really is a requirement to usher in the kingdom age. Viewed from this larger perspective, the Church age is not a static, parenthetical age.

THE CHURCH AND THE FUTURE AGE WITH A FUNCTIONAL NEW COVENANT

We've answered the first question of this chapter concerning progress in this age. Our attention now turns to the second question: why is there the millennial age that intervenes between this age and the eternal state? Historical progress *within* the Church age should be related to historical progress *beyond* the

---

[22]It may well be that angels are assigned as watchers over various local church locations as might be inferred from the addressees of the seven letters in Revelation 2–3. See the discussion in Robert L. Dean, "Identifying the 'Aggelos' in Revelation 2 & 3," available at http://www.pre-trib.org/articles/view/meaning-of-angels-in-revelation-2-and-3.

Church age. For the context of historical progress we have had to point out features in creation that are not often treated respectfully in theological studies. The creation has a metaphysical complexity of visible and invisible dimensions that interact with one another. Both of these dimensions are involved in an ethical complexity of co-existing good and evil in active conflict. This conflict is bounded between a starting and an ending point (the fall and the eternal state). Then with the ascension and session of Jesus Christ a further complexity arises: a reversal has occurred in the rank order of angels and man that directly involves the Church. It is within *that* kind of universe that the prophesied New Covenant is to come about. Two further questions need consideration: (1) what will be the characteristics of the coming age of New Covenant fulfillment? and (2) what perspective does that age give to us living in this age?

In the previous chapter we treated the New Covenant strictly as a local contract between Israel and Yahweh. Its contract format, as with all contracts, implies that the meaning of its terminology must be conserved throughout its duration. It promises Israel national regeneration, social justice like that of the Mosaic law, and material blessings of favorable climate, productive soil and crops, fertile herds, and general economic prosperity. These promises are not to be reinterpreted as symbols of individual Christian "blessings." As contract terminology they mean what they say. Prophecies of the Millennial Kingdom imply that similar blessings will extend beyond Israel – universal prosperity under the global governance of King Jesus (e.g., world peace makes costly military expenditures unnecessary, Is 2:4; 32:17-18). This is the picture of a functional New Covenant that the dispensational SCIO viewpoint obtains from the Old Testament. It differs significantly from the kind of New Covenant seen by covenant theology and apparently from various ill-defined, interim versions of the covenant seen by some dispensationalists.

To help elucidate the structure of the coming kingdom with a functional New Covenant consider the ideas of mortality and immortality. As Paul makes clear in 1 Corinthians 15 immortality refers to existence as a resurrected person. Jesus taught that there is a resurrection of life and a resurrection of judgment – everyone gets resurrected (John 5:29). Resurrection refers to the physical existence of the eternal state. It is a sobering thought that once resurrection occurs there can be no change in status from good to evil or from evil to good. However, this truth is precisely what rescues history from perpetual ethical conflict. The categories of mortality and immortality become important at this point in our discussion.

Every age until the Kingdom age can be considered 100% mortal. The corollary of mortality is the existence of temptation to evil and the possibility of repentance. Mortal culture, therefore, can never be a true utopia. *Any transformation ethically upward is reversible.* It can't escape Solomon's devastating critique in *Ecclesiastes.* This is why the Mosaic law was necessarily provisional.[23] Mortal man remains under the influence of the invisible world, but he has a conscience and an innate sense of guilt (Rom 2:14-15). He clearly perceives God's existence and some of His qualities in spite of suppressing it to varying degrees (Rom 1:19-20). For this reason Israel's prophets could hold surrounding Gentiles responsible to transcendent ethical

---

[23] See discussion of the Mosaic covenant in the previous chapter and remark there in footnote 28.

standards.[24] Although it is a mortal age, the Church age is the first age in which believers have some inkling of immortal existence due to possessing eternal life in union with the resurrected Christ.[25] How does the millennium differ?

In spite of the limitations of mortality, or perhaps due to them, the vision of the millennium continues to mesmerize political reformers. One of the leading social progressives in the early twentieth century, Walter Rauschenbusch, lamented the lack of a millennial vision: "We need a restoration of the millennial hope which the Catholic church dropped out of eschatology. It was crude in its form but wholly right in its substance. . . .We hope for such an order for humanity as we hope for heaven for ourselves."[26] He meant by the term "crude" the supernatural view of the cosmos we have discussed above. Belief in the invisible world and its evil components "will be confined to narrow circles,

---

[24] See the source materials cited in the previous chapter concerning the Reformed discussions on the Church and culture. Also Robert D. Culver, *Toward A Biblical View of Civil Government* (Chicago: Moody Press, 1974) remarks that the Mosaic law shows evidence that it incorporated previously existing statutes obtained from common Gentile wisdom. Jewish rabbis have long recognized the basic moral sense all mankind has by virtue of conscience and special revelation through Noah. See David Novak, *The Image of the Non–Jew in Judaism: An Historical and Constructive Study of the Noahide Laws* (New York: Edwin Mellen, 1983) cited in J. Budziszewski, *What We Can't Not Know: A Guide* (Dallas, TX: Spence Publishing Company, 2003), 225.

[25] John tells us that eternal life was first manifested in the Incarnation (1 John 1:2) and consists of the recognition that Jesus is the Christ (John 17:3). If Hodges is correct in his exegesis of 1 John 3:9 that the "seed" is the regenerated inner self that does not sin which is to be distinguished from the total person who does sin (much as Paul does in Gal 2:20), we have some indication that the Church age is an advance toward the future. Zane C. Hodges, *The Epistles of John: Walking in the Light of God's Love* (Irving, TX: Grace Theological Society, 1999), 140–144.

[26] Walter Rauschenbusch, *A Theology for the Social Gospel* (New York: The Macmillan Co., 1922), 88.

mostly of premillennialists."[27] Every visitor today to the United Nations building in New York City can observe the inscription of Isaiah 2:4 testifying to the continuing effect of the millennial vision on political progressivism.   Ironically, in pursuing this vision in a purely naturalistic fashion progressives actually are regressing back to the pagan dream of Babel where man imagined he could define his existence (Gen 11:1–4).

The millennial vision is thus a two–edged sword. On one hand it galvanizes hope that mortal history "should not be...brought to an end until all its known possibilities have been fulfilled within the admitted limits imposed by that which is finite and sinful...Why should there not be an age in which...unrealized dreams of humanity will at last come true on earth?"[28] In spite of being poorly understood by secular historians, this vision has been alive and well throughout American history.[29]   Many theonomists, as we discussed in the previous chapter, insist that the millennial vision must be viewed as attainable by the Church. On the other hand the vision seen in Scripture is unmistakably supernatural not just with regard to individual sanctification but also with regard to the geophysical environment and the invisible

---

[27] Ibid., 86.

[28] Alva J. McClain, *The Greatness of the Kingdom: An Inductive Study of the Kingdom of God* (Chicago: Moody Press, 1959), 530.

[29] James Gilbert, a cultural historian at the University of Maryland, commented on the cover jacket of a detailed study of American apocalyptic belief that it "amounts to the discovery of what many of us in this field have halfway understood but never quite realized, that the dominion of prophecy and 'end–time' religion is vast and of utmost importance in understanding the whole of American culture." Paul Boyer, *When Time Shall Be No More: Prophecy Belief in Modern American Culture* (Cambridge, MA: Harvard University Press, 1992).

world of evil.[30] Evidently in the complex cosmology revealed in the Bible the interaction between society, individual, environment and invisible world is so interwoven that to attain millennial conditions requires a simultaneously comprehensive system overhaul. That action far exceeds the collective abilities of mankind regenerated or not.

Here is where the dispensational SCIO view has to part company not only with postmillennialism but also with those dispensationalists who no longer hold to the Church's historic interpretation of early Genesis. Lyellian uniformitarianism simply doesn't accomplish the necessary work fast enough to explain geologic history within the time span of the Scriptural record as well as of recently-studied radiometric chronometers.[31] Eons of evolution can't explain the rapid botanical and zoological changes reported in Biblical narratives of the fall and in prophecies of the future millennium. *One cannot choose one's eschatology without choosing a compatible cosmology.* Marsden describes how this linkage has worked out over the last century or two:

> "[The dispensational] view of history is anti-humanist and anti-developmental...Change takes place almost solely through dramatic divine intervention...Modern historiography assumes that human and natural forces shape the course of history...Dispensationalists, on the other hand, start with the assumption that supernatural forces shape history...These totally opposed views of history lay

---

[30]Years ago Pentecost enumerated a long list of such characteristics. J. Dwight Pentecost, *Things to Come: A Study in Biblical Eschatology* (Grand Rapids, MI: Dunham Publishing Co., 1958), 487–489.

[31] See the multi-year, well-funded research project results by creationists: Larry Vardiman, Andrew A. Snelling, and Eugene F. Chaffin, ed., *Radioisotopes and the Age of the Earth: Results of a Young-Earth Creationist Research Initiative* (El Cajon,CA: Institute for Creation Research and Chino Valley, AZ: Creation Research Society, 2005).

at the heart of the conflict and misunderstanding between theological liberals and their fundamentalist opponents. The liberal party came increasingly to view history in the sense of natural development as the key to understanding all reality, including Scripture. Fundamentalists, on the other hand, insisted more and more that the supernatural account of things in Scripture was the key to understanding anything about natural reality, including history."[32]

It will be interesting to observe how long traditionally dispensational universities and seminaries can remain so once they have abandoned a literal view of early Genesis which many of them have already done. The Bible's promises of future geophysical events originate from within a literal view of the creation, fall, and flood.

After the tribulation judgments when Israel finally accepts its Messiah, the resurrected Lord with resurrected Church-age saints will return to implement the New Covenant locally with Israel and to establish the millennial Kingdom of God globally. This event brings into existence a new kind of age: one with *co-existing mortal and immortal people*. Its mortal component will include the (renovated) earth with an ecosystem similar to that of the antediluvian age. The administrative distinction between mortal Jews and mortal Gentiles will resemble that of the Old Testament. Mankind's world religion center dedicated exclusively to the Biblical faith will be built on Mt. Zion. The Messianic King will establish true social justice as in the ancient theocracy with its penal code and exercise global governance over all nations with the absolute authority of a "rod of iron." All demonic energization of the flesh will cease with evil removed from the

---

[32] George M. Marsden, *Fundamentalism and American Culture: The Shaping of Twentieth-Century Evangelicalism, 1870–1925* (New York: Oxford University Press, 1980), 62–63.

invisible world (Rev. 20:1–3). The immortal component will consist of Christ and all co–ruling resurrected saints as well as the New Jerusalem (apparently not yet on earth).

These mortal/immortal mixed characteristics of the coming kingdom age clearly place it in between the mortal Church age and the immortal eternal state. Why this strange age that belongs neither to the present age nor to the immortal New Creation? Evangelical amillennial proponents of "realized eschatology" object that premillennialism shares with postmillennialism the idea that the present age isn't really an eschatological fulfillment. If this age is the "last days" and an age of suffering, then what kind of victory would be significant that isn't the permanent separation of good and evil in the eternal state of complete immortality? What kind of victory is the millennium if it ends in rebellion?[33]   It seems that the problem behind these amillennial objections is an incorrect conception of the millennium due to a compromised cosmology that cannot appreciate the mixed population of mortals and immortals living together in a catastrophically altered geophysical environment.

As the bridge age between the Church age and the eternal state, the millennium reveals things about God, man and both the visible and invisible world that would never be known if the Church age were to end with Christ's return and immediate transition to the eternal state. Granted that the millennium ends in rebellion (Rev 20:7–9), but when Satan is released and re-activates evil influences from the invisible world, he can trigger rebellion because of the mortal condition of that society. The rebellion reveals that even after a thousand years of a socially just environment without what is claimed today to be causes of social

---

[33] For example, see Gaffin's response during the Reformed debate over postmillennial theonomy. Richard B. Gaffin, Jr., "Theonomy and Eschatology: Reflections on Postmillennialism," *Theonomy: A Reformed Critique*, ed. William S. Barkers & W. Robert Godfrey (Grand Rapids: Zondervan Publishing House, 1990), 197–224.

injustice – devastation and expense of wars, lack of natural resources, poverty, lack of education, plagues, corrupt leadership – ethical progress in mortal society is still fragile and reversible. With this lesson taught by the millennial age no one in the eternal state will be able to look back and impugn the just character of God. No one can plead that if God had given mankind an environment free from Satanic influence long enough for human development, man could have made a lasting and just civilization that could have withstood evil assault from the invisible world. Here once again we are back at the doxological debate over God's character.   We conclude that at least one reason for this age between the present one and eternity is to resolve any outstanding forensic issues. The doxological purpose of creation must be and will be fulfilled.

We've looked at the characteristics of the coming global millennium under the leadership of Israel's officially–recognized Messiah and a fully–implemented New Covenant. Now we want to reflect on what perspective that age gives to us who live in this age. One way to do that is to contrast specific characteristics between the two ages. By comparing the dynamics of evil in the millennium (due to depravity alone – Rev 20:2-3) with the present situation (due to both human depravity and demonic influence – Eph 2:1-3), we can see the massive extent of Satan's influence in the present age. We gain deeper appreciation of Biblical references to the unseen powers lurking around political leaders and their bureaucracies. It took only one lying spirit to delude King Ahab and his staff of hundreds of prophetic advisors (1 King 22). Isaiah's taunt against the King of Babylon exposes the Satanic arrogance in him (Is 14:4-27) as does Ezekiel's prophetic denunciation against the King of Tyre (Ezek 28:1-19). Also there are the strange words by the angelic messenger to Daniel about a very strong and evil angelic power who controlled the unseen world of all Persia (Dan 10:5-21). Satan clearly is in control of global leaders as seen by his offer to Jesus (Matt 4:8-9) and by John's proclamation that the entire world lies passively under him (1 John 5:19). When Satan is temporarily incarcerated, it is to keep him from deceiving the nations (Rev 20:3). This contrast in the dynamics of evil certainly ought to make us appreciate why we are warned to pray for our rulers (1 Tim 2:1-2). In this age there will be local jurisdictions where Satan's influence is very strong socially and politically – unlike the millennial conditions to come (Rev 2:9-10, 13, 24; 3:9).

Such a contrast gives us what military tacticians call "situational awareness" for the spiritual battle we so often ignore. The Evil One doesn't take lightly that mankind's representative now occupies the throne he longed for. Unable to assault Jesus directly on the high ground, he targets His Body that dwells within his cosmos. His strategy remains the same: drive a wedge between man and God by demeaning God's character. God's indirect strategy is to let him attack, but outmaneuver him into setting up a situation that reveals more of God's true character! That means we must pay strict attention to a clear gospel that emphasizes the perfect righteousness of Christ. We must rely on His atonement cleansing alone for our sin. And we must exercise diligence to recognize and reject every idea that impugns God's good character. In this battle human merit and self-righteousness are utterly impotent defenses against Satanic accusations. Given this situation it makes sense that the armor given to us to fight against the unseen principalities and powers in Ephesians 6 emphasizes the qualities of His nature – truth and righteousness expressed in the gospel, faith, salvation, and the Word of God.[34]

Contrasting the millennium with the Church age also gives us a perspective on how far we can realistically expect to transform culture. The last chapter showed that with the strict SCIO view of the New Covenant as not functioning today, the

---

[34] There is a striking similarity between the Christian in armor in Ephesians 6 and Yahweh in armor in Isaiah 59:15-18 where He fights against utter depravity in both Israel and the Gentile coastlands. In both cases the focus is upon God's nature.

Church operates as a Body related to Christ in heaven as Head. Rather than reigning as King from David's throne in some sort of *absentia* arrangement, Christ now acts globally in independence from Israel. Through the Holy Spirit He has an immanent presence on earth in a new sacred space where He meets those in need of salvation and those in need of sanctification. Through Christian individuals in various socio-political situations He transforms local culture as they abide in Him.

The conclusion drawn in the previous chapter is that whereas the gospel defined in Scripture has no reference to socio-political action, the very act of trying to persuade unsaved people of it will generate profound metaphysical, epistemological and ethical challenges to the cultural beliefs of surrounding pluralistic society. Though we may not appreciate this impact, the evil principalities surely do. This is why they instigate persecution of Christians all over the world. Hindu, Buddhist, and Muslim communities cannot long tolerate conversions to Christ without tacitly encouraging some demonically-inspired extremists to attack believers. In western cultures the secular elite intolerantly demands that Biblical ideas and values be excluded from all education and public discourse while all other ideas and values are acceptable.[35] The Christ-hating spirit of the cosmos is ever-present. However, the situation that especially concerns us in these chapters is the use of the political capacity of citizen "kingship" given to believers during recent centuries. What useful insights for citizenship responsibilities derive from this inter-age comparison?

We have learned that much revelatory source material for socio-political policy proposals lie available in the Bible including specific applications of God's just standards from Mosaic case-law. We also have learned that Christian citizens can follow Daniel's pragmatic approach toward unbelievers and the

---

[35] See citation in footnote 5 of the previous chapter for a glaring recent example in U.S. legal journals.

Biblically ignorant. Policies that fit creation design, i.e., that build upon human individual responsibility, integrity of language, dignity of labor coupled with respect for natural resources, private property, heterosexual marriage, family multiplication and educational authority and the value of human life, will, over the long run, have superior cost/benefit results. In spite of suppression of Creator-creature awareness, *all creatures, angelic and human, in the final analysis have to exist within the reality of God's creation, not in the fantasy of their own imagination.* J. Budziszewski illustrates how awareness of the reality, for example, of God's moral law keeps cropping up in daily life:

> Like crabgrass growing through the cracks and crannies of concrete slabs, the awareness of the moral law breaks even through the crust of our denials...[Fallen man] is like a man in a bathtub, surrounded by dozens of corks, trying to hold all of them down at once. Whenever he pushes one down, another somewhere else pops right back up. This is the reason why his worldview is inevitably incoherent, for bits of truth get into it that he does not intend, clashing with the things he does intend.[36]

Likewise, one can't read today an article on medicine or astronomy without encountering repeated use of the word "design" by those who in principle reject creation. Because of this phenomenon as Christian citizens we can use the pragmatic approach. There will be opportunities to urge Biblically based policies that we know will resolve socio-political problems which unbelievers want to fix. Nevertheless, such policies, because they implicitly glorify the Creator, will meet resistance in this age from the invisible world as well as from the arrogance of fallen man.

---

[36] J. Budziszewski, *What We Can't Not Know*, 10, 207.

This cosmic duet of fallen man and "the spirit who now works in the sons of disobedience" makes concentration of political as well as religious power in the hands of one man or an elitist oligarchy prior to the millennium problematical (Eph 2:2). The Bible always paints in a bad light concentrated power under mortal conditions from Babel, Egypt, the Israelite monarchy and Gentile empires to the coming Antichrist. Church history confirms this suspicion of overbearing power. The famous statement by Lord Acton that "absolute power corrupts absolutely" referred to the power of Roman Catholic popes and the kings they appointed.[37]

The Puritans had the best of intentions when they came to power in England and again when they led the early colonial government of Massachusetts. Trying to use political coercion to produce a just society rather than persuasion that respected liberty of conscience and that relied upon regeneration by the Holy Spirit led to their humiliating defeat in both locations. The well-known quote of Madison in defense of the U.S. Constitution echoed this same leadership truth: "In framing a government which is to be administered by men over men, the great difficulty lies in this: you must first enable the government to control the governed; and in the next place oblige it to control itself."[38] Madison's quote could be qualified by inserting the adjective "mortal" in front of the noun "men." The Bible millennia ago spoke to the problem: "When the righteous are in authority, the people rejoice. But when a wicked man rules, people groan" – Proverbs 29:2 NKJ.

---

[37] John W. Robbins, *Ecclesiastical Megalomania: The Economic and Political Thought of the Roman Catholic Church* (Unicoi, TN: The Trinity Foundation, 1999), 111.

[38] James Madison, "Federalist 51," *The US Constitution: A Reader*, ed. Hillsdale College Politics Faculty (Hillsdale, MI: Hillsdale College Press, 2012), 288.

Conceiving of the millennium as a supernatural re-ordering of creation kept the early dispensationalists from being seduced by the progressive dreams that man would "make for himself a name"(cf. Gen 11:4) They knew that the millennial vision could not be aligned with the prevailing optimism of the Progressive era that science and technology would usher in a "new order." It was precisely this insight by dispensational premillennialists that caused them to expose the shortcomings of the capitalist empires of the day. In like fashion they relentlessly criticized modernist social outreach ministries, evolution in public education curricula and government welfare programs such as the New Deal.[39] In a positive vein they strongly supported world-wide missionary outreach ministries. Judging from their actions and the angry criticism of progressive politicians and denominational leaders as well as contemporary historians like Mark Noll and George Marsden, it was dispensational eschatology resting upon Biblical cosmology that guided them. And judging from the historic results so far of progressive policies that have led to unprecedented loss of human life on battlefields and in abortion clinics and left welfare states' economies in a shambles, dispensationalist skepticism has been validated. The Progressives' usurped millennial vision ripped from its Biblical foundations has caused unprecedented global suffering.

The authentic millennial vision gives a distinct perspective to the present Church age. It leaves us with an "upper bound" on how far the Church can expect to transform mortal culture. Because of the structure of creation itself with its visible world "down here," its invisible world "up there," and the spiritual

---

[39] See more recent histories that have unearthed more favorable views of dispensational premillennialists than older works that caricature the movement: Paul Boyer, *When Time Shall Be No More: Prophecy Belief in Modern American Culture*, and Jim Owen, *The Hidden History of the Historic Fundamentalists 1933-1948* cited in the previous chapter at footnote 71.

interaction between them plus the inevitable good-evil conflict affecting both, transforming culture is not so simple as it might first appear. *Because of this cosmic background the Church cannot transform mortal culture into true millennial conditions.* Dispensational premillennialism, particularly the SCIO view, protects the Church from all versions of utopianism from "prosperity gospels" to various versions of "triumphalism" by its Biblical realism. Simply stated, we believers today in our mortal state prior to the Bema seat evaluation are not yet qualified to assume our millennial roles as judges of the cosmos and its angelic minions (1 Cor 4:4-5,8; 5:12; 6:2-3). The delta between the Church age and the millennium thus offers additional support for the gospel priority studied in the previous chapter.

Dispensational eschatology offers us yet another truth for a realistic perspective of this age. When the Body of Christ is at last completed and taken to heaven by the rapture, a short but horrible tribulation comes upon global civilization and its geophysical environment (Matt 24). This transition between the Church age and the millennium continues mortal history without the contemporary spiritual restraint. Satanic deception and influence then will be at an all-time high. The bastard millennial vision of progressivism that pins its hope upon global governance by fallen man will at last be revealed for what it is. It's a stage-setter for the mysterious Man of Sin who will attempt a cultural revolution unfettered by the Church age restrainer (2 Thes 2:7-9). The ensuing divine judgments will separate believing Jews from this new world order and prepare them, as mankind's priestly nation, to end this tribulation horror by imploring the Messiah's return to earth to implement the New Covenant (Matt 23:39; Rom 11:12, 25-26). Ironically, under the sovereign wisdom of God through this experience mankind will have a well developed understanding of what is really needed for a just and functioning global governance. Had Jesus returned, say, a few centuries ago, who would have appreciated His role as global King? Once again God's indirect strategy cleverly works out its ultimate victory.

By comparing this tribulation period with the present age, we discover a frequently overlooked truth. Premillennialism is often accused of promoting cultural passivity and impotence by conservative and liberal critics alike.[40] Such criticism, however, ignores at least two truths. First, no one knows when Jesus will return, so there is no way to evaluate when cultural decay has become uncorrectable. Thus we don't cease doing what the Lord told us which includes doing good to all men (Gal 6:10). The truth that the Lord can come at any moment is actually protected in premillennialism whereas in postmillennialism it is pushed off into the future to allow time for Christianizing the world. However, there is a second more significant truth that few have considered.

Just as the delta between the Church age and the millennium establishes a realistic *upper* bound on Christian influence on culture, so the delta between the Church and the tribulational period establishes a realistic *lower* bound or floor on this influence. That Christians in this age will always have some

---

[40] Besides later liberal progressive criticism in the twentieth century, conservatives criticized it earlier in the nineteenth century. George Ladd wrote "Premillennialism tends to let down the tone of the Christian life and to discourage ministers form feeling that they are working 'for the Ages' and 'for the race.'" Timothy L. Smith, *Revivalism and Social Reform* (New York: Abingdon Press, 1957), 235–236 (Citing George T. Ladd in Yale's *New Englander*, 33 (1874)). Presbyterian Hodge claimed premillennialism "disparaged the gospel," Charles Hodge, *Systematic Theology*, Vol. 3: (New York: Charles Scribner's Sons, 1891), 864. Baptist Strong accused, "It begats a passive and hopeless endurance of evil," Augustus H. Strong, *Systematic Theology* (Philadelphia: The Judson Press, 1907), 1012. Rutgers more thoroughly criticized, "The pessimism of premillennialism is inherent, belonging and logically related to the whole system. . .the world, church, men must grow worse. . .a gradual deterioration, retrogression on every hand must be observed. If not, then premillennialism fails as a system." William H. Rutgers, *Premillennialism in America* (Goes, Holland: Oosterbaan and LeCointre, n.d.) 157.

transforming effect is implied by the restraining influence in 2 Thessalonians 2:7. The Man of Sin cannot take over while the Church remains. Severe persecution and defeat may come locally, but it will never be global. There will always be room to migrate and regroup for another day as Paul did in Thessalonica and as missions today focus more on the Southern Hemisphere and utilize more non-Western personnel. Somewhere there will be "an open door" that "no man can shut" (Rev 3:8). *Dispensationalism thus protects premillennialism from undue pessimism by the pretribulational rapture.* The much ridiculed "fire escape" rapture is precisely what gives enduring hope for the Church age. There is no excuse, therefore, for half-hearted evangelistic and apologetic attempts other than ignorance of Scripture and/or simple laziness. Nor is there a reason for dispensational premillennialists to cease efforts at responsible Christian citizenship.

Looking back upon the present age from the standpoint of the future tribulation and subsequent millennium gives us a much-needed situational awareness. We realize that as long as the Church is here, there will be an unceasing sequence of openings for the gospel in spite of the determined opposition from invisible powers of evil. With those openings will come opportunities to do good to all men through ordinary daily living and through exercising citizenship rights. Also, we can courageously resist the opposition in such situations knowing that the tribulation isn't here yet. Jesus and the apostles give us "how to" behavior models. Jesus called believers in His day to be salt and light (Matt 5:13-14). Salt is preservative; light is illuminative. Neither is universally welcomed. As Ryrie has pointed out, Jesus did not make claiming His legal rights a priority over conducting His ministry. In the temple tax episode Jesus as Owner of the temple did not rightfully owe that tax, but paid it anyway lest He unnecessarily offend onlookers (Matt 17:24–27).[41] Peter, however, refused to comply with civil rulers' restrictions on his freedom to preach the gospel (Acts 5:29).

Paul on at least two occasions pushed back against opposition by exercising his rights as a Roman citizen. In Philippi, one of the Roman colonies in Asia, Paul cleverly took advantage of a quirk in Asian political law. When Paul's ministry shut down one of the local businesses, the angry owners pitched their case to the colony authorities that the Christian gospel wasn't legally approved in Roman law. Under mob pressure – like politicians are wont to do – they sentenced Paul and Silas to corporeal punishment and 24 hour incarceration. After the miraculous overnight deliverance from jail and conversion of the jailer, the authorities ordered their release. In response Paul refused to leave the jail in order to force the authorities to acknowledge they were the ones who had broken Roman law (Acts 16:16–39). "The rapid alteration in attitude of the authorities on discovering that Paul was a Roman citizen... illustrates how important it was for a colonial administration not to offend Rome...Failure to give a Roman proper treatment was...hazardous."[42] In Acts 22–25 in his relationships with the centurion commander of the Jerusalem army garrison and the Roman provincial governors, Festus and Felix, Paul shows clear awareness of his rights under Roman law and insists upon those rights.

On another occasion Paul appears not to demand his citizen rights but to have deliberately disobeyed Roman law for the sake of protecting a Christian slave. Onesimus was a fugitive slave having run away from Philemon. Robbins directs our attention to some crucial facts: First, Onesimus "was not a fugitive

---

[41]Charles C. Ryrie, *The Christian and Social Responsibility* (Ft Worth, TX: Tyndale Seminary Press, 2008), 60–61.

[42] Francis Lyall, *Slaves, Citizens, Sons: Legal Metaphors in the Epistles* (Grand Rapids, MI: Zondervan Publishing House, 1984) 233–234.

for a day, a week, or even a month, but in all likelihood for several months.   During all this time he was in violation of Roman law." Second, "Since Paul himself was a prisoner, not only did he not turn Onesimus in, but he also must have kept Onesimus' status as a fugitive from the Roman authorities;" and third,

> Why do all the men with Paul – Timothy, Epaphras, Mark, Aristarchus, Demos, and Luke – protect a fugitive slave? By doing so, they have become complicit in his crime. Under Roman law of the first century after Christ, anyone who harbored a fugitive slave was not only liable for reimbursing the slave owner for all the income lost because of the slave's flight (what we would call civil damages) but was also subject to severe criminal penalties.[43]

In spite of this behavior both Peter and Paul wrote exhortations to obey governing authorities (e.g., Rom 13:1-6; 1 Pet 2:13-17). Commenting on these verses in light of the apostles' actions, Robbins concludes:

> Being subject to the governing authorities does not always mean obeying them. Their authority is delegated and limited;   therefore, they are to be disobeyed when they command us to sin...A civil law is not moral simply because it is a law. 'I was just following orders' is no excuse; each man is responsible for what he does and he must use his private judgment to decide what is right. The Romans 13 injunction forbids armed resistance to governors; it does not prohibit peaceful disobedience to sinful laws...Paul does not call for a slave insurrection; he opposed it.   Nor does he call for a revolution against the

---

[43] John W. Robbins, *Slavery and Christianity: Paul's Letter to Philemon* (Uncoi, TN: The Trinity Foundation, 2007), 33-34.

362 *An Introduction to the New Covenant*

tyranny of Rome. But he did expect Christians to obey God's law, rather than man's...The reason the Roman Empire's fugitive slave law was not just is Deuteronomy 23:15–16: 'You shall not give back to his master the slave who has escaped from his master to you...' As a rabbi, Paul must have known this verse and many other verses in the Old Testament concerning slavery. That is why he did not turn Onesimus over to the Roman authorities: God's law supercedes Roman law.[44]

Here is an example of deriving guidance in socio–political matters from Mosaic case–law by using it as the historic model of true social justice. It also shows a line of reasoning that through the lives of many ordinary Christians gradually transformed prevailing Anglo–Saxon culture and finally generated ethical disapproval of slavery. But it took William Wilberforce (1759–1833) who aggressively and persistently exercised his Christian citizenship to persuade his nation to accept the Biblical design of all men in God's image.

Until the rapture, we will always be in conflict with the cosmos situated as we are in the Body of Christ. The influence of that Body will ebb and flow depending upon local receptivity to the gospel and its implications. The influence will fluctuate between a lower bound of at least some minimal cultural impact (since we are not in the tribulation) to an upper bound of maximum impact (since we are not in the millennium). And at no time can we ever retire from abiding in Christ and doing His work while casually assuming that whatever cultural transformation has occurred will remain. We don't live in the immortal irreversible condition of the eternal state.

---

[44] Ibid. 35.

CONCLUSION

This chapter has dealt with the connection between the present Church age and the future full implementation of the New Covenant in the millennium. Two basic questions were raised and answered. First, if the New Covenant indeed is a legally–binding agreement between God and Israel and will come into effect only after the Church is removed, what is the meaning of the Church age? What progress in God's overall plan is happening now? To answer that question we began with the vast work done at and following the ratification of the New Covenant, viz., the resurrection, ascension and session of Jesus Christ. We looked at the fundamental change it made in the complex creation structure of the visible and invisible worlds. From that vantage point we became aware of how the doxological purposes of God encompass His redemptive purpose – a traditional characteristic of dispensational theology.

We described the progress accomplished as God has grown the Body of Christ over the centuries with an indirect strategy of accumulating assets that reach into the invisible world rather than with a direct strategy of straightforward human cultural conquest on earth. The Church as a heavenly people becomes complete quantitatively and qualitatively. Quantitative completion occurs when representatives from every people group are at last redeemed. Qualitative completion occurs when the Church has encountered every deception, heresy, and trial thrown at it with specific victories by particular believers at particular times and places. At completion it can be said that the Body of Christ has survived every forensic challenge so that Jesus as the Son of Man is qualified to break the seals of judgment and usher in the next age.

The second basic question concerned how the Church as a non–party to the New Covenant in the dispensational SCIO view, is related to historical progress beyond this age when that covenant comes into   effect in the millennium. Using the conceptual device of mortality and immortality we examined the mixed nature of the millennium. We discovered that the millennium and cosmology are so intertwined that they stand or fall together. Thus liberal progressive attempts to borrow the millennial vision divorced from its foundation in God's design of socio-political reality have resulted in disastrous consequences over the last century. Instead of such cultural regression in the name of progress the dispensational use of the vision has kept the Church anchored in realism. By looking back on this age from both the millennium and tribulation period, we found that we can expect a variable cultural impact within reasonable upper and lower boundaries. The Church thus fits smoothly into the divinely-designed plan of God that is moving toward the eternal state. From this larger perspective, it is not just a parenthesis.

These two chapters necessarily have focused upon the Church and the New Covenant. Not discussed is another matter often criticized by non-dispensationalists: what is the purpose of mankind's advances in the arts and sciences according to dispensationalism? In a word these are part of the good things in the cosmos and carry over into the millennium and eternal state just as they have carried over from dispensation to dispensation in the past. But that is a story for another time and place!

11

CONCLUDING THOUGHTS:
THE NEW COVENANT MATTERS

Don Trest

This chapter examines three reasons why the New Covenant matters to the Church. 1) The fulfillment of the New Covenant glorifies God.   2) The Church bears forensic testimony to the efficacy of the blood of the New Covenant. 3) The restoration of Israel to God under the New Covenant brings blessing to the whole world.

INTRODUCTION

The New Covenant was made with Israel (and not the Church), as was also the case with the Old Covenant. The terms of the Old Covenant expired at the Cross with the first coming of Christ. Israel is no longer under the Old Covenant. Israel has not yet entered New Covenant relationship to God, awaiting events associated with the second coming of Christ and the conversion of Israel. The Old Covenant established Israel's inability to bring Abrahamic blessing to the world – based on a principal of works in self–righteousness. The New Covenant, on the other hand, shows that God through Christ (the Divine Son of Abraham) will restore fallen Israel in order to fulfill the initial land–seed–blessing promises of the Abrahamic Covenant – based in the blood of Christ and the righteousness of God in Christ. The failure of

Israel under the Old Covenant does not cancel Israel in the plan of God, but merely evidences the need for the New Covenant (as the means by which national Israel will be restored to vital relationship with God to bring Abrahamic blessing to the rest of the world).

Recognition of the "Israel only" aspect of the New Covenant is the single most important exegetical key to understanding the New Covenant.   This permits a consistent application of literal grammatical–historical (let–it–say–what–it–says) methodology to the reading of the text of the New Covenant (thus eliminating any need to view the New Covenant as being fulfilled by the Church in the present Church age – spiritual or otherwise).   To put the Church into the New Covenant muddies the interpretive waters and diminishes exegetical clarity (because it is based in artificial already not yet allegorical–theological hermeneutical schemes).   Moreover, any unauthorized (forced) mixture of Israel and the Church (based on a non–literal or allegorical–theological reading of the New Covenant) changes the meaning and message of the Bible and disfigures the revelation given to Man in the Bible. This does disservice to the Word of God, discounts the faithfulness of God, and dishonors His Name.

The Church does not stand in New Covenant relationship to God (as does Israel). Redemption for Gentiles and the blessings to the Church (in the church age) are based in the Abrahamic Covenant – not in the New Covenant.   The Church stands in grace (Abrahamic Promise) relationship to God through Christ Jesus (Abraham Seed).   Paul identifies the "all the nations of the earth will be blessed" aspect in the Abrahamic Covenant as the basis for the redemptive relationship of Gentiles to God: "The Scripture, foreseeing that God would justify the Gentiles by faith, preached the gospel to Abraham beforehand, saying, 'In you all the nations shall be blessed.' So then those who are of faith are blessed with believing Abraham (Gal 3:8-9)." This shows that Gentile salvation is rooted in the Abrahamic Covenant – and not in the New Covenant.

So, if the Church is not a party to the New Covenant, does the Church have any vital interest in it? It does. Christ is the Head of the Church and the Church is His body (Rom 12:4; Col 1:18; Eph 5:30). The Church is the Bride of Christ for whom He bled and died (Eph 5:24-32). The Church is destined to be glorified together with Christ at His return, and to share together with Him as co-heirs (Rom 8:16-18). Christ is the Mediator of the New Covenant and His blood is the blood of the New Covenant (I Tim 2:5-6; Heb 9:12, 15; 1 Cor 11:25-26). Therefore, the Church, as the Body and Bride of Christ, has a vested interest in the New Covenant because Christ is the Mediator of the New Covenant and His blood is the blood of the New Covenant. And, consequent to Israel entering New Covenant arrangement with God in Christ, the Church is destined to be glorified together with Christ at His coming and in His Kingdom.

THE NEW COVENANT MATTERS TO THE CHURCH BECAUSE IT IS DESIGNED FOR GOD'S GLORY

The history of the world, under the sovereign hand of God, is moving toward the climactic juncture when Christ rules and reigns over His covenant people Israel in a world that has been redeemed by the blood of the Lamb. There is a place destined for Israel in the coming Messianic (Millennial) Kingdom in accordance with the eschatological program set forth in the writings of the prophets of Israel and in the covenants made with Israel. It is a place of prominence and prestige among the nations of the world. God has chosen Israel to be His covenant people and will ultimately be glorified in Israel according to that sovereign choice.

God has publicly gone on record guaranteeing the New Covenant to Israel. The New Covenant given in Jeremiah 31 included an affirmation that secured the permanence of Israel in the plan of God and establishes Israel as the people of the New Covenant:

Thus says the LORD, Who gives the sun for a light by day, the ordinances of the moon and the stars for a light by night, who disturbs the sea, and its waves roar (The LORD of hosts is His name): "If those ordinances depart from before Me, says the LORD, then the seed of Israel shall also cease from being a nation before Me forever." Thus says the LORD: "If heaven above can be measured, and the foundations of the earth searched out beneath, I will also cast off all the seed of Israel for all that they have done, says the LORD" (Jer 31:35–37).

The glory of God depends upon God being true to His Word to Israel. "I bring My righteousness near, it shall not be far off; My salvation shall not linger. And I will place salvation in Zion, for Israel My glory (Is 46:13)." The Church honors the Name of the Lord when it believes His Word and trusts Him to fulfill His promises to Israel (as given in the covenants made with Israel). The whole world will rejoice and glorify God for His goodness and grace to Israel when Israel enters the New Covenant in relationship to Christ in the Millennial Kingdom:

The Gentiles shall see your [Israel] righteousness, and all kings your [Israel] glory. You [Israel] shall be called by a new name, which the mouth of the LORD will name. You [Israel] shall also be a crown of glory in the hand of the LORD, and a royal diadem in the hand of your God. You (Israel) shall no longer be termed Forsaken, nor shall your land [Israel] any more be termed Desolate; but you [Israel] shall be called Hephzibah, and your land [Israel] Beulah; for the LORD delights in you [Israel], and your land [Israel] shall be married (Is 62:2–4).

The Church, as the Body and Bride of Christ, should likewise rejoice in anticipation of God's glory being displayed in His future dealings with Israel when Israel enters the Millennial Kingdom of Christ under the auspices of the New Covenant.

THE NEW COVENANT MATTERS TO THE CHURCH
BECAUSE CHRIST IS THE MEDIATOR OF THE NEW COVENANT

Paul instructed the Church to observe the communion service: "This cup is the New Covenant in My blood.... For as often as you eat this bread and drink this cup, you proclaim the Lord's death till He comes" (1 Cor 11:25–26). The command to observe the communion service does not place the Church in the New Covenant, but does show that the Church is to demonstrate (during the time period between His death and second coming) the blood of the New Covenant to be efficacious – able to redeem sinners. In this, the Church is indispensable to God's plan for Israel, because the Church bears testimony to the efficacy of the blood of the New Covenant (preliminary to the establishment of the New Covenant with Israel at the coming of Christ). "For there is one God and one Mediator between God and men, the Man Christ Jesus, who gave Himself a ransom for all, to be testified in due time" (1 Tim 2:5–6).

The original statement of the New Covenant is given in Jeremiah 31. Ezekiel repeats certain aspects of the New Covenant in Ezekiel 36. The Jeremiah statement of the New Covenant is repeated in Hebrews 8. The parties (house of Israel and God) and the terms ("I will put My laws in their mind and write them on their hearts; and I will be their God, and they shall be My people....") do not change from Jeremiah 31 to Hebrews 8. However, there is a point of clarification concerning the role of the Mediator of the covenant in Hebrews 8, 9, and 12 that is important to understanding the relationship of the Church to the blood of the New Covenant. The blood of the New Covenant establishes Christ as the Mediator (executor) of the New Covenant:

> Not with the blood of goats and calves, but with His own blood He entered the Most Holy Place once for all, having obtained eternal redemption.... And for this reason He is the Mediator of the New Covenant, by means of death, for the redemption of the transgressions under the first covenant, that those who are called may receive the promise of the eternal inheritance (Heb 9:12, 15).

The blood of Christ is the blood of the New Covenant. Jesus declared it so at the Last Supper: "For this is My blood of the New Covenant, which is shed for many for the remission of sins (Mat 26:28)." God's purpose in the Church age is "to take out of them (Gentiles) a people for His name (Acts 15:14)," in order to affirm the effectual nature of the blood of the New Covenant. The Church age is declared complete only when the "fullness of the Gentiles has come" (Rom 11:25) and the required number of redeemed Gentiles has been reached; only then can "all Israel will be saved" (Rom 11:26). The testimony of all those redeemed, during the present Church age, is an important prerequisite to the establishment of the New Covenant with Israel, and the reason the Church was instructed to observe the communion service to "proclaim the Lord's death till He comes."

The New Covenant was signed at the death and resurrection of Christ in His blood: "With His own blood He entered the Most Holy Place once for all, having obtained eternal redemption" (Heb 9:12). However, the *check must clear the bank* before the New Covenant with Israel can move forward. The Church will be subpoenaed to bear forensic testimony to the redeeming power of the blood of Christ to save sinners at the scroll ceremony recorded in Revelation 5. This testimony to the blood of the Lamb is a necessary prerequisite to the establishment of the New Covenant with Israel. This is a crucial and often overlooked purpose of God for the Church wherein "[He] also made us [apostles and prophets in the Church and/or the Church] sufficient as ministers of the New Covenant, not of the letter but of the Spirit; for the letter kills, but the Spirit gives life" (2 Cor 3:6).

The scroll ceremony celebrates Christ as the One "worthy to open the scroll and loose its seven seals" (Rev 5:2), thus giving Him the authority to rule in the Messianic (Millennial) Kingdom. Two credentials are herein presented: (1) He is declared to be "the Lion of the tribe of Judah, the Root of David (Rev 5:5)" He is the descendant of David destined in the Davidic Covenant to rule and reign in the Kingdom (i.e. throne of David) forever. (2) He is described in appearance as "a lamb as though it had been slain" (Rev 5:6). Those present are redeemed by the blood of the Lamb "out of every tribe and tongue and people and nation" (Rev 5:9), i.e. Gentiles and Jews from the Church age.

Christ is deemed worthy (qualified) because He is the Lamb whose blood has effectually redeemed those in the Church. Those redeemed by the blood of the Lamb constitute the necessary evidence for the efficacy of the blood of the New Covenant:

> And they sang a new song, saying: "You are worthy to take the scroll, And to open its seals; for You were slain, and have redeemed us to God by Your blood Out of every tribe and tongue and people and nation, and have made us kings and priests to our God; and we shall reign on the earth" (Rev 5:9–10).

The whole created realm of the universe and the heavenly regions beyond resound in praise and adoration (when those redeemed by the blood of the Lamb testify to their redemption by the blood of the Lamb). An innumerable host (ten thousand times ten thousand, and thousands of thousands) of angelic beings declare:

> Worthy is the Lamb who was slain to receive power and riches and wisdom, and strength and honor and glory and

blessing! And every creature which is in heaven and on the earth and under the earth and such as are in the sea, and all that are in them, I heard saying: "Blessing and honor and glory and power Be to Him who sits on the throne, and to the Lamb, forever and ever" (Rev 5:11-13).

It is only after the required evidence is duly delivered (at the time of the scroll ceremony in Revelation 5:1-14) that Christ ascends the Davidic throne to assume Messianic authority in His Kingdom. Having been deemed qualified (on the basis of the testimony of those redeemed by the blood) Christ then proceeds to open the seven sealed scroll. When the seventh seal is pulled and the seventh angel sounds his trumpet, a heavenly chorus announces the commencement of the reign of Christ over the "kingdoms of this world" with "great power" in fulfillment of the eschatological program set forth by the prophets of Israel:

> Then the seventh angel sounded: And there were loud voices in heaven, saying, "The kingdoms of this world have become the kingdoms of our Lord and of His Christ, and He shall reign forever and ever!" And the twenty-four elders who sat before God on their thrones fell on their faces and worshiped God, saying: "We give You thanks, O Lord God Almighty, The One who is and who was and who is to come, because You have taken Your great power and reigned" (Rev 11:15-17).

The reign of Christ is a Messianic empire extending through Israel to all the nations of the earth to fulfill the Abrahamic mandate. His Messianic reign commences after the conclusion of the church age (and is separate from the plan and program for the Church in the present age). Christ is head over the Church, not the Ruler (i.e. Davidic King) ruling over Israel and the Gentile nations in a Messianic Empire. The King does not ascend to the Davidic throne before the scroll ceremony in

Revelation 5 in which is deemed qualified based on the testimony of the Church to the efficacy of the blood and after the seventh seal is pulled when the seventh angel trumpet sounds his trumpet in Revelation 11.

THE NEW COVENANT MATTERS
BECAUSE THE CHURCH WILL RULE AND REIGN WITH CHRIST

Abrahamic blessings come to the Church and to the Gentile nations when Israel is returned to relationship with God through the terms and provisions of the New Covenant. Paul contrasts the present redemptive blessings enjoyed by the Church in the Church age with those additional blessings that will come to the whole world when Israel is reinstated under the New Covenant:

> Now if their [Israel] fall [condition in the present Church age] is riches [redemption available through Christ] for the world, and their [Israel] failure [rejection of Christ at His first coming] riches [redemption available through Christ] for the Gentiles, how much more their [Israel] fullness [New Covenant blessings in the Messianic Kingdom at the second coming of Christ] (Rom 11:12).

The many blessings and benefits to Israel, mankind, and the world in the Millennial Kingdom were the themes of the prophets of Israel. However, the prophets of Israel were silent in regards to the Church in relation to the plan. The unique role of the Church in the plan of God awaited explanation by the apostle Paul:

> For this reason I, Paul, the prisoner of Christ Jesus for you Gentiles – if indeed you have heard of the dispensation of the grace of God which was given to me for you, how that by revelation He made known to me the mystery (as I have briefly written already, by which, when you read, you

374   An Introduction to the New Covenant

> may understand my knowledge in the mystery of Christ),
> which in other ages was not made known to the sons of
> men, as it has now been revealed by the Spirit to His holy
> apostles and prophets: that the Gentiles should be fellow
> heirs, of the same body, and partakers of His promise in
> Christ through the gospel (Eph 3:1-6).

The Church is identified with Christ in the plan of God as "fellow heirs" and "partakers of the promise in Christ." Thus, the Church is in the plan of God through identification with Christ – the Seed of Abraham.

There is a place for the Church, as the Body and Bride of Christ, with Christ in His Kingdom. Believers in the Church are "... joint heirs with Christ...that we may also be glorified together [with Christ]" (Rom 8:17). This means that the Church will share with Him in His inheritance (Kingdom Rule) and in His time of exaltation in the Kingdom. Christ and His Church will be inseparable once the Church Age is complete and Christ enters His Messianic rule over Israel and the world: "Then we who are alive and remain shall be caught up together with them in the clouds to meet the Lord in the air. And thus we shall always be with the Lord" (1 Thes 4:17). "When Christ who is our life appears, then you also will appear with Him in glory" (Col 3:4).

The church is slated to rule and reign (in some capacity) with Christ (over Israel and the Gentile nations on the earth since that is the dominion given to Christ). "This is a faithful saying: For if we died with Him, We shall also live with Him. If we endure, we shall also reign with Him...."(2 Tim 2:11-13). The apostle John portrayed Christ in relation to His Church as the One "who loved us and washed us from our sins in His own blood, and has made us kings and priests to His God and Father, to Him be glory and dominion forever and ever. Amen" (Rev 1:5-6). John further described the relationship of the Church to Christ in His Millennial Kingdom: "And have redeemed us to God by Your blood out of every tribe and tongue and people and nation and have made us kings and priests to our God; and we shall reign on the earth" (Rev 5:9–10). Church saints are deemed "kings and priests" because they will have authority and influence over other people groups on the earth in the Millennial Kingdom. The Church was purchased with the blood of the Lamb and will reside with Christ (as His Queen consort) and share with Him in the royal life and work of His Kingdom.

CONCLUSION

Understanding the New Covenant as an "Israel only" covenant is an important theological consideration, in light of literal grammatical–historical hermeneutics. Still, while the church is not related to the New Covenant, that covenant *does* matter to the Church because it is an important catalyst in God's doxological purpose, through the keeping of the promises He made to Abraham, Isaac, and Jacob, David, and the nation of Israel. It honors God when the Church believes His word and trusts He will keep His promises. Future blessings await the Church consequent to Israel entering New Covenant relationship to God through Christ the Mediator of the New Covenant when He comes to rule and reign in His Millennial Kingdom. Therefore, of course, the Church eagerly awaits the return of Christ and the restoration of Israel under the New Covenant – that covenant which should be as precious to the church as it is to the One who will fulfill it with Israel.